2

THE MAN FROM MARS

★ ★ ★

THE MAN FROM MARS

RAY PALMER'S AMAZING ★ ★ ★ PULP JOURNEY

Fred Nadis

JEREMY P. TARCHER/PENGUIN

A MEMBER OF PENGUIN GROUP (USA) INC. ★ NEW YORK

JEREMY P. TARCHER / PENGUIN
Published by the Penguin Group
Penguin Group (USA) LLC
375 Hudson Street
New York, New York 10014

USA · Canada · UK · Ireland · Australia
New Zealand · India · South Africa · China

penguin.com
A Penguin Random House Company

First trade paperback edition 2014
Copyright © 2013 by Fred Nadis

Most Tarcher/Penguin books are available at special quantity discounts for bulk purchase for sales promotions, premiums, fund-raising, and educational needs. Special books or book excerpts also can be created to fit specific needs. For details, write: Special.Markets@us.penguingroup.com.

The Library of Congress has catalogued the hardcover edition as follows:

The man from Mars : Ray Palmer's amazing pulp journey / Fred Nadis.
     p.   cm.
Includes bibliographical references and index.
ISBN 978-0-399-16054-7
1. Palmer, Ray, 1910–1977.   2. Periodical editors—United States—Biography.   3. Science fiction—Publishing—United States—History—20th century.   4. Publishers and publishing—United States—Biography. 5. Science fiction—Periodicals—History.   I. Title.
 PN3433.N33   2013   2013009652
 813'.0876209—dc23

ISBN 978-0-399-16884-0 (paperback)

Printed in the United States of America
10 9 8 7 6 5 4 3 2 1

BOOK DESIGN BY MEIGHAN CAVANAUGH

FOR MY PARENTS,
LORRAINE AND MARTIN

CONTENTS

★ ★ ★

PROLOGUE: IN WHICH TWO
CRIME-WEARY G-MEN VISIT
A PULP EDITOR IN CHICAGO ix

1 | BIRTH OF A FAN 1

2 | AMAZING STORIES 29

3 | THE ALPHABET FROM
OUTER SPACE 57

4 | SHAVER MANIA 87

5 | THE MAN WHO INVENTED
FLYING SAUCERS 115

6 | TRAPPED IN THE HOLLOW EARTH 139

7 | PALMER AND SHAVER INC. 167

8 | ESP, OR THE ELDER
STATESMAN OF PULP   197

9 | PROFESSOR PALMER'S
INTERGALACTIC MEDICINE SHOW   227

10 | INTO THE VORTEX   249

NOTES   265

BIBLIOGRAPHY   275

INDEX   280

PROLOGUE

★ ★ ★

IN WHICH TWO CRIME-WEARY G-MEN VISIT A PULP EDITOR IN CHICAGO

In the summer of 1947, the FBI agents in search of Ray Palmer marched through a busy publishing company, then entered the office of a small, hunchbacked man with a cheerful expression who was busy at work. Most likely he was studying a spread of futuristic science fiction illustrations or marking up manuscripts of the latest "space opera" in which brave rocketeers battled loathsome aliens in order to rescue a princess of Venus. Palmer was used to visitors, particularly pulp writers, teenage science fiction fans, business supply salesmen who slipped past the receptionist, and outright cranks. With his alert blue eyes, he offered the G-Men in their fedoras his amused attention. They no doubt greeted Palmer and his secretary civilly.

It was a hot August day in Chicago; outside the office fans whirred, typewriters clattered, and passing workers feigned indifference. The FBI men asked Palmer about his relationship with businessman Kenneth Arnold. Why had he, a science fiction editor, hired this celebrated flying saucer witness from Boise, Idaho? What did Palmer know about the alleged "fragments" from a flying saucer that he had Arnold investigate in Tacoma, Washington? What were the motives of the men who claimed to have found these fragments? The agents were questioning Palmer because a few days earlier, two army intelligence officers had met Kenneth Arnold in his hotel in Tacoma, took samples of the fragments, and were then promptly killed in an army airplane crash.

In his high, breathy voice, Palmer told the FBI agents that several weeks prior to the crash, he had received in the mail a cigar box said to hold samples of material sprayed out of a flying saucer in Washington State. The men who sent the package and claimed to be members of the Tacoma Harbor Patrol were probably hoaxers, but a science fiction editor had the right to investigate such matters. The G-Men looked over the metallic samples and then demanded to see Palmer's file of letters related to the investigation. After a few more questions, they left. According to Palmer, the next day when he showed up for work, the Tacoma file and remaining mineral samples had vanished—almost as if they'd never existed.

Palmer pondered the visit and its implications. It seemed strange that the government was impounding these fragments if the whole matter was just a simple hoax. He began to see conspiracy within conspiracy. More important, he saw a good story. It was a shame that William Ziff and Bernard Davis, his publishers, had discouraged his interest in uncovering the facts behind the recent sightings of flying saucers, especially with reports coming in nationally and internationally. In 1947, flying saucers were a genuine craze that seemed to have sprung straight from the pages of science fiction pulp magazines into the real world. Fortunately, this latest saga would be perfect for the new magazine Palmer was developing during lunch breaks a few blocks away in a drab office on Clark Street.

He drummed his fingers, sighed. Really, though, what more could he ask for? Here he was, a pulp magazine editor caught in the middle of a pulp adventure story, complete with visits from the FBI, a mysterious plane crash, a tale involving a fleet of flying saucers, and murky explanations. Can it get any better than that? Well, maybe. . . . If he was handing a manuscript back to one of his writers, he might say: "The story drags a bit here, right after the G-Men leave. Toss a body through the skylight."

Palmer liked it when the heat was turned up. And his unconventional ideas kept things hot. He loved how science fiction predicted the future—making it a force with which to be reckoned. Hadn't the FBI, during the war, visited editor John W. Campbell at *Astounding Science Fiction* in New York City to demand how he knew the secrets of the atomic bomb program? Science fiction, it seemed, often became the truth. Maybe all fiction was truth-in-waiting. Maybe people had trouble discerning the truth and deserved to be tweaked, prepared for the unexpected. And maybe, if Palmer and some of his readers were right, there really were other realms, and not just in the pages of pulp magazines.

These possibilities grounded his strategies as a pulp editor. As much as anything else, Palmer loved to bewilder his readers—for example, by making up fake author names, running stories under those names, and accompanying the stories with photographs and mock-biographies in the "Meet the Authors" column. Two years earlier, in 1945, he had really pushed the envelope when he began to run as true a series of stories by Richard S. Shaver, a novice author who claimed there was an ancient degenerate race living in caverns beneath the earth, zapping people with rays that could scramble their thoughts and lead them to murder or sexual frenzies. Something about this idea, however crazy, just felt right . . . he handled it carefully. He called these stories of Shaver's "true" but added that they were products of "racial memory." The series, which Palmer promoted as the "Shaver Mystery," became a phenomenon and boosted sales, but his publishers were getting worried over the backlash from skeptical readers.

Backlash or no, Palmer was just warming up. Flying saucers, to mention just the latest mania, seemed highly promising. Anything might turn up; a world of wonders beckoned. But at that particular moment, back in his office circa 1947, he was just a guy doing what he loved best: editing wild stories, tweaking readers, questioning their deepest beliefs. This FBI visit could only add luster to the legend. He was eager to retell it at the Friday poker game when all the writers would gather at his house in Evanston.

They'd all have a good laugh, and afterward he'd try to take their money. Palmer had heroic aspects, but he was no hero. He was an entrepreneur, always looking for an angle and constantly reinventing himself. He also was a character in search of the extraordinary. It is possible that he even made up the episode of the FBI visit—there's no note of it in his FBI file—but the main elements of the tale appear genuine. Whether the bureau had purloined his fragments or not is debatable—that summer prompted many wild speculations and Palmer contributed his fair share.

Like the white rabbit in *Alice in Wonderland*, chasing after Ray Palmer leads the baffled investigator deep into the underground history of twentieth-century America. Questing after the novel, the unheard of, and the outrageous, Palmer and his associates plunged headlong through such realms as early science fiction fandom, the pulp magazine industry, mid-twentieth-century occultism, flying saucer clubs and religions, and the convolutions of conspiracy theory. From the 1940s until his death in 1977, these various milieus intersected with one man—more often than not—sitting at the center: Raymond A. Palmer.

As the space age dawned, in publications such as *Fate*, *Mystic*, *Search*, *Hidden World*, *Flying Saucers from Other Worlds*, and *Space World*, Palmer made himself an impresario of the paranormal and shaped the sensibility of an underground community. His loyal readers embarked on an endless mystery tour careening between the real world and the pulp wilds. He offered unorthodox ideas to shake things up, overturn preconceptions, and create mystique. Year after year, to all comers, Palmer generously offered his prime commodity: tales wrapped within tales, conspiracies within conspiracies, and worlds within worlds; to use sixties' jargon, his humble goal was to "blow your mind."

BIRTH OF A FAN

Can you write a snappy, short story having some scientific fact as its theme? If you can write such fiction we would like to print it.

—*Electrical Experimenter*, May 1915

A group of men came out of a building that abutted on the wall, dragging a struggling, screaming woman in their midst. They dragged her to the edge of the wall and, as the monster saw them, it moved over to a point immediately below them. Cold sweat broke out on my forehead.

—Ray Palmer, "The Time Ray of Jandra," *Wonder Stories*, June 1930

*I*t was love at first sight. Winter had given way to March's bluster and promise and the newsstand was brimming with magazines, choked to the gills, decked out like the Fourth of July. Laid out in front, hanging, and set in the windows, the magazines were garish, brash: there were true crime magazines, true confessions, true ghost stories, movie magazines, magazines devoted to physical culture, detective stories, sports stories, weird tales, Westerns, as well as varied boys' and men's adventure yarns. But that day in 1926 brought something new: the debut of *Amazing Stories*—the first all science fiction magazine in America.

A diminutive, hunchbacked sixteen-year-old boy with thick blond hair and blue eyes that had a way of drinking in the world—he would never need glasses—goggled and stared at *Amazing Stories* on a newsstand in Milwaukee. The world came to a halt. Car horns on the street grew faint, along with the shearing sound of streetcar wheels, the shouts of news-boys, brake squeals, voices of passersby. All of it ceased when he saw the magazine cover. Daubed by former architectural illustrator Frank Paul, it revealed a strange landscape with old-fashioned sailing ships marooned on heaps of ice, while monkeylike aliens sped about on ice skates. Saturn hovered ominously in the yellow sky, the ringed planet striped red and white like a giant top. The dark lettering proclaiming the title, *Amazing Stories,* started huge on the left and shrunk to the right where it wrapped behind the ringed planet, each letter casting a white outlined shadow.

The magazine was gorgeous. The work of a proselytizing genius named Hugo Gernsback, who had left Luxembourg for America at age twenty to manufacture batteries, then to sell radio kits and imported electronic parts. He soon added to his catalog sales with a variety of magazines for radio hobbyists and electrical experimenters. Gernsback realized that the brave new world that science was opening required a new literature, a genre of fiction that he had encouraged with occasional appearances in his technical magazines such as the *Electrical Experimenter, Science and Invention, Radio News,* and *Modern Electrics,* and the genre now needed its own venue—and name. Scientific romance would not do. He dubbed it "scientifiction" but three years later changed the name to "science fiction." *Amazing Stories* was the first magazine dedicated to nurturing this literature.

At the newsstand in Milwaukee, Ray Palmer plopped down a quarter and at age sixteen became one of Gernsback's most fervent converts. Won over by *Amazing Stories'* motto, "Extravagant Fiction Today—Cold Fact Tomorrow," he began flipping through the pages, which included older tales such as Jules Verne's novelette "Off on a Comet," and stories by Edgar Allan Poe and H. G. Wells, as well as contemporary fiction such as George Allan England's "The Thing from—'Outside,'" about a horrifying alien encounter, and G. Peyton Wertenbaker's "The Man from the Atom," in which, thanks to a super science device, a man grows almost as large as the universe. As stars circle his legs, he realizes he will never go home as time has sped to the point where he sees the birth and death of stars. The table of contents noted that the next issue would include more stories by Verne and Wells, as well as Murray Leinster's "The Runaway Skyscraper" in which "the 50-story Metropolitan Life skyscraper vanishes into the Fourth Dimension."

Gernsback's editorial in the first *Amazing Stories* announced that it was "a new kind of fiction magazine! . . . We live in an entirely new world . . . many fantastic situations—impossible 100 years ago—are brought about today. It is in these situations that the new romancers find their great inspiration." The ensuing "scientifiction," he noted, offered instruction in a palatable form, as well as inspiration, and, as a stimulus to invention, a glimpse of the future. Such a story should be "a charming romance intermingled with scientific fact and prophetic vision."[1] It was also good, clean fun, avoiding the "sex appeal" of so many contemporary fiction magazines.

This all made sense to Ray Palmer. Finally something was going right in his life. As he walked away, hunched over and as short as a seven-year-old child, he could ignore the looks of surprise that passed over people's faces like the shadow of a cloud when they noticed he was "different." *Amazing Stories* had arrived. Palmer glowed with the ambition to write the new sort of romance called for by Gernsback.

In two years, Palmer would graduate from high school, take a job as a bookkeeper, and write pulp stories in his bedroom on the south side of town. While he had relished that first copy of *Amazing Stories* and knew that something new was brewing between its covers, even he would be surprised if he had been zapped by a time ray that day at the newsstand and discovered that in twelve years he would be the editor of *Amazing Stories*. With his combination of charm and ambition, Ray Palmer would also become one of the most controversial figures in science fiction history—with a taste for the unorthodox that led many to call him a traitor to the science fiction creed. Some would even suggest, not entirely in jest, that Ray Palmer, during his twelve years editing *Amazing Stories*, helped to "kill" science fiction.

Back on that spring day in 1926, Gernsback opened the door to the new field of "fandom" and Palmer eagerly entered. Several decades later, at a science fiction convention in Chicago, Gernsback was given the honorary title "Father of Science Fiction" and the exuberant Palmer a plaque calling him the "Son of Science Fiction."

The Sorrows of Young Palmer

Palmer had been a beautiful child. In fact, Milwaukee's Gridley Dairy Company printed images of the two-year-old Palmer superimposed on a milk bottle as part of their "Milwaukee's Healthiest Babies" advertising series, which included a descriptive phrase, such as "Here's a sturdy little gentlemen—a milk boy through and through," followed by the name and address of the proud parents under the slogan "Gridley's Milk Did It." The photograph of Palmer, circa 1912, showed a towheaded boy in a white blouse with a wide flat collar, white puffy knickers, and shiny black shoes standing perfectly straight (no hunchback then) near the edge of a leaded-glass window. In front of his blouse, with one hand he held the finger of his other hand, like Oliver Hardy might when getting ready to tell some uncomfortable truth to Stan Laurel; this healthy toddler faced the backlit window at a slight angle, grinning. An even earlier photograph showed him in a similar getup but with a longer pageboy haircut, a pendant on the front of his blouse, and a toy train and a set of alphabet blocks in two neat piles in front of him.

He was born in Milwaukee in the early evening of August 10, 1910, to the full name Raymond Alfred Palmer. While he formed in his mother's womb, Halley's Comet was slowly rounding the sun, and Hugo Gernsback was busy publishing his first magazine, *Modern Electrics*. The comet, which had originated hundreds of thousands of years earlier in the Oort cloud, was making one of its rare appearances (approximately once every seventy-five years) in the solar system. Shortly after the Earth broke free of the comet's tail, Ray Palmer was born.

Like the eccentric comet, which rounded the sun in the opposite direction from the planets, Ray Palmer was not standard issue—he had a puzzling turn of mind. From early on, he was curious, fascinated by how things worked, and seemed to have his own uncanny source of knowledge. He was intellectually precocious, reading the newspaper at age four in order to follow news of World War One, with the paper spread out on the kitchen floor. A self-proclaimed "wriggler," he seldom lost arguments, shifting, changing, revising his positions, then offering up baffling paradoxes. His later account of his memories of Halley's Comet establishes that approach. He recalled his grandmother holding him to a window to see the comet—but then admitted that he was born a few months after it stopped being visible. Yet, somehow, he *had* seen it.

Ray Palmer as one of "Milwaukee's Healthiest Babies" in Gridley Dairy Company promotion, circa 1913. *Department of Special Collections, Davidson Library, University of California, Santa Barbara*

Until Ray's first years in elementary school, he was happy and energetic. He recalled playing marbles with local children from the working-
class neighborhood that included African-Americans and other ethnic
groups. When Ray was born, both his parents were in their early twenties.
They later would have two more children, Evelyn and Dave. Ray's father,
Roy Clarence Palmer, listed his occupation as "electrician and machinist."
A workingman of Irish and German ancestry, he also was a fireman with
the Milwaukee Fire Department. He liked to drink. Ray's mother, Helen
Martha, a farm girl from upstate Wisconsin, was a German-American
beauty with long red hair. An early memory Ray had was of gazing through
the bars of his crib at his mother as she sat naked, brushing her long hair
in the sunlight.

Ray remembered his parents taking him to outdoor concerts in Washington Park—a large green area designed by Frederick Law Olmsted at the
turn of the twentieth century. He also recalled being able to go out into
nature on his own to hear wonderful music, music even more elaborate
and inspiring than that of a concert band. As a child, if he was quiet, he
could hear "a million-piece (or so it seemed) orchestra that seemed to play
somewhere in space around me." Although he loved books about science,
nature also spoke to him directly.

He enjoyed summer visits to his maternal grandparents, the Stebers—a
name he later adopted as one of his many pen names—on their farm 150
miles north of Milwaukee—just above Green Bay—in Abrams, Wisconsin.
As the oldest child, he had the run of the place. He loved his grandparents'
curved glass-fronted case filled with books instead of knickknacks, and the
fresh smell of baking bread when his grandmother was in the kitchen.
"Like nothing I have tasted since, or ever hope to taste again." It must have
been his grandmother's potato pancakes he sought to imitate when he
cooked them every Saturday for his family and friends as an adult. His
maternal grandparents spoke to him in German and were formal and
slightly frightening, but his love of the countryside (and decision at age

forty to leave the big city for a Wisconsin farm) undoubtedly stemmed from those visits.

Then came the accident that transfigured his life. At age seven, outside his family home in Milwaukee, Ray Palmer ran into the street past a row of parked cars; his foot got caught in the large spokes on the wheel of a passing milk truck and he was spun around on the pavement.[2] As a crowd gathered, the driver offered to take him to the hospital, but Ray's father said Ray would be fine. His spine was severely damaged, and several vertebrae were broken, nearly crushed. The medical ailments that were to plague him for the rest of his life had begun.

Two years later, a specialist operated on him, making the nine-year-old Ray the first patient in the United States to receive a spinal column bone graft. Infection set in. He recalls "gasps of horror" from nurses and doctors gathered around his bed in the morning as bandages were removed. Ray was expected to be dead within twenty-four hours. He heard the doctor whisper this news to his parents in the corridor outside his hospital room. (He claims that his senses had been sharpened so that he could overhear such whispers.) Even as he heard, he was overtaken with the conviction that he would survive. When his mother came into the room, he told her, "Don't cry, I am not going to die." Yet pain from the injuries and infection that night caused him to double up in his bed, and when he woke, he could no longer unbend his spine—nor would his doctor allow him to risk it. From that night he would be permanently hunchbacked.

Palmer spent the next five years of his childhood, from ages nine to thirteen, in hospital beds—much of it, as he recalled, strapped facedown in a device called a Bradford frame, made of canvas stretched between metal pipes, that prevented him from moving and further injuring his spinal cord. For a child, it was torture. To add another blow, his mother died during this convalescence, when Ray was twelve. He maintained a grudge against his father. In Ray's later accounts, he recalled his mother's profound sadness and weeping as she was brushing her hair when he was an infant. (Ray's children eventually learned, as adults, that their grandfather Roy Palmer had been a heavy drinker and womanizer.)

During this recuperative period, the Milwaukee school board sent Palmer a tutor, and the library also delivered to him a "large case of books every week." He read voraciously—as many as fifteen volumes a day, on topics that ranged from ancient history to archaeology, anthropology, mythology, astronomy, and the hard sciences. He also became a fan of the early science fiction and fantasy writers Jules Verne, H. G. Wells, H. Rider Haggard, and Edgar Rice Burroughs. When he was able, he attended St. Ann's Catholic high school and received his diploma in 1928. He also recalled that during his adolescence, as a result of his isolation and embarrassment over the "accident that crippled me, made me a hunchback, I became a lone-wolf, a bitterly determined, stubborn man."[3] He added that what he also had was a "massive inferiority complex" and a fear that he would never meet a girl or lead a normal life.

Science fiction became a refuge but also a place where he could nurture new friendships, continue to learn, and channel his impressive energies. Fandom was soon to become a vibrant community attracting brilliant young people. Palmer became an avid reader of *Amazing Stories* and *Weird Tales* and wrote his first story "The Time Ray of Jandra," which his high school English teacher read out loud to his class. "The whole sixteen thousand interminable words . . . I was rather pleased that they were not bored." He insisted he sent it in to *Amazing Stories*. If so it was rejected, or else sat around several years until it was eventually published in 1930 in Gernsback's second science fiction magazine, *Science Wonder Stories*, by which time the twenty-year-old author was making his mark in fandom.

The 1920s had been a good decade for pulp magazines, and many then flooded the market with their bright colored covers, large format, and interior pages printed on cheap pulp paper (often roughly cut) detailing the adventures of Western heroes, detectives, athletes, barbarian warriors, jungle kings, and space rocketeers. Aimed at working-class and young readers (as were comic books a few decades later), these magazines eventually covered every topic imaginable, including warfare (*Air Wonder Stories*), "Parisian" magazines with risqué covers, and health magazines that also often highlighted human sexuality.

Competing with other periodicals for space on newsstands, the pulp magazine field was harsh and competitive. Gernsback lost his hold on *Amazing Stories* as a result of one skirmish in the pulp wars. In addition to his electronics and science fiction magazines, Gernsback had entered the health magazine niche with the publication in 1927 of the magazine *Your Body* (motto: "Know Thyself"), and even more directly with *Sexology*, which debuted in 1930. With these health and sexuality publications, Gernsback was encroaching on the territory of Bernarr Macfadden, a health faddist and publisher who published numerous pulps, including *Physical Culture* (motto: "Weakness Is a Crime"), as well as *True Confessions*, *True Detective*, *True Romances*, and *True Story*. Macfadden operated several spas and institutes, liked to pose seminude for strong-man photographs, walk barefoot in Manhattan, and instituted the Coney Island Polar Bear Club and its winter swims.

Although Gernsback ran profitable businesses, he did not always promptly pay his bills. It was rumored that Macfadden convinced three of Gernsback's creditors to sue him simultaneously. Under then-current New York law, in February 1929, Gernsback lost the rights to *Amazing Stories* and *Radio News*. Macfadden put in a bid, but others snatched up the titles. Within only a few months, Gernsback bounced back and started his second science fiction magazine, *Science Wonder Stories*, later shortened to *Wonder Stories*.[4] Gernsback also filed patents for inventions, predicted many others for readers, and began one of the first commercial radio stations, WRNY, that later offered the first television broadcast.

Reflecting the go-getter mood of American culture in the 1920s, and the flamboyant hustling of entrepreneurs such as Gernsback and Macfadden, Palmer had no interest in playing the recluse. While he finished his degree at St. Ann's, Palmer took business courses, and, as he recalled, the "good sisters" at his school found him his first job as a bookkeeper at the sheet metal company P. J. Lavies on Milwaukee's south side. He also read voraciously, especially science fiction, and was beginning to make a name for himself in the early ranks of science fiction fans.

Fandom gained its own momentum in the 1930s, but its initial formation relied on shoves from Gernsback, who was as interested in building up his customer base as he was in ushering in the techno-future. Gernsback had begun the letters column "Discussions" in 1927 in *Amazing Stories*, and in 1928 these letters began to include readers' addresses as well so that they could contact one another. In 1928, Palmer, while still working at the sheet metal company, met with another young fan, Walter Dennis, of Chicago, who had traveled to Milwaukee to see him, and they planned their "Science Correspondence Clubs" to further connect science fiction fans and spread scientific knowledge. The creation of this club, according to SF historian Mike Ashley, "marked the birth of organized fandom."[5] One result was the first ever "fanzine" in existence, which Dennis and Palmer coedited and named *The Comet*. Its first issue was released in May 1930 and consisted of ten mimeographed pages. The main goal of *The Comet*, in keeping with the Gernsbackian vision for scientifiction was to spread knowledge of science and to encourage invention.

Under the care of Palmer and Dennis, the fanzine slowly veered from science to science fiction as its main focus. The second issue, in July 1930, was "dedicated to the Authors of Science Fiction, who have done much for the club." Despite Gernsback's wishes to the contrary, most science fiction readers did not set up home laboratories or tinker with new inventions—they just liked reading the genre. Nevertheless, the early issues contained articles such as "Recent Advancements in Television," "The Psychology of Anger," "Psychoanalysis," and "Chemistry and the Atomic Theory." For the third issue of the fanzine, published in August of 1930, the name changed to *Cosmology*. Its staid motto was: "For the furtherance of science and its dissemination among the laymen of the world and the final betterment of humanity." Experts such as Willy Ley served as director of rocketry and Clifton Amsbury as director of anthropology. Early fan, editor, and historian of SF Sam Moskowitz noted that *The Comet* "had a multiplier effect," as other science fiction groups formed and launched more exuberant fanzines that often mimicked what came to be called the "prozines," offering a mix of stories, criticism, and news.[6] Palmer was soon to contribute to *The Time Traveller*, the most influential of these new fanzines.

While fanzines and fan groups slowly gained their own agendas, through the early 1930s Gernsback remained instrumental in defining the genre and its goals and likened its spread, somewhat facetiously, to that of a new gospel. Gernsback believed that scientifiction had an important mission: to create a better world. By educating readers, inspiring new inventions, and avoiding "sex tales," scientifiction assured progress, not idiocy. Scientifiction was something new under the sun, and Gernsback urged that the gospel be shared.

In addition to Palmer, many others were converted upon seeing their first copy of *Amazing Stories*. Charles D. Hornig, who became editor of Gernsback's *Wonder Stories* in 1933, when he was seventeen, recalls seeing a copy of *Amazing Stories* in a drugstore magazine rack one summer day in 1930. The cover showed the Chrysler Building surrounded by flames; he bought it and carried it into a library but the librarian yelled, "You can't bring that kind of trash in here!" He took it home, read it, and said, "It was like an LSD experience, a sort of opening up of my mind, a feeling of awe and wonder—it was fantastic!"[7]

In this way, young fans like Palmer and Hornig replicated Gernsback's own early conversion experience. Two decades earlier, at age ten, young Hugo had read astronomer Percival Lowell's *Mars* (1895), which proposed that the planet might harbor extra-terrestrial life. The precocious youth, already a skilled electrician and inventor, was stunned, astonished, and became obsessed with the idea of life on Mars and other planets. Young

Gernsback fell into a fever for several days and raved deliriously about the fantastic technology and civilization of the Martians. He sketched out his vision of Martian life forms. The universe beckoned with fascinating promises. Interplanetary travel was inevitable.

Palmer was among Gernsback's first converts. And in June 1930 Gernsback's *Science Wonder Stories* officially lifted Palmer into the ranks of "stf" ("scientifiction") authors, publishing "The Time Ray of Jandra" complete with a solemn wood etching of the author gazing out at readers across from the title's inked letters. "The Time Ray of Jandra" is a fun yarn with the intentional Victorian stiffness of a wild adventure by H. G. Wells or H. Rider Haggard; its solemn tone persuading us that the fantastic events unfolding are credible. The story's main illustration depicts a futuristic city with zeppelins cruising overhead while soldiers on a rampart are pushing a young woman in a Victorian dress over a wall to an outlying jungle where a *Tyrannosaurus rex* rears up, eager for a morsel.

High-tech city of the forgotten past. The artist Leonard's illustration for Ray Palmer's first published science fiction story. *Courtesy of University of California Riverside Libraries, Special Collections & Archives*

The story's narrator, Sylvester Gale, is a shipwrecked sailor who stumbles upon the ruins of an ancient city in the jungles of Angola. He soon discovers a mysterious apparatus that allows him to travel back in time to witness the last days of this advanced civilization. Its populace includes two main factions, the "Interiorists," who are intent on drilling toward the center of the earth, which they believed to be hollow and full of great riches, and the wiser "Preventists," who fear the inevitable destruction that such drilling would bring to their world (hint: think lava). While the tale unfolds at a stately pace, new thrills and surprises keep the reader intrigued; stage notes might read, "enter T. rex," or, simply, "lion."

The same year that his first story was published, and *The Comet* was launched, Palmer won a fan contest in Gernsback's *Science Wonder Quarterly* based on the question, first posed in 1929, "What Have I Done to Spread Science Fiction?" Gernsback offered several rounds of prizes, with first place $100, second place $50, and third place $20. Gernsback's announcement for this contest indicates the quasi-religious or missionary zeal he sought to instill in his young followers. "It is impossible for us to succeed in our mission," he wrote, "unless our science-fiction readers preach the gospel of science-fiction wherever and whenever they have a chance to do so."[8]

With their background as codevelopers of the Science Correspondence Clubs, Palmer's friend Walter Dennis won first prize in the first round, and Palmer won first prize in the second round. With a tone of sincerity approaching the sanctimonious, Palmer noted in his own contest entry that the new genre was "pregnant with wonderful possibilities for development into a new, and infinitely beneficial type of literature." Following Gernsback's notions, he insisted science fiction not only "broadens the mind" but also offers the "incentive to actual achievement. Scientific literature, to achieve this purpose, must contain actual scientific facts and ideas not based on unfounded theory." Palmer then noted that he had started the correspondence clubs and a lending library to help writers access up-to-

Superfan Walter Dennis; some
believe he was model for Clark
Kent. *Photo courtesy Forrest J
Ackerman; scanned by Andrew Porter*

date scientific facts. He also said he would donate his prize to purchase
more books for the library.

While Palmer was in the busy whirlpool of fandom, corresponding,
hammering out stories, and posting books from the library, a new disaster
struck. At age twenty, another infection set in on Palmer's spine, a form of
tuberculosis called Pott's disease. The bone graft that had bridged several
of his vertebrae was disintegrating, along with six vertebrae. In September
1930, he was sent to Muirdale Sanatorium, located seven miles outside the
city. The 1919 directory *Public Tuberculosis Sanatoria in Wisconsin* stated, "It
may be reached from Milwaukee by taking the Wells-Farwell car marked
Wauwatosa to the end of the line." For many, Muirdale was indeed the end

of the line. It was a large, imposing facility set on huge lawns with surrounding woodland. Fitting for a facility named after naturalist John Muir, patients followed a regimen, according to the directory, based on "the therapeutic value of cold, dry air."

When Palmer arrived late in 1930, a year after the stock market crash, this tuberculosis sanatorium was understaffed and Palmer was among the patients who were paupers—he was unable to pay the $5 to $10 weekly fee (at the sheet metal company he had been paid only $15 each week). He was told he was there "To die—an event the very blunt German doctor in charge assured me was only a matter of six months away."[9] According to this prognosis, offered either by Dr. George Ernst or Dr. Harry Cohn, the infected bone would collapse, damaging a vital section of the spinal cord, leading to paralysis and death.

Palmer had another hunch. He bet the doctor $5 that he would get better within six months. He then set about a vigorous program of self-healing that involved creating a mental image of every step that would be necessary to "seal" the damaged area of his spine in cartilage and bone—as if getting a new graft. While he studied the X-rays of his spinal column and went about visualizing this process, Palmer saw "hundreds die . . . I was not one of the doomed, but had to watch them moved into my room one week, and die with their blood gushing over me the next." He recalled embracing an African-American roommate as he died, because there "was no orderly on the floor that night to help him."[10] Many of these patients ended up buried in the nearby potter's field.

Two years later, either the "cold, dry air" or Palmer's own healing visualizations had brought miraculous results. The delicate area of his backbone was encased in new bone. The staff marveled.

Workingman of the Wild Cosmos

In 1932, Ray Palmer was released from the sanatorium. More than likely, the sanatorium orderlies drove him to the streetcar stop, wished him luck, and offered subdued handshakes. Then came hugs and tears from those family members who had taken the train out to bring him home. He returned to P. J. Lavies and did the bookkeeping, but he also began to go on site as a sheet metal worker, installing furnaces and clothes chutes as well as climbing ladders to install drainpipes, gutters, and roofs. His desire to prove himself as a workingman despite his crippling infirmities indicates his lifelong attraction to the creed of rugged individualism. He would have nothing to do with the labor radicalism prevalent in the industrial north during the Depression years. His goal was not to cheer on strikers, harass scabs, join marches, or sing rousing union songs. Instead, he noted, his work in the sheet metal industry included "battling the then CIO union to maintain an open shop." While he shared Gernsback's vision of progress that included a future world of peace and new possibilities, Palmer's fervor for rugged individualism often placed him politically to the right of center.

After his stay in Muirdale, Palmer returned to his typewriter, a holiday present from his family, with whom he was temporarily living. He was determined to forge ahead as a writer of science fiction and adventure tales. He also quickly reinstalled himself in the center of the fan world. He became one of the founders of *The Time Traveller*, a fanzine that debuted in 1932 and included many destined for science fiction prominence, including Allen Glasser, the editor Forrest J. Ackerman (also known as "4E," "4SJ," or "Forry"), and two science fiction fans who later became prominent editors of science fiction and comic books: Mort Weisinger and Julius Schwartz. Palmer also became the literary editor and a columnist for this same group's next fanzine *Science Fiction Digest*. His column was called "Spilling the Atoms" and signed "Rap" (a nickname based on his initials that had been cooked up by fellow "trufans" Forry Ackerman, Julius Schwartz, and Aubrey Clements). The nickname stuck.

While *Science Fiction Digest* was among the most polished of the early fanzines, the product of a printing press not a mimeograph machine, many rivals began to appear. By the late 1930s, these tended to be compendiums of chatty letters from fans; assessments of books; reports on visits, outings, and science fiction club meeting minutiae, all rendered in a slowly developing SF slang, often based on abbreviations: "scientifiction" became "stf" (then later "sci-fi" and the more current "SF") and some fans called themselves "trufans," or "actifans," or simply "fen" ("fenne" became the plural for female fans). The fanzines also featured amateur artwork—frequently depictions of naked young women. Geeks, yes; repressed, no.

Rap was anxious to encourage the flourishing of stf. In January 1933, in his column "Spilling the Atoms," he launched the Jules Verne Prize Club with plans to name the three best science fiction stories of the year. He urged readers to send in nominations and 25-cent contributions to cover the cost of trophies. He wrote, "Join the JVPC and do your part in carrying the torch ignited by the immortal Jules Verne. Help make the world science-fiction conscious." There were plenty of readers willing to vote,

Palmer at his typewriter, "Spilling the Atoms," in *Fantasy Magazine*, 1934. *Courtesy of University of California Riverside Libraries, Special Collections & Archives*

but no one contributed the requested twenty-five cents—so the year's three winners, finally named in 1934, could not collect the handsome cups envisioned as awards.

While literary editor at *Science Fiction Digest*, Palmer arranged one of the unique stunts of early science fiction, the novel *Cosmos*, which consisted of seventeen chapters assigned to different authors, printed as a serial. Palmer loosely set up the plots of chapters and adjusted them as new sections were turned in, giving authors plenty of room for invention. The authors included some prominent pulpsters and SF writers such as Ralph Milne Farley, John W. Campbell (soon to become the famed editor of *Astounding Science Fiction*), Abraham Merritt, and P. Schuyler Miller. Palmer also contributed chapters under his own name and as Rae Winters.

Cosmos was pure space opera—a pejorative term borrowed from the term "horse opera," indicating these were simply Wild West stories with good guys and bad guys battling in outer space. The space opera, perpetually criticized, once its basic elements were recognized, would nevertheless rocket on through the decades, spawning hit television series, new religions, and a steady flow of Jedi to doorways on Halloween. The first bans on space operas were announced in the early 1930s. In December 1933, F. Orlin Tremaine, then editor of *Astounding Stories*, announced a new emphasis on stories that provided "thought variants." In January of 1934, close on the tails of Tremaine, the new editor of *Wonder Stories*, Charles Hornig, now the ripe age of eighteen, announced that he was banning space operas—or at least stories with worn-out plots. Nevertheless, space operas abounded, and continued to be fun. *Cosmos* was one. The first chapter was called "Faster than Light," other chapters had titles such as "The Murderer from Mars," "Tyrants of Saturn," "The Last Poet and the Robots," and "At the Crater's Core."

Palmer was having a blast. He was dashing off letters to create *Cosmos* while also working as a sheet metal installer, writing his own pulp stories, sending out books from his lending library, and corresponding with at least twenty authors and other fans. In the spring of 1934, on *Science Fiction Digest* letterhead, Palmer wrote to weird tales author Lloyd Arthur Eshbach with his assignment for one of the concluding chapters of *Cosmos*, "The Horde of Elo Hava." Palmer tapped out his instructions, "As for your part, you are to rescue the Neptune fleet, or ship, from the trap they have fallen into. You are out in space on the way to the battle-front as your part opens. You have just received a message from the commander of the earth ship saying that you are to proceed no further along your course, as it is also a death trap. (The lunarian, who has taken control on Luna, and is impersonating Dos-Tev, has sent these false courses.)"[11] Palmer noted other difficulties that would plague the rescue and asked Eshbach to await word from another contributor to find out what "trap" the other space crew had fallen into. After succeeding in the rescue, "together you search space via radio for your brother and sister ships of the solar system, and meet nothing but dead silence! That ends your part." He concluded his instructions with, "And now, go to it, and the sooner you finish, the better. Miller will be at it in a hurry too, so you won't have long to wait."

Palmer soon got a response from Eshbach, along with the new chapter, and a note declaring, "It's finished—and I'm not one bit sorry! Between Flagg's jelly characters and my desire to write something a bit out of the ordinary, I had one sweet time." Eshbach encouraged Palmer to adjust the chapter as necessary to fit in with the rest of the narrative and went on to praise the chapter written by Abraham Merritt, "The Last Poet and the Robots." Establishing himself as a fellow fan, Eshbach then complained about the latest issues of *Amazing Stories* and their reliance on reprints of Verne and Poe rather than fresh material. He also provided Rap with a frank physical description that included his own reportedly "thick lips." (One suspects the science fiction fan's tendency toward stark scientific objectivity was at work.) Eshbach added, "Now it's your turn."[12]

Palmer's response was on the new letterhead for *Fantasy Magazine*, the successor to *Science Fiction Digest*. He noted, "I too, have thick lips, and

Haggard suggests that all authors (on a majority) have thicker lips than other people. I agree. I've only met one author (bona-fide—not one timers.) who hasn't thick lips, and that is Farley." Rap goes on to say, "I weigh 90 lbs at present. About thirteen pounds under weight. Blond, blue eyes, 4′8″, small feet, (size 6½), hands that look small, but are deceiving, since I can cover hands that look much bigger than mine, long fingers."

Knowing of Eshbach's taste for fantasy, Palmer next described his meeting with the editor of *Weird Tales*, Farnsworth Wright, at that horror and fantasy magazine's Chicago office. Wright had an uncontrollable tremor (most likely from Parkinson's disease). He spoke in a low voice, forcibly making the effort to be heard despite his tremor and the distraction of an office boy clacking away on a typewriter. Palmer said, "I was beginning to sweat in sympathy with him. There's an editor who has a real handicap to his work. But how appropriate to a 'weird' magazine."[13] And indeed, the science fiction and fantasy community welcomed "weirdness" or "difference"—perhaps explaining Rap's own feeling of being at home, and the appeal of this early fan culture to individuals who might otherwise have felt marginalized due to ethnicity (numerous participants came from Jewish backgrounds), physical handicaps (as with Palmer), or those who were, as with the classic geek, Clark Kent, too shy or overly intellectual. The SF fan community, which imagined a future in which current taboos were seen as quaint, eventually spawned several leaders of the much later gay liberation movement, but such differences were unlikely applauded in the early decades. The very low participation of African-Americans in the early SF writing and fan community indicates that prejudice circulated in the SF fan community as fiercely as that in society at large; nevertheless, the prevalent intellectual curiosity and willingness to examine unorthodox points of view provided an uneasy refuge to outsiders.

In *Fantasy Magazine*, Palmer again served as literary editor, along with Julius Schwartz as managing editor, and Forrest J Ackerman as "scientifilm editor." In the June 1934 issue of *Fantasy*, Palmer brashly announced himself and his intentions to the science fiction world at large through an autobiographical sketch that includes an allusion to his time spent at the sanatorium:

> At the age of seven . . . I jousted with a truck in the middle of the street. The truck won; and landing on my head, folded me up to a permanent height of 4′8″. I'm still folded. Followed years and years in hospitals. Passed the time reading thousands of books. Acquired a vocabulary thereby, and the deed was done. All I needed was a typewriter. Santa Claus brought that. Wrote "The Time Ray of Jandra" and went to the sanatorium for another year. That brought 1932. . . . Sharpest memories of this period were: the ghastly face of a dead room-mate staring up into the full moon from where he had fallen on the floor in a flood of blood, the 1800 fish I caught in a lake where "there were no fish," and the rendezvous with a dream I actually kept—to my horror upon realisation of the truth. Intentions: to make my living by writing, and by writing alone. (Editors please note.) And to ferociously endeavour to turn out fiction worthy of comparison with the best.

As he had in *Science Fiction Digest,* in *Fantasy Magazine* Rap published stories, sometimes under his own name, and other times under pseudonyms, serials such as "The Vortex World" (run in 1934), and his column "Spilling the Atoms." He also loaned his story "Whispering Space" to the pioneering comic book team of Joe Shuster and Jerome Siegel (even then devising *Superman*) to serialize in comic book form. He also continued to come up with new contests, including "Which interplanetary story is best for filming?" and a request that fans submit "the most original slang list of the future." (Forry Ackerman won this last contest with a list that included phrases such as "Go Oil a Robot—take a jump in the lake"; "She's 87—she's hot stuff"; "Esperant—come to the point"; and "that's gravitude for you—space rocket pun.") In *Fantasy*, Rap also displayed his irreverence, taking joy in promoting spoofs of the genre. Under the pseudonym "Omnia," he ran Milton Kaletsky's "Skylaugh of Space," a satire of the popular Edward E. "Doc" Smith novel, *The Skylark of Space*, serialized in the 1920s, that had helped establish the template of the "space opera."

In "Skylaugh," the jaded antihero Fauntleroy auditions beautiful young heroines, and when he spots the most comely of them, he inquires:

"Is your father a decrepit old scientist and you his only child and assistant?"

The fatal words came "No."

Fauntleroy staggered.

"Sorry, you don't fill all the qualifications," he choked. (But very unfortunately not to death. Ed).

"Oh, but it is only my uncle who is the decrepit old scientist, etc."

"Fine," sneered Faunty. (You see, dear reader, this story is different. Here the hero does the sneering. Ed)."

The story continued to spin out its "scientifictionarration," with dialogue and commentary such as:

"Now for a trip to Mars."

"Don't we have to build the space ship first?" asked Geraldine. [Who is Geraldine? How did she ever get into this story? The person who answers these two questions correctly will receive a handsome fur-lined 4th dimension. This contest is over.][14]

Ray Palmer's Scarlet Adventures

To remedy the difficulties of writing and then selling science fiction stories while based in Milwaukee—far from the editorial offices of New York

City—Palmer became one of the early members of the "Milwaukee Fictioneers," a group established in 1931. Robert Bloch, who joined the Fictioneers in 1935, noted of Milwaukee, "The number of pulp magazines published there could be counted on the fingers of one sardine. Milwaukee writers had no editors to buy martinis for, or the money to buy them with—a statement which, however ungrammatical, happens to be true."[15]

The Milwaukee Fictioneers, a group of about ten writers, met twice a month on Thursdays to read and discuss their stories and to help each other with plotting and marketing. Its members included journalists, professors, advertising copywriters, the then-teenage Bloch (later to pen *Psycho* and make his escape from pulps), as well as the Harvard-educated lawyer Roger Sherman Hoar, who as a hobby wrote for *Weird Tales* and other pulps as Ralph Milne Farley. (Farley wrote a series of "Radio Man" novels, inspired by Edgar Rice Burroughs's John Carter novels, that were published in *Argosy All-Story Weekly* in the 1920s.) The Fictioneers also included the highly regarded Stanley Weinbaum, who wrote about a dozen classic science fiction stories with an enormous impact on fellow writers and then died young in 1935. Another member, as Bloch recounted, was Lawrence A. Keating, who "specialized in western stories, presumably based upon his own career as a cowboy in La Grange, Illinois." Bloch added that three other members of the Fictioneers, Leo Schmidt, Bernard Wirth, and Dudley Brooks, "were university professors, but otherwise decent, law-abiding citizens."

They alternated in meeting places, from Farley's manor to Palmer's family home. Bloch remembered his first nighttime meeting with Palmer at a streetcar stop on the near South Side of Milwaukee. "Here, stepping out of the shadows to escort me to the meeting site, was a dwarf. At least that was my first impression of Raymond A. Palmer, an impression quickly dispelled by the warmth and wit of his personality. Actually he was diminutive rather than dwarfed. . . . The evening meeting took place at his family's home."

While Bloch, who joined as a teenager, insisted that the meetings did not involve alcoholic drinks, Palmer later reminisced about the excellent hot toddies served in winter by one of the members. He also dubbed Fictioneer Leo Schmidt as the man who came up with a thousand plots but never bothered to write any of them. Palmer didn't fall into that trap, particularly since he didn't have a university job; he was desperate to publish and earn his penny-a-word rate. He also, wisely, was publishing the works of some of his fellow Fictioneers, notably Ralph Milne Farley in the polished fanzine *Fantasy Magazine*.

Farley proved to be an important contact for Palmer. About twenty years older than Palmer, Farley was not only a successful corporate attorney representing the steam shovel manufacturer Bucyrus-Erie, but also a former assistant attorney general in Massachusetts and former state senator. He was from an elite family that included Roger Sherman, a signer of the Declaration of Independence. As a lawyer, and under his birth name, Roger Sherman Hoar, he published works such as *The Tariff Manual* (1912), *Constitutional Conventions, Their Nature, Powers, and Limitations* (1917), and *Patents; What a Business Executive Should Know about Patents* (1926). As a politician he championed progressive causes such as women's rights. Apparently imbued with the energy of a Teddy Roosevelt, he also was a mathematician, and, in addition, loved dictating wild tales in his spare time, using his pen name. His fellow Fictioneers always referred to him not as Hoar but as Farley. Hoar may have worked as a lawyer, but Farley not only hobnobbed with downtrodden pulp writers, he enjoyed paying calls on pulp publishers.

In 1934, Farley learned that the Philadelphia-based Shade Publishing Company was getting ready to launch a new magazine to be called *Strange Adventures* that would include fantasy and science fiction. The publishers were old acquaintances of Farley's, as he had previously contributed to their crime magazines and such stories as "The Man from Ouija Land" and "The Hieroglyphic" to their short-lived magazine *Mind Magic*, which offered "thrilling, gripping, startling, psycho-mystic stories!" Farley called on the publishers and recommended Palmer as an editor for the new pulp. By 1935, however, after learning of Gernsback's financial problems with *Wonder Stories* (which he sold off in 1935), Shade decided the science fiction field looked shaky and canceled the planned *Strange Adventures*. In the meantime, their magazines *True Gang Life* and *Murder Mysteries*, launched the year before, needed more material.[16]

Shade decided instead to add to their crime line with *Scarlet Adventuress* and *Scarlet Gang Stories*. (The word "scarlet" was code for racy, sexual material.) The pulps only slowly went "scarlet." Writer and publisher H. L. Mencken, better known for his highbrow magazine *Smart Set*, had also made a lucrative foray into pulp publishing in the 1920s with magazines that mixed crime and salaciousness, such as *Parisienne, Black Mask* (a detective journal that ultimately launched Dashiell Hammett and, later, Raymond Chandler), and, more to the point, *Saucy Stories*. It competed with *Pep!*—another early girlie magazine that promised "Snappy, Spicy Stories and Art."

Magazines that highlighted sex and crime could barely go wrong. Shade had entered the pulp field in the 1920s with a girlie magazine called *Paris Nights*. Shade's new magazines of 1935 would serve as rivals to the *Spicy Detective* line launched earlier that year and already wildly popular, with its sexually charged stories and covers that featured maidens in flimsy lingerie roughly treated by criminals, rogues, and mad perverts. Such magazines were often the target of reformers. In the late 1930s, the Spicy line (which also included *Spicy Adventure, Spicy Western*, and *Spicy Mystery*) added a star to the cover to indicate a tamer, self-censored issue, starting with the cover art. (Most likely the racier versions were hidden away for customers who asked.)

On one of his many business trips of early 1935, Farley dictated a letter to Palmer and several other Fictioneers, including Weinbaum, enlisting them to help provide material for Shade's detective magazines. Palmer had gotten a kick out of bossing the authors of *Cosmos* around, and Farley took similar relish. Farley instructed his fellow writers how to proceed in writing ten-thousand-word episodes of the Jim Grant series that he had created earlier for *True Gang Life*. The magazine's new editor, J. Bruce Donahoe opined "the Grant series must be sped up. Less talk and description. More fast action." When last seen, Grant had been attacked and left for dead by "the Man on Long Island," "in the latter's castle on Long Island." He wouldn't be resurrected until an opportune time. New episodes would revolve around the adventures of G-Man Walter Scott, who would face off with enemies such as "Slim Hammond," and, yes, "the Man on Long Island." The G-Man might fall in love with Mary Smith and engage with other characters from the Grant series.

As to the writing, Farley noted, "The magazine has become frankly pornographic, and hence will probably feature other stories than ours on the cover." He also noted that another new Shade magazine, *Scarlet Adventuress* would be "featuring (as I judge) vampires in either or both senses of the word, and very sexy." He signed off by noting that "Farley and his pals still appear to stand ace-high with the management," and then urged Palmer to write two episodes of the Jim Grant series with one month writing time for each.[17] Palmer was not the only Fictioneer to contribute to the Shade line. Stanley Weinbaum, who died in December 1935, and who remains well-respected as a SF writer, had the dubious posthumous honor of appearing as a coauthor with Farley of "Yellow Slaves" in the February 1936 *True Gang Life*.

Weinbaum was best known in SF circles for his 1934 story "A Martian Odyssey," which destroyed the standard depiction of aliens as Bug-Eyed Monsters (or BEMs), and instead offered a unique, even sympathetic non-human character Tweel. Weinbaum's brief SF career included a little more than a dozen stories published in *Astounding*, *Wonder Stories*, and the fanzine *Fantasy Magazine* (most likely stories he then was unable to sell to the top magazines). His writing had been much admired. Palmer wrote a feverish condolence letter to Weinbaum's widow, "When I consider my own sense of heaviness, depression, and sorrow . . . I am struck by the enormity of your own suffering." Later in the letter he added, "I think we all agree that Stanley was one of the chosen ones of the muse." He wasn't just going through the motions. The following year, at Palmer's instigation, his friend Conrad H. Ruppert, who ran the Science Fiction Digest press, published *Dawn of Flame: The Stanley G. Weinbaum Memorial Volume* in an elegant edition that included a foreword by Palmer. Weinbaum's widow later demanded the foreword be removed for being "too personal." (A crater on Mars has since been named after Weinbaum. Gernsback has one named after him on the moon.)

As the Depression ground on, Palmer moved from his family home to a rented room, continued to work days at the sheet metal company, and at night put paper in the typewriter and knocked off stories for Shade Publishing. In addition to the "Jim Grant" series that he helped with in 1935, the story "Hot Lipstick" by "Rap" appeared on the cover of the March 1936 *Scarlet Adventuress*, and, sticking to the color scheme, Rap's "Crimson Heart," appeared in September 1936. The January 1937 *Scarlet Adventuress* included Raymond A. Palmer's "A Rose in Her Hair." He published several others and recalled that he turned in some stories that were deemed "too scarlet" even for Shade.

Yet the cover art of these magazines made it clear that the "adventuress" was frequently in charge and not a victim; unlike the helpless females at the mercy of sadistic villains as depicted on covers of *Spicy Detective*, these adventuresses coolly gazed out, bemused by the mayhem around them. The adventuress on one cover sits on top of a desk, her skimpy red dress hitched up, leaning back and coolly watching as two thugs assault each other and knock over furnishings. These women might have been underdressed, but they often held a pistol to fend off Fu Manchu–style assailants. Palmer's heroines, Carla Romaunt and Fay Langdon, also fit the magazine's story specifications, as these heroines were "pitting their wiles and wits against the world."[18]

By his own account, Palmer also had a contract with Shade to fill several issues of their crime magazine on his own, using his full arsenal of pseudonyms, a list which would eventually grow to include: Rap, A. R. Steber, Frank Patton, G. H. Irwin, Henry Gade, Morris J. Steele, Rae Winters, Alexander Blade, Wallace Quitman, and Robert N. Webster. This pulp writer might easily have sung along with Walt Whitman, "I am large, I contain multitudes." Besides his efforts for Shade Publishing and the fanzines he edited, in the 1930s he also contributed stories to *Wonder Stories*, *Marvel Tales*, *Astounding Science Fiction*, and *Amazing Stories*.

In 1938, Palmer quit his job at P.J. Lavies & Company. He insists that he went to his rented room "and simply waited. I was waiting for a specific event to occur. I was waiting to be called to the editorship of *Amazing Stories* magazine which was published in New York and had an editor who had no intention of relinquishing his job . . . I fixed in my mind that this was my 'destination.' In short, I pre-destined it! . . . If I could do what I had already done in winning a $5.00 bet, I knew that I could do anything I wanted. I could make it happen."[19]

He may have had some cosmic Judo working for him. Or he may have had another patron—Roger Sherman Hoar's pulp doppelgänger, the well-connected Ralph Milne Farley.

AMAZING STORIES

Scientifiction . . . is designed to reach that portion of the imagination which grasps with its eager, feeble talons after the unknown. . . . Scientifiction goes out into the remote vistas of the universe, where there is still mystery and so still beauty.

—G. PEYTON WERTENBAKER QUOTED IN *AMAZING STORIES*, JUNE 1926

His mind, hardened to terrific acceleration by his years as a Space Guard, was already clearing when the ray gun fired its last bolt and the robot controls whipped the cutter away in a flaming curve.

—JOSEPH J. MILLARD AND A. R. STEBER (RAY PALMER), "THE LONE WOLF OF SPACE," *AMAZING STORIES*, MAY 1941

I n 1937, Ralph Milne Farley journeyed to the twenty-second-floor office of Ziff-Davis Publishing in Chicago to pay a call on editor in chief Bernard Davis. Ziff-Davis owned the slick magazines *Popular Photography*, *Popular Aviation*, *Popular Electronics*, and *Modern Bride* and had just acquired *Amazing Stories* along with *Radio News*—both former Gernsback publications that had changed hands several times. In his posh office with walls lined with tan leather, Davis confided to Farley that he needed a new editor who really knew science fiction.

The editor at *Amazing*, T. O'Conor Sloane, who had remained with the magazine even after Gernsback had lost ownership, was then eighty-six years old. White-bearded, slow-moving, cordial, he had a sign on his desk in Manhattan that quoted the show tune "Ol' Man River": "Tired of living and scared of dying." A former professor of physics and mathematics as well as an inventor, Sloane was the author of *Liquid Air and the Liquefaction of Gases* (1899). Gernsback liked to hire science PhDs and Sloane had been his first. By the 1930s, though, Sloane's tastes were antiquated. Regarding the dream of space flight, he stated, "We do not believe in the possibility of interplanetary travel, but the subject has given many good stories."[1] When other science fiction writers, fans, and editors—notably David Lasser at *Wonder Stories*—had started the American Rocketry Club, Sloane noted, "But what could man do if chilly Mars or cloudy Venus were his destination? The time of the journey might run into years."[2] Writers also found submitting to *Amazing Stories* a long journey—Sloane was notoriously slow in getting stories into print. One writer called him "old fuzz-ball."

Living up to the slur, Sloane began each issue of *Amazing Stories* with a long, thorough, but rather dull treatise on a topic such as the history of printing technology or the chemical composition of the earth's atmosphere. And while he could be affable, and even joke in his responses to readers, his tone was courtly and reserved. To letters to the editor he accorded plodding titles such as "A Very Good and Amusing Letter from a Young Correspondent, We Presume," or "An Irish Boy Writes a Most Friendly Letter" as well as "A Scolding Letter from an Esperantist." Unlikely to move from New York City to Chicago even if invited, Sloane simply had to go. The pioneering magazine's circulation was down well below forty thousand readers and the magazine was in critical condition. In Davis's posh office, while he and Farley took in the view from on high at 600 S. Dearborn Street, Davis invited Farley to take over *Amazing*.

The thin-lipped Farley's only interest in *Amazing*, however, was to place a few stories—when he had the time to dictate them to a stenographer. An easy way for Farley to cultivate this new market would be to recommend a crony. He suggested Ray Palmer as a young, energetic candidate for the job. Davis put in a phone call to Milwaukee and Palmer was there the next day, passing through the plate-glass doors of the reception area with its modern chrome furniture, then across the editorial offices that took up the entire twenty-second floor of the Transportation Building.

As he made his way to Davis's corner office, Ray Palmer shook off the February cold (along with his overcoat) and drank in the scene. Depending on who was describing them, the Ziff-Davis editorial offices had either the hushed ambience of a cathedral or the mad activity of a newspaper press-room. Another commented on the fact that "every secretary was well under thirty and a beauty pageant finalist." Palmer felt right at home. Brash, witty, and confident, Palmer gave Davis, seated behind a semicircu-lar desk, an earful of what he wanted to hear. He, Ray Palmer, had been "spilling the atoms" for years; that is, he knew science fiction inside out. He also knew what made readers turn pages.

With great glee, like a cackling mad scientist in a B-movie, Palmer later described that first meeting with Davis in a Chicago fanzine edited by Wil-liam Hamling: "I succeeded in deluding him into committing the magazine into my tender care. So I went to work, determined to make the worst magazine (who knew better than I how it stunk?) the best in the field. You can imagine how I felt. Here at last I had it in my power to do to my old hobby what I had always had the driving desire to do to it. I had in my hands the power to change, to destroy, to create, to remake, at my own discretion."[3]

Davis was impressed with Palmer but made it clear to him that *Amazing* would have to be a crowd-pleaser—and aimed at young readers. As the writer and cartoonist Earl Binder soon after informed his brother, Otto, "One thing he [Davis] will insist upon firmly; THERE MUST BE MORE STORY AND HUMAN INTEREST THAN SCIENCE! . . . He wants . . . stories in which a likable group of characters took the reader to some delightful and engrossing adventures with just enough science to make it legal. Savvy?"[4] The new motto, "Every Story Scientifically Accurate," disappeared from the cover after the first two issues with Rap as editor. Not only the substance but also the style morphed. Rap's editorial, "The Observatory," following the format he had developed in "Spilling the Atoms," was brash, silly, and chummy. The Sloane era was over.

In Rap's first "Observatory," which he later called "rather stiffly" rendered, he insisted the stories would be "founded upon scientific research," yet offer the "tenseness of adventure and romance." He also noted, "As we took over the management of *Amazing Stories*, we stepped into a mighty big pair of shoes, when we stepped into those of Dr. T. O'Conor Sloane. . . . It is with humble hope that we can fill them to as satisfactory a degree as he did."[5] Within a few issues, Rap had settled into a new tone and format. "The Observatory" became a series of snippets, offering introductions to stories, tidbits about life behind the scenes at Ziff-Davis—he insisted frequently that he did no work whatsoever and was a complete cad—lolling about while his beautiful secretary Elaine labored away at the manuscripts; then there were excerpts from particularly derogatory letters to the editor, as well as anecdotes, profundities, and scientific "fun facts" to ponder. In July 1939, for example, he mulled over an artist's back-cover rendition of what was then a novelty, a "space suit." Rap wondered what a space explorer, in such a getup, would do to scratch an itch. "It might easily become a torment worse than Dante's Inferno and who knows whether or not we'll run into a patch of itching powder walking around on another world." The bizarro-world version of Sloane had arrived.

Palmer's early salary was contingent on sales, and Ziff-Davis planned to end the life of the then-struggling magazine if Palmer could not significantly increase its circulation. Palmer set to work with gusto. He tossed out the bulk of the backlog of stories that Sloane had kept and scrambled for new material that would be lively and fun for juvenile readers. As Earl Binder advised his writing partner and brother Otto (or "Otter") Binder that first year, "Ray picked stories like, Moon Mines, The Green Cloud of

Space, Thieves from ISOT, high adventure and lots of story. You will find they are easier to write than the conglomeration of scientific crapo that requires a text book in one hand and the mag in the other."

While chasing down good stories, Palmer also puzzled over appropriate art for the Ziff-Davis pulp covers. In 1928, when still an eighteen-year-old fan, Palmer had written to Gernsback complaining that he had interested a friend in *Amazing Stories* but his parents demanded his friend stop reading it when they saw the garish cover and deemed it "trash." Yet covers with sensational paintings in glorious, blaring colors were critical to drawing attention to the pulp magazines, whether detective pulps, true confessions, Westerns, air adventures, or science fiction. Despite the young Palmer's letter of concern, the covers of the science fiction magazines of the 1920s and 1930s, even if viewed as "trashy," were not as highly sexually charged as those in other pulp genres. Early on, Gernsback had insisted that scientifiction offered a clean alternative to sex stories. This template, briefly, held. At *Astounding*, for example, according to the lore, John W. Campbell's assistant Catherine Tarrant removed all sexual content from stories, leading writers to joke that "It cannot be too errant for Tarrant."[6]

The cover art in other pulp genres gloried in eroticism. Near-pornographic covers had long been a staple of *Weird Tales*, the fantasy pulp published in Chicago since 1923. Its very first issue showed a fully clothed woman enwrapped in giant tentacles, while a Gatsby-like hunter with slicked back hair tried to rescue her. Such scenes became far more risqué in the 1930s when bohemian artist Margaret Brundage took over the cover art. On Brundage's covers, semi- or fully naked women were threatened by giant pythons, elaborately tied up, offered to gods as human sacrifices, enraptured by sorcerers' spells, shown whipping one another, or bowing to weird idols. Brundage recalled having the *Weird Tales* editor Farnsworth Wright simply commenting after one of her first efforts, "Make the breasts bigger in the future." Brundage's women were not always victims—she

empowered some of her heroines, who posed languidly with black pan-
thers, cracked whips, led wolf packs, and bedazzled otherworldly creatures,
including the Devil.[7]

While the covers of *Weird Tales*, *Spicy Detective*, and *Scarlet Gang Stories*
were very racy in the 1930s, science fiction cover art still had a somewhat
stilted Victorian aspect in its renditions of weird-adventures-in-space. Artist
Frank Paul set the standard. Ghastly, tentacled aliens (aka BEMs) were
more likely to threaten crouching all-American men on most science fiction covers until the 1940s when science fiction gave up on protecting ju-
veniles' eyes and offered sexier fare.

Ziff-Davis owned *Popular Photography* and the proud new owners of
Amazing Stories made an odd experiment—instead of using painted artwork, they tried out color photography on the covers of the first two issues
that Palmer edited in 1938. The June photo cover featured a Buck Rogers–
type hero climbing up a rope ladder to a spaceship while supporting and
looking down at a swooning damsel, as if performing a tango in midair.
The next issue, in August, showed a barebacked man (it is rumored that
this was Palmer's friend, the horror and fantasy author Robert Bloch)
plunging a laser sword into a chained up woman. Neither of these women,
however, was unclothed à la Brundage nor could the photographer give
the images the zany energy that pulp artists guaranteed. The reader response was tepid.

Ziff-Davis returned to painted covers. It was not until the World War
Two years, when providing servicemen with pinup girls became a patriotic
duty, that science fiction (and *Amazing Stories*) began to turn regularly to
highly sensual covers, with renderings of erotic space damsels in peril al-
ternating with covers that featured bizarre landscapes or high-tech fight
scenes. Nevertheless, even as early as the late 1930s, *Amazing Stories* took a
more lurid turn with the hiring of artist Harold W. McCauley. Like Brundage, McCauley had studied at the Art Institute of Chicago. One of his
teachers was J. Allen St. John, who was well known for his misty covers for

Edgar Rice Burroughs's novels, including the Tarzan series. In addition to advertising work in Chicago, McCauley painted covers for Ziff-Davis's *Amazing, Fantastic Adventures*, and *Mammoth Detective*. His November 1939 cover for *Amazing* is a portent of things to come: a mad scientist poses at the giant dial of a strange device in front of two capsules that contain identical bathing beauties in red swimsuits—in a somewhat macabre strip-tease, one reveals all of her body—up to her bust—as a skeleton; presumably she is being X-rayed as the hunched-over madman works the dial.

The April 1941 *Amazing Stories* became the first to show a quasi-bare-breasted woman—in this case being attacked by a Siberian tiger on the steps of an Angkor Wat–inspired temple compound. Ironically, the story it illustrated, L. Taylor Hansen's "Lords of the Underworld," was written by a woman who masqueraded in print as a man—one of many female writers whom Palmer patronized.

Some of the sexier *Amazing Stories* covers in the 1940s, in addition to those by McCauley, were by Robert Gibson Jones, a commercial artist in Chicago who, in addition to advertising work, had illustrated Catholic cal-endars. Brundage's languorous doe-eyed beauties were out—as were the quasi-Victorian heroes and heroines in jodhpurs that once graced *Amazing*; by the mid-1940s, women wearing shiny brass bikini tops leaning on astro-nauts with ray-guns who zapped space aliens began to be common on the covers at *Amazing, Startling Stories*, and *Planet Stories*.

To increase *Amazing*'s allure, Palmer also added to each issue a back cover illustration instead of an advertisement—an innovation in the world of pulps. These back covers had an educational bent and many were by Gernsback's former stalwart Frank Paul. At first, Palmer insisted on culti-vating Chicago artists who were convenient to work with, but fans kept demanding that Paul be brought back. (Paul had concocted that first cover of *Amazing* with the view of Saturn from a comet, and he was exceptional at depicting strange worlds and stylish rocket ships but derided for his in-ability to draw appealing human figures, let alone space sirens.) On these back covers he did what he did best—primarily alien cityscapes such as "Life on Ganymede," "City on Venus," and "A City on Pluto." Paul also contributed renderings of imaginary aliens—such as "The Man from Mars," "The Man from Venus," and "Life on Mercury"—for the back covers of Ziff-Davis's companion pulp *Fantastic Adventures,* but these were eventually discontinued as the magazine shifted from soft science fiction to pure adventure. Palmer stuck to the educational back covers on *Amazing Stories.* In addition to Paul, local artists contributed renderings of carefully labeled devices of the future, such as the future ocean liner, future rocket train, an undersea salvager, the space devastator (shades of *Star Wars*'s Death Star), the "Stratosphere Airliner of 1988," and an atomic power plant (conceptualized fairly accurately in 1939).

With each issue, Palmer added readers. Early letters thanked him for bringing back some "pep" to *Amazing.* Although the magazine had a downscale reputation, this didn't stop up-and-coming teenage SF fan Isaac Asimov from sending in letters—he was quick, in November 1938, to comment on the first two covers' "super-ultra-horrible photographs." In the same letter, Asimov also criticized Palmer for featuring anti-Soviet propaganda. "Entirely too many stories are being printed part or all of whose theme is the reaction against some form of despotism." This criticism didn't stop Asimov from sending in work, and, in *Amazing,* Palmer ran the teenage Asimov's first two stories to see print. While some gave Palmer an E for effort, many of the era's "actifans," like space opera villains, sneered at Palmer's efforts. John W. Campbell had taken over the editorship of *Astounding* a year earlier and was pleasing highbrows with his demands for literary quality.

Palmer, admittedly, simply wanted to find stories that would sell. He printed some innovative stories, including Otto and Earl Binder's Atom Link series—the first story of which was "I Robot." It is told from the point of view of an anguished robot in search of acceptance, who notes, "You call me a monster, but you are wrong. Utterly wrong!" (Isaac

Palmer and associates at Ziff-Davis office, circa 1939. Walter
Dennis may be to Palmer's left. *Cushing Memorial Library and
Archives, Texas A&M University. Estate of Sam Moskowitz*

Asimov's publisher later insisted on borrowing the title "I Robot" for a
short story collection.) Likewise, Palmer published the work of Asimov,
Stanley Weinbaum, Ray Bradbury (one of whose early stories was titled "I,
Rocket"), and Edgar Rice Burroughs. Circulation built. Ziff-Davis put
Palmer on a regular salary rather than on a commission basis. In addition
to *Amazing*, Palmer soon after added the sister magazine *Fantastic Adventures* to intrigue the *Weird Tales* audience. In addition, Palmer began to
manage Ziff-Davis's new *Mammoth Western*, *Mammoth Adventure*, and *Mammoth Detective* pulps.

To fill all these magazines, Palmer slowly built up a stable of writers,
relying on his friends from the Fictioneers, as well as the fan ranks and
references from agents such as Julius Schwartz—his old contact from the
Science Fiction Digest who, with Mort Weisinger, had founded the SF literary
agency Solar Sales Service. (Weisinger, meanwhile, had moved on to edit
Thrilling Wonder Stories and a full line of other pulps for Standard Magazine.) In the early days, Bernard Davis would overrule Palmer on some

story choices, but Rap was given more freedom as circulation built and the magazine began to turn a profit.

Confession of a Happy Hack

Amazing Stories printed the sort of high-action stories with super-science (i.e., impossible gadget) content that Gernsback had grudgingly allowed to become the standard by the late 1920s in *Science Wonder Stories*. The sort of writing that Palmer liked was, in his own words, "hack"—without poetic phrasing. That all had to be "hacked" away. He told one writer, Robert Moore Williams, "Your stories all are a lot of 'pretty' writing. . . . If you'll take your next manuscript, blue-pencil *every* phrase that you consider to be *good* writing, I'll buy it."[8] He urged his stable of writers to peel off the fancy language and tell the story. Some of these stories, as was common practice at New York City pulp houses, were based on paintings that artists such as McCauley had already concocted. To unsure writers, Rap offered advice such as "Gimme bang-bang," or "When a story stops moving, that is the exact spot where the writer should drop a corpse through the roof"— pulp lore slowly changed this latter dictum to the even zippier, "When the action slows, throw another body through the skylight." (One of the first writers to report Palmer's "corpse through the roof" advice, Robert Moore Williams, suggested it was not to be taken literally, but meant, "Work that twist, brother.")

In October 1938, his first year on the job, Rap sent a call to writers for Ziff-Davis's new pulp *Fantastic Adventures* to be positioned in the weird field, noting, "Swift, dramatic action, with plenty of suspense and the anticipation of the fearful will be the keynote of each story. . . . The wild, or the utterly gruesome, or disgusting, is not wanted. . . . There will be a tinge of sex, but nothing obnoxious or suggestive. Sex may be used only where it is not dragged in just for effect."[9] After the success in 1939 of Nelson S.

Bond's "The Amazing Invention of Wilberforce Weems," about a babysitter and a magic potion, Rap pushed the *Fantastic Adventures* editorial policy toward similar whimsy—an approach that was the near antithesis of that of fantasy authors such as H. P. Lovecraft or Robert E. Howard (author of the Conan series, among others). Other stories were developed in a similar light vein, such as Bond's "The Unusual Romance of Ferdinand Pratt," Robert Bloch's "The Weird Doom of Floyd Scrilch," and Leroy Yerxa's "Freddie Funk's Madcap Mermaid."

Palmer's friend Robert Bloch was a skilled hand at such whimsical fantasy and lampooned an editor very much like Palmer in "The Man Who Walked Through Mirrors," a story published in the August 1939 *Amazing*. It opens with its hero, the pulp editor Stanhope, exhausted from the office visits of a stream of crackpots. Gazing into an office mirror, Stanhope concludes that he looks "like the devil." Then still another crackpot, Volmar Clark, visits. This writer is furious because Stanhope had rejected his story "Fourth Dimensional Mirrors" as it did not fulfill the magazine's motto: "Every Story Scientifically Accurate." Clark grabs hold of a magazine and says, "You call this stuff science? Robots and Martians and fungoid beings and opium-smoker's visions." He goes on to assure Stanhope that he, Clark, is a great scientist and would never make something up. Stanhope turns the crackpot from his office, but later switches on a device Clark left behind and ultimately the editor gets trapped in the mirror, a fact he only realizes when the logo of his magazine "Every Story Scientifically Accurate," reads backward on the front cover.

Ziff-Davis continued its foray into pulps, and, in the process, squeezed as much work out of Palmer as possible. After adding *Fantastic Adventures* they planned two new pulps for 1939, *South Sea Stories* and *Air Adventures*. *South Sea Stories*, which only survived for a few issues, was to "be strong in both romance and adventure. . . . Manuscripts must open with action. . . . Descriptive, slow-moving openings are out. . . . There should be plenty of the exotic south sea atmosphere, with beautiful girls and sex treated in a decent manner."[10] (It would appear that Joseph Conrad with his trancelike opening descriptions of foreign locales wouldn't have a chance in this publication.) Rap assured writers their manuscripts would be read quickly, and payment would be prompt—golden words to writers in any era, but particularly during the Depression.

Palmer, as a proud hack, was walking a tightrope. Serious science fiction fans looked at the revived *Amazing* with disdain—remarkably snobbish letters might arrive from fifteen-year-old readers—but this egalitarian element was part of what made the science fiction fan community so unique. The sober interests of the early science correspondence clubs had changed into something rich and strange. The days when Palmer could call himself "Fan No. 1, 3, and 4" were long gone.

Dozens of fanzines had arrived by the early 1940s, with titles such as *Agenbite of Inwit, Alchemist, Beyond, Cosmic Dust, En Garde, Fan-Dango, Polaris, Polymorph, Purple Flash, Satellite, Saturnalia, Shangri L'Affaires, Spaceways, Vampire, Voice of the Imagi-Nation, Vulcan, Wavelength,* and *YHOS (Your Humble Obedient Servant).* Regional fan societies, many of them quite formal, with regular elections, campaigns, fund-raising, and nitpicking arguments, were on the scene. National and international conferences were held, with the first World Science Fiction Convention, or Worldcon, held in Manhattan over the Fourth of July weekend, during the 1939 New York World's Fair. Artist Frank Paul was the guest of honor; 4E (or Forry) Ackerman attended in a "futuristicostume."

Fans' obsessions ranged from serious politics to outright silliness. At the first Worldcon, Sam Moskowitz and James Taurasi, two beefy leaders of the "New Fandom" group sponsoring the event, refused entrance to members of the "Futurians." This latter SF group was an offspring of the era's Popular Front politics (in which Communists were encouraged to work with other left-wing groups and liberals), and included members with varying progressive agendas, including Communist members who adhered to "Michelism." One of the Michelists had earlier announced,

"MICHELISM is the belief that science fiction followers should actively work for the realization of the scientific socialist world-state as the only genuine justification for their activities and existence."[11] The Futurians also published anti-Fascist statements that fit the contours of the Popular Front. The faddish Technocracy, Inc. and Alfred Korzybski's General Semantics movements also had converts among fans, or "fen," as did the Esperanto movement, which sought to promote a global language to further world unity and peace.

At conventions, meetings, and in fanzines, the fen engaged in the mock-heroic effort of creating a new universe as well as hatching new identities. Bright young women who appeared among the fen—and often took on nicknames such as Pogo (Mary Gray), Morojo (Myrtle R. Jones—a nickname based on her initials in Esperanto), and Tigrina (Alicia Aria)—were treated with near reverence. Fans' efforts in world building also involved developing new slang and founding mock religions, the first of which, Ghughuism, appeared in 1935. Ghuists worshipped as their "ghod" a beetlelike monster named "Ghughu" who lived on the planet Vulcan. Followers created a "Ghuist" calendar and drank "bheer," while its high priests were "ghuardians of the gholy ghrail." Ghughu was challenged in 1938 by the "Sacred Order of FooFoo," invoked at times as "by the Grace of Foo, of the fanish lands king, lord of the Obsequious Manor, etc." The female fan Pogo helped found Foo, whose followers became Foomen. Later came the Rosconians, who worshipped Roscoe, a god in the shape of a beaver, first revealed to fans in 1947. One of Ray Palmer's later assistants, Bea Mahaffey, swore her allegiance to Roscoe in a fanzine.

Fans who didn't just read science fiction, but also engaged in the world of fanzines and further participated in fan culture (and fannish religions) were known as "actifans." The new category of "stefnist" (likely derived from "scientifictionist") also evolved in the 1940s and referred to people who rarely bothered to read SF or fantasy but simply dedicated themselves to fan culture. By the late 1940s, fans prided themselves on holding a "long view" that placed human affairs in their appropriate galactic perspective. Perhaps, some suspected, they were a new breed entirely. With the popularity of A. E. Van Vogt's *Slan*, a story of a mutated super race hunted on Earth and first published as a serial in *Astounding* in 1940, "Slan shacks" began to open as places where fans might live together or find shelter while traveling.

Midwestern fans tended to be kinder to Palmer, one of their own, but serious SF readers generally had little sympathy for the all-action formula to which he adhered. As Howard Browne, a writer who later joined the Ziff-Davis staff, noted of the typical Palmer tale, "A raygun was a raygun, a space warp was a space warp, and no scientific details need apply. Alien invaders from west of Sirius were beaten back by armadas of Earth's spaceships commanded by steel-thewed heroes; bug-eyed monsters pursued lovely Earth maidens. What they intended to do with them was never made clear. The appeal was almost entirely visceral."[12] These tales, however, hooked less sophisticated readers—pleasing Rap's publishers. *Amazing*'s circulation climbed until it would eventually be the best-selling SF magazine of the 1940s, although it would always trail behind *Astounding* as second-string in terms of respectability and impact.

The usual, crude distinction made to describe SF's development in American pulps is that the genre began with Gernsback-flavored science fiction focused on science education and futuristic gadgetry. Literary quality was overlooked. A second early category of SF focused on action, in the vein of Edgar Rice Burroughs, author of *Tarzan*, *John Carter of Mars*, and similar romantic adventures. These high-spirited romances (i.e., adventure stories) ignored "serious" science altogether, but occasionally merged with the Gernsback gadget-filled tale. This was, undoubtedly, the vein that Palmer favored. But the third category, supposedly originating with Campbell, paid more attention to character and literary qualities and emphasized speculation on the possible social consequences of new technologies or beliefs. While Campbell did encourage excellence, such stories had been around from the beginning and had appeared in Gernsback's *Amazing Stories* and *Wonder Stories* as well. One accurate distinction is that Campbell's stories avoided sex whereas Palmer was encouraged to allow "tasteful" sex in his stories.

While *Amazing* was never as bad as its critics declared, and often published stories that exceeded its basic requirements, Palmer was aware of the emerging hierarchy and admired John W. Campbell, who had become editor of *Astounding Science Fiction* in 1937. (*Astounding*'s publisher, Street and Smith, which began as a nineteenth-century dime novel publishing house, did not necessarily gravitate toward the "intellectual" or "literary"; in addition to thousands of dime novels, story magazines, and numerous pulps, they published *Doc Savage* and *The Shadow*.) In science fiction histories, Campbell is depicted as the guiding spirit of SF's "golden age." According to Browne, when Palmer visited Campbell at the offices of *Astounding* in New York, he was utterly deferential. Campbell was apparently disdainful—feet up on his desk, puffing away on his cigarette in its holder, but willing to chat with his energetic, if jejune, rival.

At times, Palmer could be combative. Although one of his own stories was printed in an issue of *Astounding* edited by Campbell, Rap made fun of the "pretty writing" that Campbell favored and the pretentious titles of *Astounding*'s stories, noting, "I am afraid I can't imagine what a story titled: 'Xnix-4 Plus Quintessence' would be about. . . . It is, to put it plainly and simply, gibberish." Rap wrote in 1940, "I even admit that sometimes I read a story in *Astounding* with keen enjoyment, because I too, was once only a fan, and still like to go through a bit of mental calisthenics. . . . Why should *Amazing* invade *Astounding*'s field? The result would be two identical magazines. . . . Campbell would be a fool to imitate me. Thank God we are individualistic enough to stick by our own tenets."[13]

If not trying to win a battle of the minds with Campbell, Palmer certainly offered himself as the antidote to the "fuzz-ball" Sloane, who had edited *Amazing Stories* from its founding until its sale to Ziff-Davis. Unlike the elderly Sloane, Palmer was neither reserved nor courtly. Nor did he have a PhD, or indeed any college education. Instead, he bragged of getting bowling tips from pro bowler Ned Day. In literature and philosophy, Rap had a taste for the unorthodox, and in manner he was "one of the gang." His readers enjoyed his inside jokes, chummy editorials, columns with fan club announcements, and his regular-guy answers to letters. And they liked that he abbreviated his name to "Rap," which helped set an informal tone picked up in comic books' editorial pages as well. In "The Observatory" Palmer used the pronoun "we" to allow his fans to feel they were sharing the editor's chair, as seen in this comment about a new story: "We've seen his time machine ourselves, and believe us, it's quite a gadget. We once took a trip in it."

Palmer liked to pull tricks. As in this time machine report, he liked to put himself in the pulp action and to scuff the line between truth and fantasy. In a 1941 "Observatory," he noted: "Only this editor, and his new Buick, could sneak past a man with a flag in West Virginia, and get within a hundred feet of a charge of dynamite in the roadbed (which was under construction) before it went off. Having faced Martian invasions, and monsters on the moon, our usual courage asserted itself and we found ourselves crouching under a steam-shovel while rocks showered down." He later added, "At least that's how we explained the smashed fender to the rest of the office force! They don't have to believe it, if they don't want to. You don't either."[14]

Revealing his trickster streak visually, the July 1943 issue of *Amazing Stories* features Palmer's likeness on the cover as the evil scientist at the heart of the action of that month's "Carbon-Copy Killer." A syringe near his hand, he hunched over a recumbent, possibly drugged, beauty, whose head was flung back. Behind him stood a girl in a vaguely futuristic golden outfit pointing a gun at him. Just to add to the pulchritude, in the background a naked woman writhed in a giant, somewhat phallic test tube. Artist Harold W. McCauley was at it again—making his "boss" into a pulp villain. In that issue's "Observatory" Rap noted of the cover "a particularly obnoxious creature is being held at bay by a particularly good looking girl." He then told readers that he served as the model for the obnoxious scientist, while his secretary, Elaine, was the girl with the gun. (This was not her first appearance on the cover, either.) As for the recumbent figure in the clingy white dress: "McCauley just smiles when we ask him."

Ray Palmer, evil scientist, as rendered by Harold W. McCauley for the July 1943 *Amazing Stories. University of California Riverside Libraries, Special Collections & Archives*

Another favorite Rap trick was to write and print stories with pseud-onyms and then to talk up or malign these imaginary authors in "The Observatory" and run their fake biographies in the "Meet the Authors" feature. Some of the mock biographies read as "straight": the August 1939 presentation of Manhattan resident Alfred R. Steber (actually Palmer) in-

dicated that he was an average Joe, not yet thirty but tending toward bald-
ness, who, when not writing science fiction, liked to bowl, fish, and play
pinochle. He also admitted to being a soft touch and so claimed to usually
be broke. In October 1942, the saga continued, as Rap mentioned how
Alfred R. Steber had insisted of his latest story, "Don't give me a buildup.
If the yarn can't stand on its own feet, don't put it on a pedestal; immerse
it in concrete and dump it in the Chicago drainage canal."

Other hoax biographies took slapstick turns to signal the trick to readers. In 1943, Rap ran the biography of Frank Patton, another of his aliases.
Under the photograph of a rather dashing man with a slight mustache ran
text that indicated Patton had trained as a chemist and worked briefly at
the California Institute of Technology, "under the tutelage of the General
Electric scientists, but they finally decided I couldn't add anything to their
refrigerator, except maybe gas, and they had enough of that." The sketch
became even more farcical when Patton discussed his future plans. "After
the war, I plan to open my own little chemical 'works' and have a labora-
tory where I can putter around at a few things I've had in mind for a few
years. Maybe I'll be able to make plastics out of hot air, or rubber out of
clouds—who can tell."[15]

Lone Wolf as Pack Leader

While Rap had landed his dream job, he found life in Chicago difficult.
During his first months in the big city, when he was working on commission, his existence was precarious and, undoubtedly, lonely. While Milwaukee was not exactly a small town, Palmer missed "that heaven that is
Wisconsin." Chicago has never been an easy city and this would be particularly true in the 1930s, an era of bread lines, high unemployment, cor-
rupt politics, and powerful rackets. Though Rap was a tireless worker, who
put in late nights at 600 S. Dearborn laboring over manuscripts, examining

artwork, and tapping out his own stories to be published under pseudonyms, he was uncomfortable with the city. He was also poor.

According to Rap, following his rushed move to Chicago, he had to eat
"in cockroach-ridden hashhouses for six months" and to lodge "among the
drunks and dopes of a Clark Street rooming house." He later added, "I
came there as an abandoned person. I had no family, no friends. I often, late
at night, wandered through Chicago's south side, and often stopped at a
Negro restaurant for coffee. . . . The Negroes, from my very clothing, and
my lack of money to spend for a doughnut to go with the coffee, knew I
was 'one of them' in that I had nothing. They were very friendly."[16]

But Rap was a sociable man who did not long remain abandoned in the
city that Nelson Algren referred to as "the true jungle, the neon wilder-
ness." Slowly he built up a stable of regular artists and writers who were
required to turn in a set number of words per issue for a guaranteed
monthly paycheck. He would insist they show as a group on Fridays to
receive their checks and to play poker at his home, first in Chicago, then
later Evanston. For a while, he played on the Ziff-Davis softball team and
its bowling team. He also had a "coffee club" and could hoist a beer. He
let writer Otto Binder stay at his apartment when visiting from New York
City in 1940 and likely made his home available to other traveling members of the SF community.

Rap's twenty-second-floor office, number 12, also was open terrain for
SF writers and fans. Teenage fans would wander in and converse sincerely
about the merits and weaknesses of each issue of the magazine. They
would stare longingly at the stacks of original pulp art, including covers
by J. Allen St. John, who had helped shape the image of Tarzan, and Palmer
would send them home with one or two such handouts. Palmer liked to
"rap." One visiting writer recounted calling on Rap at Ziff-Davis and spending an "interesting four hours together. I took him out to lunch and then
steered him to a foam emporium. And never were words as closely crowded
per minute." In the early 1940s, Frances Deegan, an aspiring writer, decided

on a whim to visit Ziff-Davis. She recalled that the "reception room was elegant. But it was very informal inside. I simply walked in and said, 'Do you mind if I write something for you?' And Mr. Palmer said, 'No, go right ahead.' I went home and wrote a story, and he bought it."[17] (The resulting story, "The Martian and the Milk Maid," was published in *Fantastic Adventures*.)

In 1942, Howard Browne, an excellent writer of detective stories and a good imitator of Edgar Rice Burroughs, joined the staff—specifically to oversee *Mammoth Detective*, but also to help out on the other pulps. A new desk was added to office 12. Shortly after his arrival, in "The Observatory," Rap bragged about Browne's skill as a bowler and the brilliance of his Tarzan-inspired "Tarn the Caveman" stories and noted that as he typed his praises Browne kept reminding him that he spelled his name with a final *e*.

Browne—who had grown up in a foster home and a reformatory and previously worked as a bill collector—was delighted to join the fiction magazines at Ziff-Davis, but he noted that they were at a lower caste level than the editors of Ziff-Davis's slick magazines. "They wore Brooks Brothers suits and Sulka ties and tucked away three-martini lunches at the Tip Top Inn; our wardrobes came from Goldblatt's and we dined on hamburgers and cokes at a nearby beanery. But would we have traded places with them? Yes."[18] Like a true hard-boiled detective writer, Browne recalls of the "stunning" Elaine, "I was to spend a lot of time planning ways to get rid of her husband."

During his bachelor years in Chicago, the space opera stories that Palmer wrote, such as "Outlaw of Space"—under the pseudonym of Wallace Quitman—and later, "The Lone Wolf of Space," by A. R. Steber and Joseph J. Millard, indicated his general state of mind. The "Outlaw of Space" (published in August 1938) featured as its antihero a lonely, angry man, with a hard-boiled sensibility. This gruff outlaw, who has been cheated out of patent rights, turns renegade and leaves Earth to roam outer space,

Palmer with Howard Browne, mystery writer and assistant editor at *Amazing Stories*, 1944. *Copyright © Locus Publications*

determined to gain vengeance. He disables a spaceship and nearly molests a fetching young woman he later realizes is the fiancée of his only son. Recognizing the error of his ways, he helps the young lovers reunite without ever revealing his identity.

The "Lone Wolf of Space" (May 1941) offered a similar outline: "The Martians blasted all that was dear to Buford and he became a raging wolf of space to get revenge." Buford was a skilled member of Earth's Space Guard, hardened in the wars against the Martian Tigermen. Buford's fiancée, Diana, is kidnapped. He gives chase. The Tigerman he duels resembles a Mexican bandit in a Western. As the Martian strokes his feline whiskers "with a furry, clawed hand," he offers macho insults such as "But you must be tired after your flight, pupo." (A footnote explained, "Pupo is a martian worm, the lowest form of life on the planet.") Eventually Buford prevails. Together with Diana—or "shoulder to shoulder, partner," as she says—they bravely plan an attack to save Earth from the Martians and their human collaborators.

Rap needed someone to stand "shoulder to shoulder" with. The lone wolf was still on the prowl. Through the young Chicago science fiction fan and fanzine editor William Hamling—who later became the publisher of *Rogue* magazine—Palmer was introduced to Leroy Yerxa, who wrote and published crime and science fiction stories. One afternoon in October 1942, Frances Yerxa, Leroy's wife, invited Palmer to their apartment on Chicago's north side for dinner.

Rap drove up in his bright red 1941 Buick convertible with white sidewall tires. In October, Chicago would be at its finest, the leaves on trees yellow, red, brown. The skies blue. Leaves skittered near the curb as he pulled over and checked the address. A handsome young woman was holding two babies and leaning over a station wagon loaded with more small children. The driver looked bored. The woman in the midst of all these young children enchanted him. Like a goddess with her charges. Pulp editors knew a hot dame when they saw one. To Rap, she was a dream come true.

Later in his visit, the same young woman, Marjorie Wilson, appeared in the Yerxas' apartment to get some milk from the refrigerator. He learned that along with Frances she ran the day care center on the first floor. She had been born in Indiana, but her family moved shortly after to a Michigan farm where she and Frances had attended high school together. Before she left the room, Ray invited the Yerxas and the young woman to a play. They agreed. Perhaps winks were exchanged.

A skilled card player, Rap could not hide the defects that kept the draft board from urging his entry into the military, but he could highlight his strengths, which included wit, charm, intelligence, drive, and the red convertible—a stylish car, high set, that had traces of rocketry in the flare of its fenders and its chrome streamlining. The night of the play, Ray showed up in the convertible with only two tickets and whisked a bemused Marjorie away. She realized that he was a bit of a show-off, but also, deep down, a gentleman. They hit it off. Although diminutive and hunchbacked, after the first wave of shock, people always just saw him as Ray, tough-minded but with a gentle heart.

They began dating. Marjorie enjoyed his company. She was an accomplished pianist, and her family had a taste for the unconventional—her older sister, Mildred, would eventually write essays for *Amazing Stories* on weird science topics such as "Inside the Earth" and "Death Trap for Giants." Her life had not been easy. In order to attend high school, Marjorie, as well as her friend Frances, had had to leave their family farms and board with and work for families in town near the school. Marjorie graduated high school in 1935. She recalled days of looking for work when she would have soup for lunch and then save the crackers for her dinner. For two and a half years she worked at an orphanage in Lake Bluff, Illinois. During the war years, many of the able-bodied men were in uniform, women were working factory jobs, and the need for day care was intense. Frances had persuaded Marjorie, then working as a nanny in Michigan, to come to Chicago to set up a day care center. Marjorie's organizational skills helped them navigate the many regulations required.[19]

The man in the red Buick with a ready grin and the toughness of a pulp editor entered her life with a blast of determination. He was certain she was the woman for him. After two months, on Christmas 1942, they were married and soon after purchased a house in Evanston, one of Chicago's leafy northern suburbs that allowed an easy El train ride downtown. She accompanied Rap on one of his many trips to New York City, and he introduced her to his science fiction colleagues. They took in some Broadway shows (Rap complained that smoking was allowed in New York City theaters) and witnessed an early demonstration of television in their hotel. He was a lone wolf no longer. Before the war's end, their first child, Linda, would be born—on Christmas Day 1943. Two more healthy children, Jennifer and Raymond Bradley, would follow her. Rap doted on them and was delighted, however irrational the concern, that they had no deformities.

Fighting the Nazis from Office 12

On December 7, 1941, the Japanese attacked the U.S. fleet at Pearl Harbor. The following day the United States declared war on Japan, and three days later added declarations of war against Germany and Italy. Comic books and pulp magazines that hadn't already joined the war effort now did so. In a *Look* magazine article from February 27, 1940, nearly two years before the United States entered the war, in a short comic strip, Superman brought both Joseph Stalin and Adolf Hitler to the League of Nations and demanded they be tried as war criminals. Also prior to Pearl Harbor in March 1941, the first *Captain America* debuted with a cover showing Captain America punching out a cowardly Adolf Hitler while the captain's young ally, Bucky, in an inset, gives the reader a snappy salute. Both *Superman* and *Captain America* continued to feature their heroes working with the United States armed forces to defeat foreign tyrants.

The pulp magazines also went patriotic. While scenes of contemporary warfare were only rarely splashed onto the cover of *Amazing Stories*, Palmer's editorials frequently highlighted the war effort. He would use the guise of science fiction to speculate on new weapons or methods of solving shortages. As the young Isaac Asimov had pointed out in his letter, Palmer had never been shy about promoting the superiority of the American way, and now *Amazing Stories* became a vehicle for direct propaganda. Palmer had particularly harsh words for the Japanese following Pearl Harbor. In April 1942, he wrote in "The Observatory," "Speaking of the Japs, not so long before the Pearl Harbor treachery, we received a protest from Japanese sources against the use of the term Jap in referring to the coward-race.

Therefore, knowing that is it insulting to them we shall hereafter refrain from using any other term."

The following month, while speaking appreciatively of the United States's efforts to arm for war, Palmer mused over the possibility of enlisting super science weaponry, "What we wouldn't give for a fleet of those Martian rocket ships, or a couple of D-ships powered by atomic power, and bristling with disintegrator rays!" He went on to praise the new gadgets that American ingenuity was offering the military. The next month he argued that powerful explosives could be made from the chemical inositol, which could be extracted from waste corn, and added, "Let's blow up the joint!"

With the government's encouragement, in the pulps women were featured as aiding the war effort in varying guises. In August 1942, Rap facetiously mentioned that "The Mac Girl will not be in the army after all, because maybe someone noticed how many of the boys have her pasted up over their bunks, and she's worth more to morale on our cover than in a tank." The September 1943 issue followed a "women in war work" theme that the government had requested that magazines highlight. To pitch in, Rap used the Frank Patton alias for the story "War Worker 17": "Mary's job was helping to turn out the weapons of war—but then suddenly she found herself snatched into a world where the menace of war had no end."

Palmer frequently expressed plain, simple patriotism. In the September 1942 issue he announced, "V for Victory! That's the battle cry of this issue of *Amazing Stories*." The cover story, "Blitz Against Japan," showed a somewhat futuristic bomber jet targeting a squadron of battleships. The August 1943 issue, in honor of the Fourth of July, included a story by Frank Patton, "A Patriot Never Dies." The cover superimposed Colonial soldiers holding an early American flag with futuristic soldiers wearing gas masks behind streamlined machine guns. Its blurb: "Like a ghost he came onto the battlefield. But no ghost fought as this man did. Who or what was he?" Patriotism also could be incorporated into everyday life. In January 1943,

Rap noted that drivers who insisted on exceeding the 35-mile-per-hour speed limit urged in order to conserve gas should be beeped at to get them to slow down. That was "the way to regulate that wasteful speeding without the necessity of a flock of policeman. V for Victory! Give it to 'em, right on the horn!"

Then there were war-themed contests. In March 1944, *Amazing Stories* ran the results of one in which readers were asked to prepare a story based on an illustration that depicted Adolf Hitler in a futuristic vehicle next to a bug-eyed, lizard-skinned monster in armor. The prize was a $1,000 war bond, which would be doubled to $2,000 if the winner was a member of the armed forces. Rap remarked that he had been surprised at how many women had prepared entries. He noted that the stories tended to be grouped around four premises: (1) Hitler kidnapped by aliens; (2) Hitler taken on a tour of hell by the devil; (3) A Nazi lab monster (secret weapon) turning on its master; (4) a god of war taking Hitler on a tour of wars past.

As another wartime stunt, the September 1944 *Amazing Stories* was a special "service-written" issue. Members of the military contributed all of the stories. The authors included some former members of Rap's stable, since drafted, including Lieutenant William Lawrence Hamling ("Overlord of Venus") and Sergeant William P. McGivern ("The Thinking Cap"). McGivern's frequent writing partner, David Wright O'Brien, whose story "Private Prune Speaking" also appeared in that issue, died in the war that year during a bombing raid over Berlin. Much of the issue's art also came from servicemen, including Private First Class Julian S. Krupa, who painted dozens of front and back covers for *Amazing Stories* during the Palmer years. Such an issue wouldn't be complete without at least one decoy, in this case Rap (or Leroy Yerxa) took on the name Sergeant Morris J. Steele and wrote "Weapon for a WAC."

O'Brien's death shocked Rap. Soon after, Rap's younger brother, Dave, was killed during the Battle of the Bulge in the winter of 1944–45. Palmer first received a letter from his brother saying that he would be coming home as a result of an injury. But the note was written in a woman's handwriting, probably by a nurse. Sometime after, Ray received the message that his brother was dead. His left leg had been blown off. Long before this family tragedy, however, Rap had begun to develop war weariness. His thoughts took a utopian turn while trying to picture the postwar world. In a position that he would utterly repudiate in later years, he began to imagine the value of a world government that would prevent such wars.

In January 1943, he remarked, "It's time, we think, for Democrats, Republicans, Socialists, Communists—everyone with any idea of freedom in their heads, to begin planning just what kind of world state we are going to vote in when this is all over. . . . No 'party' is going to be responsible for winning this war . . . this Victory is for free, united, equal men." He followed this thought, in the summer of 1943, with a desire, at the very least, for greater solidarity in the Americas. He wrote that world solidarity could be greatly advanced "by beginning to weld the two American continents into a unit that will become a peaceful leader toward a future civilization that will stagger our imaginations. Scientific miracles will be accomplished. . . . The greatest barrier to the super civilization that is to come after the war is understanding."

Like the followers of Esperanto in the 1930s, who hoped to create a unified world, this dreamier Rap believed in human potential and progress—primary tenets of the science fiction "faith." Yet at the war's close when he began promoting what he called the Shaver Mystery, and presenting it as another fulfillment of human potential, many actifans blamed him for "killing" not only *Amazing Stories* but science fiction.

THE
ALPHABET
FROM
OUTER SPACE

3

I'm nuts about science fiction, and can't help messing around
with it.

—RAY PALMER, *IMAGINATIVE TALES*, NOVEMBER 1955

Since you are one of the few people who ever troubled to exercise
his brain enough to understand my antique alphabet, I'm hoping
you will do the same with this tale.

—RICHARD SHAVER, DECEMBER 1943

Several writers were in the office that early winter afternoon
of 1943. Howard Browne, Rap's hefty assistant editor, was
rummaging through letters, looking for samples to publish in
"Discussions"—the letters page. As Robert Bloch's story about the editor
Stanhope had illustrated, crank letters were common at Ziff-Davis's fiction
group. Yet such letters, from way out in left field, can enliven an editor's
day. Browne read aloud excerpts from one crackpot's correspondence for
laughs and then tossed it into the garbage can. When he was done, Ray
Palmer fished the crumpled pages out of the garbage, saying, "You call
yourself an editor?"

The six-page letter was from a Pennsylvania steelworker, Richard S. Shaver, who likely had serious mental problems and believed he had discovered the key to an ancient alphabet, part of a language that he subsequently named "Mantong" (man tongue). The letter opened, "Am sending you this in hopes you will insert in an issue to keep it from dying with me." Shaver claimed Mantong was a universal language, rather like an Esperanto for an ancient race that predated mankind, noting of it, "This language seems to me to be definite proof of the Atlantean legend." Each letter and/or phonetic sound of the Western alphabet corresponded to a concept from this root language. (In Shaver's language, for example, A represents "Animal," E "Energy," and P "Power," so the word *ape* forms the meaning "animal with power and energy.") After offering the entire alphabet, he added, "It is an immensely important find, suggesting the god legends have a base in some wiser race than modern man. . . . It should be saved and placed in wise hands. I can't, will you? . . . I need a little encouragement."[1]

Palmer handed the crumpled pages back to Browne, and said, "Let's run the entire thing in next issue's letter column."

Browne's response: "As a fledgling editor anxious to learn the trade, I'd love to know why you want it run."

Palmer smiled and said, "One of these days, I'll tell you why."[2]

Rap had a hunch. It was early winter in Chicago. Out on the streets puffs of fog came from people's mouths as they hurried in overcoats to jobs. Similar puffs came from the mouths of cattle herded by cowboys at the stockyards to the west. Out in Rap's neighborhood of rambling houses in Evanston, the elm trees were bare. Nights were cold and stars sharp in the skies. Frost etched the windows. Thoughts deepened. Marjorie was pregnant and due to have their first child—only weeks after the letter arrived, their daughter Linda was born. Could he support an even larger family? Yes. Rap was commanding a good salary: $10,000 a year—far more than he had as a pulp writer. He was a lucky guy.

As always, though, Rap was restless. He was teeming with ideas and one of them was to more clearly connect his interests in things mystic with science fiction. Or more precisely, he wanted to connect science fiction with an unexpected reality. Why had people believed Orson Welles's Mercury Theater broadcast of *The War of the Worlds* on Halloween 1938? As Rap, then the fledgling editor at *Amazing Stories*, had explained it a few months later, it was because science fiction had stretched people's minds, preparing them. "They accepted the reality of the danger because they believed in the possibility of invaders from other planets. No longer is man earth-bound, except in body. His mind has already recognized other worlds in addition to his own." Later that same year, hadn't he, Rap, noticed a strange light in the sky from the office's twenty-second-floor window? "It remained for maybe ten minutes, then faded. A mirage, you might say, but your editor got a great kick out of announcing the arrival of the Martians to his fellow editors on the staff of *Radio News*, *Popular Photography* and *Popular Aviation*."³

Five years later he was prepared to chase down this mirage. This strange letter from Richard Shaver gave him a feeling of promise. He had a hunch about Shaver and his bizarre alphabet. Just as a reporter could sniff out a story, Rap sensed a treasure trove in the recesses of his strange correspondent's imagination. The letter would be a trial balloon. And if he was wrong, so what? He had printed one letter from a crackpot.

Shaver's "alphabet" appeared in the January 1944 *Amazing Stories*. It included an editor's note asking readers to try it out and see what percentage of root words made sense when the alphabet was applied—would it be higher than pure chance? Rap told readers, "Our own hasty check-up revealed an amazing result of 90% logical and sensible! Is this really a case of racial memory, and is this formula the basis of one of the most ancient languages on Earth?" Dozens of readers responded. Many discussed the philological value of Shaver's discovery while others scoffed, curious why the interstellar root language depended so highly on English-based phonetics to impart its concepts.

If Palmer is to be believed, what began as a lark—or a dare—soon was to create a genuine personal crisis—with some paranoid overtones. It also marked the beginning of a long and trying friendship. Even prior to printing the alphabet, Rap asked Shaver to send in a story. They mailed letters back and forth. Within weeks, Rap received a ten-thousand-word manuscript called "A Warning to Future Man." Shaver introduced it with the note, "I would like to work for you, if you like any of my writing tell me what you want. I am a little rusty, I have been roaming for ten years, not writing. I have trouble typing, both mental and from frozen hands."[4]

Palmer found "A Warning to Future Man" fascinating. The rambling text described the outlines of a secret world Shaver had accessed. There were few characters, except for the letter writer, and a vague story line. The prose was weak, yet the story indicated a wild imagination at work. Shaver, a fan of fantasy authors Edgar Rice Burroughs and Abraham Merritt, knew his underground civilizations.

Beneath the earth, Shaver asserted, were vast caverns and remnants of ancient races. Interstellar beings, the Titans and the Atlans, had come to earth millions of years ago but had fled once they realized the sun's rays damaged their health. Some remained behind, underground, along with technological artifacts. Many of these "abanderos," affected by the detrimental energy from the sun, degenerated into evil *deros* bent on destroying mankind with evil ray machines. Others, the *teros,* were trying to help people with beneficial rays. These elder races were also the ancestors of modern humans.

Shaver's strange world had imaginative flair and a curious logic. Perhaps less flair than Edgar Rice Burroughs, but more logic. It opened possibilities. Palmer wrote to Shaver on January 14, 1944, and said, "I am certainly going to buy it, and I will do much re-writing." With some amusement, Palmer put some fresh paper into his typewriter and recrafted the letter of warning into the thirty-thousand-word pulp story "I Remember Lemuria."

Palmer placed great hopes in "I Remember Lemuria." It offered a new course for *Amazing Stories*, a new mutation for science fiction, and a way to bring in a wider audience. Palmer held on to the new story for a while, as he wanted to build it up and persuade Ziff-Davis to give him free rein in its promotion. By May 1944, he was ready to start the hype. Rap noted, "For the first time in its history, *Amazing Stories* is preparing to present a true story. But it is a story you won't find in the newspapers. . . . We, the editors believe the story. . . . We may bring down a hurricane of debate and perhaps even scorn on our heads. But let it come!" Browne and the rest of the staff had little faith in the "truth" of "I Remember Lemuria," but Palmer insisted he was running with it. When he promised to cloak the "truth claims" in a reference to racial memory, Bernard Davis gave the go-ahead.

While Shaver had referred to an Atlantean civilization in his letter, in his revision of "A Warning to Future Man," Palmer more firmly set the narrative in the underground realm of Lemuria. Lemuria, or "Mu" for short, to followers of Theosophy, is one of the great lost civilizations—an ancient continent swallowed by the Pacific, a twin of Atlantis. Tales of the lost civilizations of Atlantis and Lemuria intrigued Madame Helena Blavatsky, who in 1875 had founded the highly influential Theosophical Society. Her teaching, purportedly, recaptured the lost wisdom of these root races.

Nineteenth-century scientist Philip Sclater first proposed the idea of Lemuria as a sunken continent. He was unsure why there were fossil remains of lemurs on mainland India and also on Madagascar, just off the coast of Africa, but not in Africa. In his 1864 article "The Mammals of Madagascar," he proposed the existence of a once great continent that had broken up into smaller islands and dubbed the hypothetical landmass Lemuria. Other scientists considered the notion of a land bridge or continent to explain other similarities in flora, fauna, and geological formations. Even before plate tectonics emerged, the Lemuria concept fell into disrepute and was interwoven with pseudoscience. Photographer and amateur archaeologist Augustus Le Plongeon claimed that his translations of Mayan writings confirmed the existence of Lemuria and Atlantis and the influence of refugees from these lost continents on other civilizations. British inventor and occultist James Churchward published several books in the 1920s describing the wonders of the civilization of Lemuria and examples of its written language.

When Palmer titled Shaver's story "I Remember Lemuria," he sought to attract readers who would know of Theosophy and Churchward's works. The content of the story had little to do with occultist theory though. Its sources were standard space opera added to the pulp writings of H. P. Lovecraft, Robert E. Howard, Edgar Rice Burroughs, and Abraham Merritt.

"I Remember Lemuria" was featured in the March 1945 *Amazing Stories*. Readers sent in what became an enormous stack of letters to Ziff-Davis offering both praise and denunciation. It was phenomenal. More Shaver stories were to come. Shaver had worked out an entire universe adequate as a setting for a pulp saga. From 1945 to 1949, at least two dozen Shaver stories were published in *Amazing*. Most of them made the cover. Some were long enough to be published as novels. They were a strange amalgam: pulp science fiction that Palmer hyped as thinly veiled versions of the truth. While the Shaver stories amused some as good yarns and infuriated others as outrageous nonsense, Shaver's paranoid vision beckoned to many as genuine. That he could convince so many to start looking in caves to search for abandoned technology and confront evil dero indicates the very permeable boundary between creativity and madness.

Palmer's decision to pull Shaver's letter out of the garbage can became fateful. A year later, Palmer would lose his younger brother at the Battle of the Bulge, but in Shaver, he gained not only a writer whose stories could sell magazines, but a friend who became the most important figure in his creative life for the decades that followed.

Mr. Shaver's Universe

Shaver, born in 1907 and just a few years older than Palmer, had led a knockabout existence. Richard Shaver was the second youngest of five children.[5] According to Shaver, during his childhood, his father, Zeba Shaver, bought, sold, and operated restaurants, moving the family from town to town. (Zeba, of Dutch descent, apparently had a prominent seventeenth-century ancestor, Jean Mousnier de la Montagne, a Huguenot émigré to the Netherlands, who served as a physician and vice director of the Dutch colonies in North America.) Census accounts suggest that Zeba Shaver's family did their moving among different towns in Pennsylvania, with Zeba variously employed as a steel mill press operator, jeweler's clerk, furniture salesman, and as a chef at a college in Philadelphia.

The family had literary leanings. Taylor Shaver, one of Richard Shaver's older brothers, churned out stories for *Boy's Life*, and his mother, Grace, contributed poetry to women's magazines and wrote "True Confession" style stories. His younger sister, Isabelle, later became an advertising copywriter. Shaver had been an early science fiction fan and like Palmer and others had bought the first issue of *Amazing Stories*. Shaver told Palmer that he "had a genius IQ in high school," and that before turning to writing, he had been "an artist, rigger, tramp, etc."[6] As a young man, Shaver worked stints as a meat cutter and with a landscaping company that specialized in moving large trees. In 1930, when he was in his early twenties, he left Philadelphia. With financial help from his brother Taylor, he moved to Detroit and attended art classes at Wicker School of Fine Arts, worked as a life model for art classes, painted portraits on commission, and was possibly involved in bootlegging.[7]

As the Great Depression deepened and FDR's blue eagles (the National Recovery Administration insignia) and the NRA motto "We Do Our Part" appeared on business windows to improve morale, radical politics became more popular throughout the country. Violent strikes were common, both in agricultural and industrial areas, such as Detroit. In 1932, John Schmies, a popular Communist candidate for mayor of Detroit, organized a march from Detroit to the Dearborn Ford factory to present worker demands; the protest ended in a riot and the deaths of at least four marchers. Identifying with labor, Shaver joined the John Reed Club in Detroit in 1930, made fiery speeches, and admired the notorious murals of leftist artist Diego Rivera completed at the Detroit Institute of Arts in 1932–33. By 1933, New Deal legislation had decriminalized strikes, and organized labor gained new strength.

The same year, while employed as a spot welder at the Briggs Auto Body Plant, Shaver married one of his art teachers, Sophie Gurvitch. Sophie was an accomplished local artist who gained recognition at annual exhibitions in Michigan with canvases such as *Morning* and *Composition: Diana.* The following year, their daughter, Evelyn Ann, was born. As Shaver described this period, "I had studied writing and science and art, was married, almost owned a seven thousand dollar home and was well pleased with myself and the world."[8]

Shaver, then, was not simply a working stiff, but a bohemian intellectual of sorts. While visiting the art exhibits at the 1933 Chicago "Century of Progress" World's Fair, he might easily have ventured to the Dill Pickle Club near Bughouse Square in Chicago; the club had been started as a speakeasy by an IWW (International Workers of the World, or "Wobblies") member, but lasted beyond Prohibition, providing a venue for freethinkers, radicals, prostitutes, lawyers, and hoboes to gather between bouts of haranguing the passersby in the park. The door of the alley entrance was painted with the slogan: "Step High, Stoop Low, Leave Your Dignity Outside." Inside, pulp artist Margaret Brundage, who daubed racy covers for *Weird Tales,* had met her husband, IWW member Slim Brundage, a Dill Pickle bartender.

Shaver's life fell apart in 1934 when his brother Taylor died suddenly.

Distraught, Shaver, still a young man in his twenties, became convinced that a demon named Max was responsible for Taylor's heart failure. "The thing that killed him has followed me ever since—I talk to him—many times every day. . . . He has killed many people. . . . Others are holding him [Max] in check."[9] Taylor's death crushed Shaver, who said their plans were "intertwined." He told Palmer, "I drank a pint of whiskey right down after my brother died—and I guess it helped—but it was agony anyway for we were very close. I prefer the embalming fluid experience if I had my choice."[10] What others might call a psychotic episode began soon after when Shaver was on the factory line. One workday, when his welding gun was on, he began to overhear the thoughts of his fellow workers. He then realized their thoughts were influenced by very destructive, mocking voices that he could also detect. For example, he overheard one worker wondering how he could tell a girl that the guy she was dating was no good, then wondering whether bothering to tell her would do any good. The destructive voice wickedly quipped, "Put him on the rack. It'll pull him apart in an hour."

Shaver later deduced that these mocking voices that plagued all of humanity belonged to the underground civilization of the dero, or "detrimental robots"—descendants of the star settlers who had absorbed so much "*dis* particle" energy from the sun that they could only do evil. In Shaver's mind anyone locked into a repetitive life pattern was a *ro*—a sort of organic robot—or, to shift metaphors, a zombie. New growth of thought was needed to break from the ro state. All this was hard-won knowledge, born of years of confusion and disorientation. In an earlier time, Shaver would have stuck to the vocabulary of demonology and witchcraft. By the 1940s, he gift-wrapped his worldview in science fiction. First came awareness of the demon named Max, then the voices and visions, and then the final revelation of the dero underground. It all proved too much. He could no longer function coherently.

In 1934, at the height of the Depression, Shaver's wife, Sophie, had him

institutionalized in the Ypsilanti State Hospital. As if a scene from a melo-drama, when he was released two years later, he learned that his wife was dead. She had accidentally electrocuted herself in the bathtub by touching the power wire on a new electric heater, a gift from friends. His young daughter, Evelyn Ann, now lived with his in-laws, Benjamin and Anna Gurvitch, who wanted nothing to do with Shaver. The following year he was declared "mentally incompetent" and the Gurvitch family was granted custody of his daughter. When she was growing up, they told the girl that her father was dead.

So began for Shaver a period of drifting that included at least one stint in jail in Canada—apparently after he had stowed away on a freighter—and at least one more visit to a mental hospital.[11] He slept in flophouses and tramped through the woods. He recalls being thrown off a bus at a border crossing on the way to Montreal for lack of fare. It was a cold night. With only a bedroll, he headed into the woods, made a fire, and hung up the blanket to reflect heat his way. In the morning he kicked earth over the fire. His loneliness was aided by voices that occasionally praised him at this time saying, "You are certainly a woodsman, you are as comfortable out here as the people in their warm homes—and you put out your fire too."[12] Good rays also sent *stim* his way, offering sexual pleasure and pain relief following different injuries, such as a broken leg.

Shaver eventually recast this dark period of his life, which resembled an allegorical descent into hell, as a literal journey underground, a variant on a shamanistic initiation ending in illumination. First came a period of confusion and disorientation. Addled by the dero, "the subtle energy of the telepathy machines" and their "rays and forces," he made bad decisions and admitted that he ended up in a state prison—although this more likely was an institution for the criminally insane. Alternately, he said he had been kidnapped and imprisoned by the dero underground for what he claimed was a period of eight years (which might cover 1934–42). There, or through the aid of mysterious projecting machines, he witnessed some of the deros'

depravities firsthand: in a letter to Palmer he mentioned how the dero would treat kidnapped women. "A beautiful girl is draped over a special kind of divan and wired full of sex stim [sexual stimulation devices]—then used casually as ornamental upholstery—to sit on—for it is pleasant to feel the stim through her body."[13]

Shaver on his Wisconsin farm in the late 1940s, after his wandering years. *Hidden World*, Fall 1962. *Department of Special Collections, Davidson Library, University of California, Santa Barbara*

Yet there was hope for Shaver in this bleak descent. In much of religious vision literature, whether chronicling the mystic experiences of ascetic monks, nuns, or shamans, the more fortunate seers, when they enter the underworld, are attended by a *psychopomp,* or guide, to lead them through hell's horrors then on to glimpses of heaven. Shaver's psychopomp also arrived. While serving a twenty-day sentence in jail in Newfoundland for stowing away on a ship, a *ray* (that is, a tero) named Sue came to him. "Sue brought every animal and insect into my cell to make mystic love to me." Heavenly pleasures mixed with hellish visions. He recalled a woman with a spider's body visiting him in his cell, offering both horror and ecstasy. He reported, "It mounted me and playfully bit me—its fangs shooting me full of poison—tobacco juice you know—with appropriate sexual sensations of impregnation. After a time my skin began to pop with little spiders and they swarmed out of me by the million."[14] Sue, his kind visitor, also had a blind daughter with whom he fell in love. He called her Nydia. They became lovers. Nydia helped teleport him to an underground cavern where he saw amazing machinery and a chamber where the thought records and history of the Elder Races were recorded.

The Elder Races, before fleeing into outer space, had left behind fantastic machinery—or "antique" *mech*—that could be used for good ("integrative") or evil ("detrimental") purposes. These included *telaug* (thought augmentation) devices that could provide telepathic contact and project or influence thoughts. The dero controlled much of this technology. They often captured humans as slaves, roasted and devoured them, and enjoyed orgies with human captives prompted with *stim-ray* machines that evoked sexual arousal and could be adjusted to varying levels. Teros, descendents of the same races (as, apparently, were humans), yet still possessing some decency, tried to hold off the deros from their twisted plans. Two key words in the Shaver lexicon were dis to represent "disintegrative" energy, and *tamper*. No act was too petty for the deros to tamper with. If you were in a car crash, this was a result of tamper. If you could not find your keys in the morning, this was an act of tamper.

As in a worldview based on witchcraft, there were no accidents. Everything was the result of intent. All problems could be traced to the dero, while the tero could help fend off such attacks. (When Shaver wanted help from his tero friends he would make a ruckus, throw his shoes on the floor and yell to get their attention, then ask for their help.) This general vision of life on earth—that Shaver slowly amplified into a grand scheme that included a cosmology and new sciences—became the basis for the Shaver tales that began to appear in *Amazing* for the next five years.

His wanderings ended with a long stay at Ionia State Hospital, an asylum for the criminally insane in Michigan. In May 1943, he was released into the custody of his parents, Zeba and Grace, in Barto, Pennsylvania.

His father died the following month. Shaver began work as a crane operator at Bethlehem Steel and remarried in early 1944. The marriage lasted only a few months; soon after, in October 1944, he met and married a young local woman, Dorothy "Dottie" Erb. This marriage helped ground him and ended his wandering—although he admitted at times to bouts of wanderlust. In this period of calm, he sat down and wrote a letter to the editor of *Amazing Stories* that ended with the plea, "I need a little encouragement."

In the months and years that followed, he got plenty of encouragement. Palmer made him one of his better-paid authors, eventually upping his pay from the standard one cent a word to two cents.

Admiral Steber's Devious Ploy

A year in the works, the first collaboration between Shaver as visionary and Palmer as rewrite man, "I Remember Lemuria" was published in March 1945. In his column "The Observatory" for that issue, Palmer boldly introduced Shaver's tale as the first of a new type of story that would save science fiction. He began the column with reflections on the genre's short history and then added to the long history of manifestos about how to save the genre. (Such fan preoccupations were common since expectations for this genre were that the ordinary always must be extraordinary. In a 1934 "Spilling the Atoms," for example, Rap praised young editor Charles D. Hornig for promoting a new genre "mutation" labeled "visionary fiction" that would save science fiction from its then current rut.) In 1945, Palmer promoted a new mutation. He began by reminding readers that the underlying purpose of SF had been to serve as "a stimulus to the imagination, a seeking out of unknown mysteries that may someday become fact." Hugo Gernsback had sought to "tell stories of tomorrow, of rocket trips to other planets, of strange new inventions and their effects upon civilization, of other dimensions, of time-travel, of evolution. His new magazine was the magazine of the future."

This dream of chasing the future had ended. "On the threshold of 1945, we have finally realized that the future has caught up with us. Today rockets are no fantasy of the mind; the super civilizations dreamed of in the past are with us. Travel to the planets has not been accomplished, but . . . many groups have plans for ships that are to be built in the more-or-less near future." He argued that the magazine that Gernsback started, *Amazing*, had merely become "the magazine of today . . . outstripped in its fiction by fact." Palmer then noted, "For several years we have been wondering as much as you what that new evolution in science fiction would be." He proposed a powerful direction would be to print speculative articles about past mysteries.

Robert Gibson Jones's cover for "I Remember Lemuria," *Amazing Stories*, 1945. *Department of Special Collections, Davidson Library, University of California, Santa Barbara*

What he really appeared to be suggesting was to blend science fiction with the occult. *Amazing*, he said, would begin to explore stories that relied on "racial memory"—a faculty that offered up uncanny knowledge to provide new insights into history and its stranger episodes. Writers would be a different sort of visionary, indicating, for example, what "happened" to Cro Magnon man, to the lost civilizations based at Angkor Wat or Easter Island, to reported races of giants or "little people," and so on. The first example of the use of racial memory would be "I Remember Lemuria." Palmer insisted that Shaver's story was about to set the standard for all new science fiction.

The story originated, Rap assured his readers, and quite truthfully, in "one of the most mysterious corners of Man's mind." Of Shaver's productions, Rap simply stated, "he insists [these] are true stories of ancient Lemuria and of the Elder and Lesser Gods, with the added flavor of fiction to make them acceptable to our magazine." He concluded his discussion of Shaver and announced that five other Shaver stories would follow, all based on enormous letters Shaver had sent him. "It could be a hoax! If MR. SHAVER WERE THE CLEVEREST MAN THE WORLD HAS EVER KNOWN! . . . We confess we are bewildered, impressed, and excited . . . delighted at the series of stories from the typewriter of Mr. Shaver." Was he sincere? Or was this all simply a carnival spieler's patter offered to the assembled rubes?

"I Remember Lemuria" included a foreword by Richard Shaver, in syntax that sounds suspiciously like Ray Palmer's, stating, "I myself cannot explain it. I know only that I remember Lemuria! . . . What I tell you is not fiction! How can I impress that on you. . . . I invite—challenge!—any of you to work on them; to prove or disprove, as you like. . . . I care only that you believe me or disbelieve me with enough fervor to do some real work on those things I will propound."

The actual story, a collaborative creation, shows some imaginative flair, a sweetness of tone, and as is expected of pulp, some over-the-top moments. Based on the "thought records" that Shaver accessed, it is set thousands of years in the past before the Titans fled the earth and its poisonous sun. The narrator, Mutan Mion, is a "lab product," i.e., one of Sub Atlan (just below Atlantis) civilization's test-tube babies. Mutan is a mild-mannered art student who presents a failed masterpiece to a teacher and is urged to descend deeper into Mu for wisdom and "true growth." The way is via a giant elevator with an entrance shaped like a fanged beast's mouth—the classic hell gate of medieval mystery plays. Deeper in the earth, in Tean City, Mutan marvels at all the new species or "variforms" that Technicons have created from intergalactic hybridizing projects. "Creatures of every shape the mind could grasp and some that it could not. All were citizens; all were animate and intelligent—hybrids of every race that space crossing had ever brought into contact, from planets whose very names are now lost in time." He feels privileged to visit the realm where the Titans and Elder Atlans live.

On a telescreen, the six-armed Sybyl of Info, a forty-foot Titaness, directs Mutan to the Hall of Symbols, once again with a fanged serpent's mouth as its entrance gate. There he contemplates amazing artworks and is interrupted by the "sound of a pair of hooves that clicked daintily to a stop beside me." He meets Arl, a fawn-girl. This young and attractive medical student serves as his guide and becomes the story's love interest. (In a drawing he sent to the Ziff-Davis art department, Shaver conceived Arl as a full-bodied showgirl with a tail that might just as well have been a hootchie-kootchie dancer's fan.) Mutan sits in on a lecture with her and learns that Tean City's scientists have determined that radioactive metals from the sun have poisoned not only the upper atmosphere but also the water. An exodus is planned to a new star. But an evil group within the government, under the sway of degenerate dero, is preventing the migration.

Pretending to only be going on a holiday cruise, Mutan, Arl, and other students escape to a sunless planet inhabited by the Nortans, an interstellar and "pure" species of handsome blond giants. There, the colony's giant and sexually stunning Princess Vanue, with her powerful life force and erotic energy, gains the immediate allegiance of all males. Vanue takes the escaped students to a conclave of Nortan Elders to plan the rescue of the Sub Atlans. Vanue also commissions Mutan to create a "Message to Future Man" to warn them of the dangers of the sun's poisoning.

In order to break the sexual spell that has entrapped Mutan, the Nortans place Mutan and Arl in a tank of warm liquid, where they splash and play; Vanue's maids then wire the couple together. "Fastening breathing cups over our mouths; thrusting needles into our veins and attaching them to the ends of thin tubes; placing caps of metal with many wires connected to generators and other machines on our heads; covering our eyes with strangely wired plates of crystal." The couple then experiences an ecstatic communion that leads to spiritual growth. "So it was that Arl and I were married by an actual mingling of the seeds of our being, and not by any foolish ceremony." In this mech womb they sleep and wake as if gods. After this mechanically aided wedding ceremony, the Nortans launch their invasion of the inner earth.

Battles ensue underground. The invaders discover ruined cities and evidence of weird atrocities, such as butcher shops full of "Atlan girl breasts." Mutan, who apparently shared Ray Palmer's libertarian politics, remarks, "So much for our illusion of benevolent government! How long had it been composed of hideous, grinning cannibals. . . . I saw now the fatal weakness in centralized government." Although the Nortans drive out the evil deros, it is not certain that all have been defeated. As the story ends, the Elder Races are evacuating the planet, and Mutan prepares his warning to future man on "timeless plates of telonion." The keynote of this warning was to beware of the sun's rays, and to be aware that disintegrant and integrant energies were locked in a never-ending battle.

The story included nearly forty footnotes to clarify Shaver's thoughts and the validity of his statements. It appeared to typical science fiction readers that either Rap with his theories of "racial memory" had finally gone over the deep end, or that he was creating an elaborate hoax. Not even he was sure. Yet careful readers of this *Amazing Stories* could see that throughout Rap was playing with the categories of truth and fiction. In the same issue, Rap published his story "Moon of Double Trouble" under his pseudonym A. R. Steber. At the back of the volume, in the "Meet the Authors" column, a fresh biography of Steber ran alongside a goofy photo of Rap wearing a monocle and posed in an oversized admiral's uniform.

The counterfeit biography began: "I was born in a log cabin on the frozen steppes of Siberia, July 4, 1867. . . . My youth was largely spent in the pursuit of wolves, not because I loved the beasts, but because their fur was necessary to provide me with warm trousers." The yarn continued to detail Steber's stint as a soldier in Russia and his subsequent espionage work for the French that ended when the Gestapo chased him out of Holland. With surreal logic, it continued, "Almost immediately I joined a salmon canning company's technical research staff and became part of an expedition into the Pacific." The essay mixed further international intrigue with banal details then concluded, "One phase of my life I have thus far neglected to mention dates from February 14, 1938, at which time I became the editor of *Amazing Stories*, in which position I have been ever since, and which accounts for all the foregoing fiction—for which I hope I will be forgiven!" Did the phrase "all the foregoing fiction" refer only to the biography, or to the entire issue with its Shaver story? Further muddying the waters was the tagline on the table of contents for Steber's story "Moon of Double Trouble": "If one of the babblings of a madman turns out to be true, does that mean all the rest must be so?" Palmer would have had to run a giant advertisement saying, *I'm messing with you, folks*, to make the doubled message any clearer.

Despite these cues, most readers took Palmer's breathless introduction about clearing up unknown mysteries as dead serious. In offering Shaver's work as racial memory, Palmer was essentially calling it "channeled" material. (More precisely, mysterious ray projections from underground thought records.) In doing so, Palmer had crossed the line separating weird fiction from occultists' tales of Mu. Yet Shaver's channeled material had none of the high-sounding diction of most Spiritualist or occult publications. Violating the codes of both fantasy and the occult, the piece was their bastard offspring—a kind of prodigy, or monster.

A. R. STEBER

Palmer, dressed in admiral's garb, posing as imaginary author A. R. Steber. *Amazing Stories*, March 1945. *Department of Special Collections, Davidson Library, University of California, Santa Barbara*

It made a sensation. Apparently at Shaver's urging, and his insistence that he would bring in the help of the tero, Palmer had persuaded Ziff-Davis to commandeer some of the valuable pulp paper planned to be used in *Mammoth Detective* and instead print an extra 50,000 copies of *Amazing*. They all sold: 180,000 copies in total. Readers were fascinated and appalled. Bernard Davis went from being furious to mightily pleased. Circulation increased for the next issues with the promised Shaver stories, and it remained high. *Amazing* was flooded with letters either denouncing Shaver and Palmer or backing up this product of racial memory. Some letters that Palmer printed, on both sides of the issue, he likely wrote himself. Palmer continued to tend to the Shaver Mystery in issues that followed. Letters poured in. Circulation spiked. Palmer, choreographing this non-hoax/hoax, was having a great time.

The Mountains of Madness

Neither Ray Palmer nor Richard Shaver was the first pulp science fiction writer to conjure up the "weird" or to borrow from and dabble in the occult or in vision literature. The field had always encouraged wild imaginations. Edgar Rice Burroughs not only invented Tarzan, but also the adventurer John Carter, who traveled by astral means to Mars. Alien races or mutant humans were frequently endowed with telepathic and other "psi" (i.e., psychic or paranormal) powers. In *Slan*, A. E. Van Vogt wrote of a heroic super race with telepathic tendrils hidden in their hair; when it was published in *Astounding* in 1940, the *Slan* saga sparked fan fervor, and some fans experimented with new hairdos to imitate Slan tendrils.

The wild premises of science fiction and fantasy required writers to borrow ideas liberally from science, mythology, religion, and the occult. Some of these authors, such as L. Ron Hubbard, were deeply involved in magic rites. Others, like Harold Sherman, who published the somewhat tepid comic adventures of a man from outer space, "The Green Man" and "The Green Man Returns" in *Amazing*, also quietly pursued arcane studies of occult materials such as the *Book of Urantia*.

The hollow earth narrative with roots in myth and science was a natural for SF authors to adopt. Virtually every culture includes tales of journeys to the underworld. The Greek myth of Orpheus's descent to the underworld is only one pagan version of this ordeal. In the Christian tradition, in the twelfth century, the Venerable Bede's *Ecclesiastical History* (1149) includes the "Vision of Drythelm" in which a bright being escorts the apparently dead Drythelm (a family man who had fallen ill) through the afterlife. Drythelm walks through a valley with roaring fires on one side, and ice and hail on the other. He then travels through darkness to the mouth of hell where he sees demons drag sinners into a burning sulfurous pit; other souls shoot up like sparks and fall back again. Demons attempt to drag Drythelm in as well, but his guide intervenes. The angelic guide then boosts Drythelm up a wall where he glimpses a garden that is a foretaste of heaven. He is allowed to walk through the meadows but not to approach an area of bright light from which comes angelic music. The supposedly dead Drythelm woke up the next day, frightening the wits out of his mourning family, and then promptly left to live the life of a monk.

Drythelm's tale and further vision literature embellishing the landscape of the afterlife provided the map for Dante Alighieri's epic poem, *Inferno* (1314), and numerous mystery plays that featured hell and its denizens. With the onset of the scientific revolution, hell lost some of its fury and encouraged new literary depictions, chief among them, the "hollow earth" saga. The notion that the Earth might be hollow gained a serious patron in astronomer Sir Edmond Halley. In 1691, Halley presented to the Royal Society his theory that beneath the surface of the earth were three nested, hollow spheres, each turning independently on its axis, with light sources and life potentially inside each. This far-fetched theory was based on a desire to explain the bewildering variations in the earth's magnetic fields that made navigating by compass far from cut and dried.

Halley's theory and the older lore of the underworld became fodder for new romances. Baron Ludvig Holberg's *Journey of Niels Klim to the World Underground* (1741) describes a hero who, while exploring a cavern, falls for miles and miles, begins to float, encounters flying monsters, and then lands on the inner planet of Nazar. On Nazar, he wanders through various bizarre countries on an adventure like Gulliver's. Between assignations, Giacomo Casanova de Seingalt penned his own tale of the inner earth, *Icosameron Or, the Story of Edward and Elizabeth: Who Spent Eighty-One Years in the Land of the Megamicres, Original Inhabitants of Protocosmos in the Interior of Our Globe* (1788). In the tale, an incestuous brother and sister are swept below the earth in a watery maelstrom. Underground, they meet hermaphroditic dwarves who live in a complex society and depend on suckling on each other's breasts for nourishment. The brother and sister become, like the dwarves, nudists and set about populating the underground land with human offspring.[15]

In the nineteenth century, as the colonial enterprise filled in many of the blanks on the map of the world, dozens of novels employed narratives in which brave explorers discovered utopian societies hidden inside the hollow earth. In a circular dated 1818, American soldier John Cleves Symmes proposed an expedition to the North Pole to find the entrance to the hollow earth. He sought funds for an enterprise involving "one hundred brave companions" to set out from Siberia, using reindeer and sleds, and insisted they would find "a warm and rich land."[16] Using the pseudonym Adam Seaborn, Symmes also published the novel *Symzonia* (1820). In it, a sealing expedition finds an entrance near the South Pole and sails into the inner earth. Eventually the doughty crew lands among utopian, vegetarian farmers and learns of the order of their society.

By the late nineteenth century, such utopian novels began to overlap with science fiction and occultist tracts. Dozens of inner earth novels were published, including Jules Verne's influential *Journey to the Center of the Earth*, in 1864, translated into English in 1872. John Uri Lloyd's *Etidorhpa* (1895) offered to an initiate named "I-Am-the-Man" a visionary tour of an inner earth that bloomed with mushroom forests and occult wonders. This protagonist was led by an eyeless, sexless, gray-bodied being who communicated by telepathy and would have been viewed as an alien if presented in a narrative half a century later.[17]

Within the science fiction/fantasy genre, immediate predecessors to Richard Shaver include Edgar Rice Burroughs, Abraham Merritt, and H. P. Lovecraft. Edgar Rice Burroughs had almost single-handedly made pulp magazines a successful medium with the publication of his John Carter of Mars stories in 1912 in *Argosy All-Story*, followed by the first of his Tarzan of the Apes stories that same year. His Pellucidar series, printed in the 1910s and 1920s, featured the rather dully named but steadfast duo of mining millionaire David Innes and inventor Abner Perry who drill deep into the earth with a corkscrewlike vehicle, the Iron Mole, to discover the mysterious prehistoric land of Pellucidar. There they battle dinosaurs, dragons, and demonic men who control wolf packs and live in trees. Worst of all, however, are the telepathic lizards, the Mahar, an all-female species that keeps human slaves for food and cruel entertainments. Innes, the true hero of the book, rescues a fair maiden, Dian the Beautiful, from a dragon and mounts a liberation movement. The book, however, ends with a cruel twist. Attempting to return to the surface with Dian, Innes is trapped with a Mahar on the Iron Mole and the book ends with this odd couple lost in the wastes of the Sahara Desert.[18] Palmer, a huge fan of Burroughs, persuaded him to write for *Amazing Stories*. *Amazing* offered new works by Burroughs, including "The Return to Pellucidar," which appeared in the February 1942 issue—only one year prior to Palmer's discovery of Shaver.

Of his predecessors, Shaver spoke most highly of Abraham Merritt. Comfortably wealthy from his income editing William Randolph Hearst's mass circulation magazine *The American Weekly*, Merritt was an eccentric collector of the primitive arts who raised orchids and psychotropic plants, married twice, and wrote florid fantasy stories, heavy on atmosphere, in the manner of L. Rider Haggard with titles such as "Through the Dragon Glass," "The Moon Pool," "The Face in the Abyss," and "The Snake Mother." Often they involved journeys into netherworlds. Science fiction historian Mike Ashley insisted that in Merritt's fantasies, "There was always the hint that the strange worlds were governed by an alien science unknown to humans."[19] Shaver claimed that Merritt's tales, published in *Argosy All-Story*, *Famous Fantastic Mysteries*, and *Weird Tales*, were true, as, clearly, Merritt too was an initiate of the underground civilizations.

H. P. Lovecraft also wrote stories of strange civilizations living beneath the planet, one of which, "At the Mountains of Madness," features an exploration party to the Antarctic that comes across the ruins of an alien city, and then the entrance to caverns and tunnels where the "Elder Things" had departed for an underground ocean. Only two of the explorers escape, in an airplane, and one, turning back, catches a glimpse of some unspeakable horror and goes mad.

None of these early SF authors claimed their wild concoctions were true. To Shaver, though, Lovecraft's "mountains of madness" were real. Speculating on Shaver's likely schizophrenia is not unreasonable. In 1919, psychoanalyst Victor Tausk published the now-classic article "The Origin of the Influencing Machine in Schizophrenia," apparently with patients such as Richard Shaver in mind. Tausk identified a unique group of schizophrenic patients. These patients all were convinced that distant enemies were victimizing them through the use of "influencing machines," or strange devices whose workings could not entirely be explained. The machine, Tausk reported, was generally of a "mystical nature. The patients are able to give only vague hints of its construction." As technology advanced, new developments were incorporated into these delusional apparatuses. These devices could flash images creating 2-D hallucinations, they could interfere with thoughts and feelings or remove them "by means of waves or rays," they could create "sensation that in part cannot be described, because they are strange to the patient himself," as well as "erections, and seminal emissions, that are intended to deprive the patient of his male potency and weaken him." Whatever the gender of the patient, the enemies, in all cases that Tausk knew of, were identified as males and were "predominantly physicians by whom the patient has been treated."[20]

Tausk suggests that such diseases moved through stages beginning with a recognition of change, specifically of "abnormal sensations" that ultimately led to a sense of "estrangement." The patients, he wrote, "become strange to themselves, no longer understood themselves." This awareness of unpleasant changes and "strangeness" eventually crystallized in a notion of an outside force creating the changes, and usually that force is regarded as an "influencing machine manipulated by enemies."

This general outline fits Shaver's pattern of first hearing voices, alongside his developing sense of estrangement. Only later did he trace his disturbances to the distant, underground, dero civilization and their amazing *ray mech* with which they disrupted thoughts and caused other mayhem. Likewise, Shaver identified psychiatrists as a species of dero. He warned Palmer on various occasions never to get locked up in a prison or mental hospital. "DON'T GET IN ONE. You can't get out. Your friends can be very sly and evil—if they think you are cracked—they—your own wife will lie to you—and say she met the most wonderful doctor—and she wants you to see him and she insists—you can't refuse your dear wife. . . . The hospitals—mental are one of their favorite hells where they [dero] torment their victims for years without anyone listening to the poor devil's complaints."[21]

Tausk's insights into schizophrenia provide a key to understanding one aspect of science fiction's appeal—its offerings of mysterious, even disorienting technologies. Tausk notes of the influencing machines, even if the "patient believes he understands the construction of the apparatus . . . it is obvious that this feeling is, at best, analogous to that of a dreamer who has a feeling of understanding, but has not the understanding itself." This makes the patient analogous to the science fiction reader (perhaps being led around a warp-drive spaceship), who luxuriates in descriptions of influencing machines (aka "super science") shaping the universe in unexpected, alien ways. The science fiction reader, however, does not find such prophesied technology hostile but comes to grips with it and so is inoculated against "future shock."

In Shaver's case, science fiction (via editor Palmer) could be said to have helped him negotiate his own likely schizophrenia. Shaver's cosmos of integrative forces in a never-ending battle with disintegrative forces mirrored his inner landscape. Science fiction was his chance to name and come to terms with what he sensed as hidden manipulators—whether distant rays, voices, or chemicals run amok in neurons. Science fiction offered hope. In the marriage scene in "I Remember Lemuria," when Mutan and Arl are placed in the vat of liquid and wired together, they gain bliss and deep wisdom. Opposites are integrated. The influencing machines, in this case, are not detrimental but integrative, bringing the couple into communion, providing a sense of spiritual growth as well as sensual pleasure.

Similarly, the story "I Remember Lemuria" helped to some extent to "cure" Shaver and win him a wife. While courting Dottie, Shaver reports that with her dog next to her in bed she fell asleep reading the manuscript of "I Remember Lemuria." She promptly dreamed that she was the fawn-girl Arl, and woke up startled, feeling the tail of the dog sleeping next to her and thinking she "still had a tail." A private world ceases to be private when shared. Shaver conquered Dottie and Palmer first, and then the readers of *Amazing*. While some depict Palmer as exploiting Shaver, or encouraging his delusions, Palmer in fact helped Shaver reengage with the world, bringing out the artistic products of his own vibrant imagination.

Years later, Palmer divulged that Shaver had spent up to eight years in a catatonic state in the state hospital in Ypsilanti, Michigan (this long stint was more likely in Ionia State Hospital). During this time, according to the staff, "he had removed himself from reality, living in a shadowy imaginary world in his own mind. He even had to be fed. All his adventures in the caves were in his own mind. So they said."[22] Characteristic of Palmer, this "fact" only further proved the validity of Shaver's claims. Palmer argued that the catatonic Shaver had left his body for another realm. Metaphorically and perhaps psychically, Shaver went underground. There he discovered a hidden battleground, sought integration, and in dramatizing his struggle, managed to carry on a creative life—and ultimately influence popular culture.

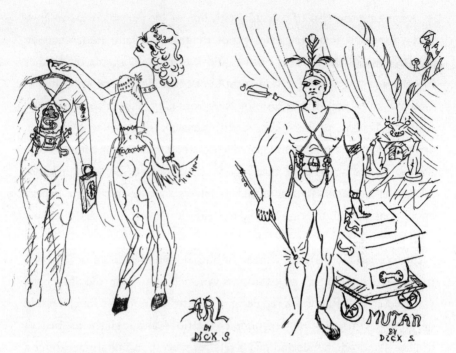

Richard Shaver's sketches of Arl, the fawn-girl, and Mutan Mion the hero
in "I Remember Lemuria." *Hidden World,* Summer 1964. *Department of
Special Collections, Davidson Library, University of California, Santa Barbara*

The Bard of Barto

Several months prior to publication of "I Remember Lemuria," Palmer
and Shaver arranged Rap's visit to Barto, Pennsylvania, so that the two
coconspirators could finally meet. Shaver had admitted that both he and
Dottie were nervous, commenting, "Dot, who is keeping house for me,
says she don't know whether to act like a lady when you come or act normal. But if she makes chicken and waffles like I just had for dinner, you
won't care what she acts like."[23]

Arranging the visit to coincide with one of his periodic trips to New York City, in late February, Palmer took the train to Manhattan, where he stopped at Ziff-Davis's small office and met editors, agents, and other members of the science fiction community, including stops for coffee in Greenwich Village. After a taste of New York City, Palmer took the train to Pennsylvania and then proceeded to Shaver's isolated home in Barto, arriving at around midnight. He had felt the best way to gain Shaver's confidence was to act as if he thoroughly accepted all of Shaver's premises about the universe. Rap admitted in letters that he had never experienced contact with the rays but did not question Shaver's constant contact with them.

Shaver and Dottie made a meal for him, despite the late hour. The two men talked and Dottie's awkwardness vanished. (She later told Shaver she was pleased that Ray was a regular guy.) Dottie did not have much faith in her husband's ideas of underground civilizations, although she did believe in ghosts and witchcraft and had a relative who spun out stories about a hex doctor with a weird machine as well as underground beings. Still, as Dottie later told a Shaver fan, "We differ slightly on things." But she was devoted to her husband and pleased at his new writing career. During his visit, Palmer learned more of Shaver's past. They discussed their idea of creating an organization dedicated to the Shaver Mystery and of writing a book. Palmer inspected a few of the many manuscripts Shaver had in the works, and they talked about Mantong and related matters. Just as important, Palmer encountered uncanny evidence that Shaver was not just a deluded maniac.

Late that night, in his room at the Shavers' house, his thoughts perhaps drifting to his wife and their toddler, Linda, Palmer was disturbed to hear five distinct voices conversing with his host in the neighboring room. He heard them informing Shaver that about four miles beneath the earth and four miles away, a woman had been torn to pieces. The voices concurred that it had been "horrible" and such things "should not be." Like a character in an Edgar Allan Poe or H. P. Lovecraft story stuck for the night in a haunted mansion, Palmer sat up and cried, "What's this all about?"

The voices switched to a foreign language. Then the little girl said of Palmer, "Pay no attention to him. He's a dope!" No one called Palmer a dope. He couldn't explain what he'd heard, but Palmer wasn't about to reject it just because that was what a normal person would do. After a sleepless night, he searched the next day in Shaver's room for hidden devices but didn't find any. He was no dope. This could be something. He spent another day with Shaver and an eventless night. Shaver commented, "They think you're pretty much of a dope . . . but that's because they don't know you well enough to realize you're one of the insiders."[24]

Palmer returned from Pennsylvania to Chicago on the train, passing through the barren winter landscape while puzzling over the reality of Shaver's inner life. Should he have called it racial memory? Had Shaver really been in caves? Perhaps in a parallel dimension? He had been privately showing Shaver's stories to many correspondents and getting their reactions for months. Some, like the typist Shaver had hired to help clean up his handwritten manuscripts, Bob McKenna, wanted to march down into the caverns. Others thought they were both nuts.

Although not the merry party in the woods that Shaver would have liked to offer Palmer, the visit had been a quiet success. Soon after, Shaver wrote how pleased he was that "now that we know each other better the last doubt of each other has been finally resolved, is the way I feel about it."[25] He also exclaimed at how great the cover of *Amazing* looked with Robert Gibson Jones's rendition of "I Remember Lemuria"—he insisted it was far better than that month's cover of *Planet Stories*. In the same letter he also apologized for any awkwardness in the visit, commenting that neither he nor Dottie were "fifth avenue" types. "You were the first visitor I and Dot have had—that is—a visitor whose critical eye we had any respect for. So put our deficiencies down to our lack of a social life—and remember our intent. Dot and I mean the best by you." Perhaps recognizing that

Palmer needed reassurance, he complimented him on his bravery in finally revealing the secrets of the caverns and added, "I see the firm, intelligent idealism activating you in your thought as I read your work woven around mine."

"I Remember Lemuria" was in *Amazing*. The gates had opened. Shaver, serving as Palmer's psychopomp, was leading him and fans of the Shaver Mystery deeper into the inner earth.

SHAVER MANIA

Incidentally, as you read this, men are lowering themselves into a cave in Texas. They are taking cameras along. The cave may prove something, or it may not. It is a tremendous cave. It has much "shaver-mystery" about it. Queer things happen in it. BUT, the truth of the matter is, SOME of our readers are SINCERE enough about Amazing Stories' great "hoax" to risk their lives to prove it isn't a hoax because THEY *know* it isn't a hoax.

—Rap, "The Observatory," *Amazing Stories*, April 1947

Lastly, sir, and without facetiousness, I do truly believe that many of your authors and correspondents are neurotic people to whom occult and related subjects are merely an escape mechanism.

—Bart Goldman, *Mystic*, December 1954

Palmer had been courting the outrage of SF fans—but it was a long time coming. In early 1945, he wrote an article for *Fantasy News*, saying, "The greatest thing ever to happen to science fiction has happened, and the 'fans' have missed it entirely—because they did not read it! . . . If they had read it, they would have been forced to write me about it. . . . I am referring to Richard S. Shaver's 'I Remember Lemuria,' which is two things—1) the 'new' science fiction; 2) not fiction! . . . Shaver tells the truth!"[1]

Eventually, the Shaver Mystery gained notoriety as one of the great controversies in 1940s science fiction. Just not right away. Other events, such as the final phases of World War Two, the liberation of the Nazi death camps, elections in various fan organizations, and the atomic bombing of Japan intervened before SF fans, including many of Palmer's old colleagues such as 4E Ackerman and Sam Moskowitz, united to declare the Shaver Mystery heretical—nay, unclean. Yet the Shaver Mystery opened the way to a mutant form of science fiction that was to bear fruit as imaginary narratives of the weird gave way to actual sightings of flying saucers, reported visits to underground caves, and encounters with alien beings. By the 1950s, a group of SF fans had embraced what fan historian Harry Warner Jr. dubbed "Psi-Fi"—a subgenre that mixed mainstream SF with interest in telepathy experiments, the Shaver Mystery, and, often, Dianetics—the creation of SF writer L. Ron Hubbard championed by, among others, *Astounding*'s John W. Campbell and *Slan* author A. E. Van Vogt. Slowly, popular culture veered toward a deep abiding interest in the paranormal. With his grand act of chutzpah, Palmer was elbowing the field of science fiction into the Twilight Zone.

In the 1940s, the Shaver stories became a minor industry, filling entire volumes of *Amazing Stories*. Shaver had help at first but was eventually to become a capable pulp writer. (His help was not only at Palmer's end—Shaver hired at least two typists to clean up his manuscripts and sharpen his early submissions. One of these was Bob McKenna, a KDKA radio station news announcer and a SF fan who fell under Shaver's spell.) While Palmer took the lead in revising and amplifying Shaver's first pulp story, "I Remember Lemuria," Shaver became far more active in writing the stories as the months passed.

A typical and lighthearted letter from Shaver to Palmer in 1944, as they were just beginning to shape up his stories, began "Dear Boss" and referred to the story enclosed along with reflections such as: "If there is anything you don't like, send it back or fix it yourself. Parts are good and I guess some parts are pretty lousy. I confess I can't figure out what speed a ship should travel to get around from sun to sun and back again. Acceleration should be— you fill it in, it's too much for me. Some of those writers do it so beautifully too." Shaver disliked typing, but even more, he disliked the scientific nitpickers. After then thanking Palmer for a reference book on astronomy, he added, "I figured out a rather new idea for a space drive— with a touch or two from you they should like it, those math hounds that write the letters on how it couldn't be done."[2]

After "I Remember Lemuria," more than twenty Shaver stories followed in the next four years. Shaver's pay increased from one cent a word to one and a half cents, and then to two cents a word. But it is clear that many of his submissions underwent serious revisions. In June 1944, a half year after the Mantong alphabet letter had been published, and while the Ziff-Davis crew was still working over Shaver's raw submissions, he wrote to Rap, "Naturally I am overjoyed that you can use my stories and am sorry that they must be rewritten—but believe me I know why—for I have been through much and it is work for me to write."[3]

Because of paper shortages, only four issues of *Amazing* ran in 1945, but each featured Robert Gibson Jones covers for a Shaver story: "I Remember Lemuria," "Thought Records of Lemuria," "Cave City of Hel," and "Quest of Brail." Of the nine issues published in 1946, six included titillating cover art for a Shaver story. The pattern continued in 1947 and 1948, with either Shaver or Shaver-inspired stories in the majority of issues as Palmer began to assign regular writers such as Chester Geier and Roger Phillips Graham (pen name Rog Phillips) to write in the Shaver mode. The all-Shaver issue of June 1947 was undoubtedly the high point—or, to critics, the low point—of the mystery. Throughout this period, Shaver also published fantasy in Ziff-Davis's *Fantastic Adventures* under his own name and pseudonyms.

Advertisements for Shaver's "The Quest of Brail" called it "the fourth of the new type stories based on the mysterious background of the thought records of the caves beneath the earth's surface where mysterious beings still live."[4] As with his other work, the story is uneven, but surprisingly sweet, and at times has an over-the-top Nietzschean energy; a Shaver tale always included a high erotic quotient and, when referring to the activities of the dero, a solid dose of sadomasochism. Palmer noted that he often had to tone them down. The stories unfolded against a background of the hellish scenes that Shaver described in his letters.

Shaver's vision of the dero cavern wedded the hellish visions of sixteenth-century Dutch artist Hieronymus Bosch to the modern factory, "Men hung swinging from hooks, boiled in fluids, writhed on rocks, thirsted in the stocks, sat on spikes tugging to get off, lay under hammers that crushed them inch by slow inch, or slid inexorably into machines that sliced them gradually with the thinness of microtone."[5] Shaver noted in a September 1944 letter to Rap that in addition to orgies and simple torture devices the dero entertained themselves with what they called an "organ of the opposites." Two people are wired to apparatus, one "giving off pain vibrants" and the other "giving off pleasure vibrants." A single keyboard controls both apparatuses. "It is one of their greatest delights to hook up a man and woman who are in love to this apparatus and the conscience-stricken lover finds himself desiring pain for his mate in order to get the inordinately sweet delight. . . . This is one of their great pleasures, to watch our despised conscience in such a predicament." The "program ends in a crescendo of pain—fatal pain for one and infinite ecstasy for the other."[6] Shaver commented in another letter, "That Hell still exists is very true, in many places, and I have seen some of its parts in operation. It is not good for the stomach, an inverted hospital, where scabs always enlarge, the well always become sick, and the sane insane."[7] Of the dero, Shaver commented, "Something has taken the real life out and left a thing that is not human at all. Their only pleasure is torture."[8]

Shaver was a metaphysician with his own theory of the universe and its workings. Good and evil, pleasure and pain, disintegration and integration were forever in conflict. Yet he strived to create stories that gave pleasure. Shaver's criticism of John Campbell's editing of *Astounding* makes clear his tastes. Shaver wrote to Rap in July 1944, "Just looked at *Astounding* and remembered I wanted to tell you I think he emphasizes science just a little too much. Campbell's stories don't contain enough sex and some of them are almost dry though laid in space and adventures. But . . . it is a good magazine."[9]

Shaver's stories had enough sex and adventure and were not dry. The artwork for the Shaver issues of *Amazing Stories* indicate the stories' strengths. Robert Gibson Jones's cover for "The Quest of Brail" depicts a reclining woman in quasi-Grecian garb that includes a skimpy dress, a metal belt plate, and Spartan-styled helmet. Through the helmet, she is wired for stim. She is in a dreamy ecstasy: her eyes are closed, and arms draped overhead. Near her divan, incense billows from a burner, its fumes supporting a handsome golden-haired Buck Rogers sort who hovers over her in a futuristic craft.

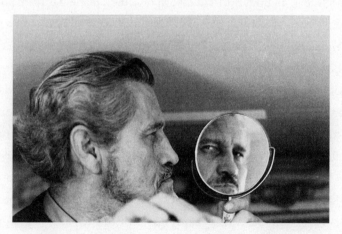

Shaver in a reflective mood. *Photo courtesy Brian Emrich*

The story features two heroes. The first, Brail, is the noble leader of planet Helgo (as in "gone to hell") turned "puppet leader" as his civilization is secretly ruled by evil dero called the "Fat Ones," who rely on torture and thought-aug rays to maintain their rule while endlessly seeking pleasure.

The second hero is Lori, a warrior at odds with the ascetic values of his leaders who is also one of the pilots of the invading Horde now attacking Helgo. Brail captures Lori and other Horde pilots and plies them with drink and grateful women he has saved from the Fat Ones and their stim and torture devices. Brail convinces these invaders to help him in an escape from Helgo past the attacking Horde's ships to found a new world. On the journey, Lori meets a green-skinned woman he has long dreamed of, Norla. As with Mutan Mion and Arl, Norla wires him with magnetic devices to ensure they will be each other's slaves and enjoy a techno-erotic meeting of souls. The ensuing godlike raptures transform him and usher in a weeklong honeymoon that begins when "He crushed her body to his and knew that such a mating could come to Gods only."

After helping Brail found a new planetary outpost where justice rules, Norla and Lori set off to meet the Dark Goddess who dwells with her peers in deep space in an underground cavern on a dark planet far from any suns and their detrimental rays. "Her skin was black as night itself with a purple iridescence rippling over it like heat lightning, her lips were a scarlet flame about her sharp teeth." She and her company have learned to free themselves of the "deadly little sun seeds which gather in the body and kill all life near a sun." The goddess offers the same treatment to her visitors. The novelette ends with Lori proposing a toast "to the new immortal race we will build with our new found friends, the Gods who dwell in space-dark."

The Shaver stories continued to hit the newsstands: "Invasion of the Micro-Men," "Earth Slaves to Space," "The Sea People," "The Mind Rovers," "Witch of the Andes," and "Slaves of the Worm." Palmer would carefully distinguish those that were "real" from those that were simply "yarns." Shaver mania continued. Hundreds of letters poured in to the Ziff-Davis office. Some readers howled their outrage, but many others linked Shaver's ideas to favorite occultist notions of astral planes, of sightings of mysterious inhabitants inside Mount Shasta (a people sometimes called the Telos), and reports from the lost civilizations of Atlantis and

Lemuria. Several insisted that Mutan Mion's "telonion plates" were not lost at all, but guarded at various sites. Others, who had no clear connection to occult groups (but likely to influencing machines), insisted that they too had been in the caves.

Palmer was delighted. He alternately tried to stoke the flames of the "Mystery" and to appear indifferent, above the action. In the third issue to contain a Shaver yarn, that of September 1945, Rap's column, "The Observatory," was a bit aloof. He promised a terrific Shaver story and then commented there had been "odd reactions" to the Shaver Mystery. He was fascinated that a fan group had promised "to 'expose' our 'hoax' (which was a compliment, by the way, as it was termed the 'biggest ever attempted in modern science fiction history.')" He insisted he was looking forward to seeing how they would proceed.

Sounding eminently reasonable, Rap added, "We realize that a lot of our readers find it difficult to believe that we ourselves believe one single word of what Mr. Shaver tells us in his stories, but we'll keep presenting the evidence as it comes in, and you can judge for yourself. However, aside from that, these stories are good science fiction stories. . . . We confidently predict, that disregarding hoax or truth or fiction angles, these stories will be remembered by readers for many years to come."

Yet deeper in that same issue, Palmer began a feature named "Report from the Forgotten Past," with an over-the-top essay noting that the whole affair was more than "puzzling." Hoping to get to the bottom of the Mystery, he had invited readers to share their experiences if they confirmed Shaver's allegations. Then he added "THERE HAS BEEN EVIDENCE ADVANCED OF A VERY STARTLING NATURE!" He insisted that this evidence involved hundreds of letters from readers who didn't want their names disclosed who also indicated they'd had experiences with "cave people, or with strange humans." Many warned Rap to end the entire campaign, as it was risky.

Rap then added that many of his correspondents sensed an enormous change coming and then he gave the report an odd spin, as if suddenly writing a pamphlet encouraging people to join a utopian commune. Many of his correspondents, he said, were convinced they were on Earth for a secret purpose, and had "spent their lives so far in perfecting themselves in certain trades." Their skills were practical and concrete. All united could pool their knowledge to do amazing things on the planet. He wanted to hear from all people who believe they are part "of a great plan," and know "things today unknown to science." Palmer added that *Amazing*'s editor was "ONE OF THOSE PEOPLE! THE TIME HAS COME FOR ACTION!" It is not quite clear what sort of action Rap was suggesting. In 1944–45 he and Shaver had corresponded about setting up an organization of some sort. A further clue comes in a letter from a reader in 1947 who proposed starting a cooperative community on the lines of the recommendations of *Oahspe*, a Spiritualist bible, channeled in 1882. Palmer's response: "Sounds like a good idea.—Rap." At all costs, he was trying to rally on the Mystery.

Boarding the Mystery Train

Palmer's development of the Shaver Mystery provided a meeting place for the fantastic visions of science fiction and the separate but oddly similar components of occultist narratives—two strains that have played leapfrog over the years. Jeffrey J. Kripal, a scholar of religion, has argued, "The paranormal needs the popular culture form in which to appear at all. The truth needs the trick, the fact the fantasy."[10] Occult theories and popular culture have long sustained each other. The occultist tastes of the 1940s can be traced back to earlier trends that also mixed entertainment—even titillation—with earnest inquiry such as mesmerism (suppressed in America until the early nineteenth century), Spiritualism, New Thought (or positive thinking), and Theosophy.

Spiritualism, which began in the 1840s, was a diffuse and very popular movement in which people held séances or attended public performances in which mediums contacted the spirits of the dead to convey knowledge or comfort. Inspired female Spiritualist speakers became akin to rock stars in the 1850s when they braved the public sphere to offer inspirational speeches and support feminist thought. Spiritualist performers such as the Davenport Brothers, who toured the variety stage circuit offering spooky effects, and anti-Spiritualist performers who reproduced their tricks, competed for audiences.

Mesmerism, begun in the late eighteenth century, in the popular mind occupied a spot midway between science and black magic. Popular novels of the early nineteenth century often featured mesmerists as demonic seducers. The forerunner of hypnotism, mesmerism also had its lighter side, with demonstrators amusing audiences by convincing a spectator that he or she was a rooster and should peck at food or let out a crow. As an early version of psychotherapy, mesmerism also set the foundation of the still-influential positive thinking or New Thought movement with its basic notion that one's attitude can change one's reality. From mesmerism eventually sprang Christian Science and the hundreds of books and audiobooks to be found in airports today that assert that affirmations—or auto-suggestions—can lead to happiness and success in business, love, and life.

The key movement shaping twentieth-century occultism, however, was Helena Blavatsky's Theosophy. Born to an aristocratic Russian family, and attracted initially to Spiritualism, in her Theosophical teachings Blavatsky drew from Spiritualist writings that insisted the cosmos involved a hierarchy of nested planes of reality, each inhabited by beings with increasing spiritual aptitude. The universe was a giant "university" in which souls slowly learned key lessons and graduated to higher planes. Theosophy wedded such views to Blavatsky's own version of the "wisdom of the East," which included notions of reincarnation and a theory of the mythic origins of the human race. Blavatsky claimed to have traveled to secret areas of Tibet to gain esoteric knowledge. Much of her philosophy was culled from Hindu thought. In 1875 she began to share the wisdom of her masters, both earthly and from higher planes of reality. In its early days, her movement gained the support of prominent creative thinkers, including Thomas Edison, Alfred Russel Wallace (co-originator of the theory of evolution), composer Gustav Mahler, authors Lewis Carroll (Charles Dodgson), William Butler Yeats, and L. Frank Baum, and artists Piet Mondrian, Paul Gauguin, and Paul Klee.

As a teacher of hidden or occult knowledge, Blavatsky was fascinated by the theory of Atlantis as a lost continent, an idea popularized in the writing of politician and author Ignatius Donnelly. His book *Atlantis, the Antediluvian World* appeared in 1882, seven years after Blavatsky founded the Theosophical Society. She also admired the fiction of Edward Bulwer-Lytton, whose oeuvre included the hollow earth romance *The Coming Race* (1871). Its hero wanders underground and contacts a race of superhumans who, through the use of wands, control "Vril," a mysterious energy akin to the life force. Vril could blast through rock or heal the sick. The Vril-ya, alternately of Atlantean or Aryan descent, were destined to emerge from underground and destroy and supplant human civilization. (The book later became a favorite of the Nazis.)

In her own works, such as *Isis Unveiled* (1877) and *The Secret Doctrine* (1888), Blavatsky propounded a theory that humanity went through evolutionary cycles related to root races. Two other root races had preceded our present Aryan, or fifth root, race: Atlantis as fourth, and Lemuria (or Mu) as third; these two sunken civilizations had both featured highly technological and spiritually advanced beings. In the early twentieth century, mystics also whispered about one other subterranean outpost, called Agarthi, a peaceful, utopian civilization with an entrance in a remote area of Asia, whose inhabitants number in the millions. According to scientist and seeker Ferdinand Ossendowski's *Beasts, Men, and Gods* (1922), a "King of the World" ruled Agharti and would ultimately emerge to battle evil and save the earth.

Indicating the game of leapfrog between pulpsters and occultists, Palmer picked up on this theory and ran first "Tales from Tibet" in the February 1946 *Amazing*, which presented Agharti as a realm of evil. When readers complained, he followed this with "King of the World?" in the May 1946 *Amazing*. In this article, Rap changed the king into a miracle man from Venus—anticipating Venus as the favorite planet of origin for the Space Brothers that flying saucer contactees would begin to report in the 1950s. In the same issue another author insisted that the spiritually advanced people of Agharti could influence thought, for the better, on the planet's surface.

Occultists' chronicles of underground initiations, difficult to distinguish from pulp narratives, gathered momentum in the twentieth century. Guy Ballard, along with his wife, Edna, who ran an occult bookshop in Chicago and began as Blavatsky disciples, created their own breakaway group, the "I Am" movement. Ballard reported that in the early 1930s, while searching the slopes of Mount Shasta in California, he encountered Saint Germain, an Ascended Master, a "Magnificent, Godlike figure in a white jeweled robe."[11] Saint Germain brought Ballard to caverns beneath Shasta to meet the wise beings of the Mu civilization who offered him great knowledge. The Ballards gained followers and in the 1930s spliced their teachings of higher awareness with far right-wing thought and aligned themselves with fascist groups. Prosecutors hampered the movement with mail fraud charges in 1940, a year after Guy's death.

Simultaneous with Ballard, another seeker, Maurice Doreal, claimed that in 1931 while lecturing in Los Angeles, he met not Lemurians but Atlanteans who conjured him to caverns beneath Mount Shasta. Doreal founded the Brotherhood of the White Temple in Denver. He later traced much of his knowledge to his translations of Emerald Tablets discovered in the Great Pyramid. These tablets were the work of Thoth, an Egyptian god of wisdom. Emerald yes, telonion no.

In his desire to plumb the Shaver Mystery, Rap gleefully published

THE KING OF THE WORLD?

Is there an underground cave city called Agharti ruled by a Venusian who holds our future hopes?

ALL through the world today are thousands of people who claim to have knowledge of an underground city, not specifically located although generally assumed to be in Tibet, called Agharti, or Shambala. In this city, they say, is a highly developed civilization ruled by an "Elder" or a "Great One" whose title is among others "The King of the World." Some claim to have seen him, and it is also claimed that he made at least one visit to the surface. It is also claimed that when Mankind is ready for the benefits he can bring, he will emerge and establish a new civilization of peace and plenty.

To quote the words of a "witness": "He came here ages ago from the planet Venus to be the instructor and guide of our then just dawning h u m a n i t y. Though he is thousands of years old, his appearance is that of an exceptionally well-developed and handsome youth of about sixteen. But there is nothing juvenile about the light of infinite love, wisdom and power that shines from his eyes. He is slightly larger than the average man, but there are no radical differences in race."

Apparently the ruler of Agharti is a man; apparently he possesses great power and science, including atomic energy machines. Apparently also he is dedicated to bring to us great benefits. Apparently he has power to end warfare on the surface at will. We, the people of Earth, ask: What man can judge another? Wars must end now! Judge not, Great One, lest you be judged. For we ARE ready for peace!

Pulp artist Robert Fuqua's depiction of Agharti's enlightened underground leader indicates how, by 1947, *Amazing Stories* had shifted to occult topics. *Department of Special Collections, Davidson Library, University of California, Santa Barbara*

letters from members of specific occult societies such as the Brotherhood of the White Temple as well as freelancers who simply had had odd, frightening experiences. Shaver filled the unlikely role of the only sane person in the house, frequently declaring in letters and articles that he did not believe in other planes of reality or spirits. As he wrote to Rap, "I didn't want you to persist in the idea that I too am touched by the religious bug or 'hearing things or seeing things.'"[12] When people died they were dead and gone. His experience had not involved another dimension or an astral plane. He had been in the caves. The deros actually pulled people apart. This was not a mystical matter.

Amazing Stories' readers cheered on the Mystery. One reader in September 1945 told of a recurring dream in which he rallied his people, an underground race, to go into battle once again against their enemies, the people of the upper world, who relied on specimens of *Tyrannosaurus rex* to aid their armies. His fellows were not impressed until he announced that he had a new weapon: a mechanical dinosaur. "For a moment there was no sound, then a shout of joy, like the sound lost souls might make when finding they are rescued."

In that same issue, another writer, who noted she could communicate with all manner of beings physical and astral, spoke with pity of Shaver. "I can say I know, not believe, but know that Shaver merely wore down his normal, natural outer defenses which all people have and he laid himself open to lower astral entities. . . . Wiser men than Shaver have been duped. . . . The insane asylums are full of people who are taken over with this sort of thing." The writer went on to note that the Aquarian Age had commenced and "this coming age will be an opening up of all kinds of seemingly new knowledge, new isms, systems—both good and evil."

Other letter writers wanted to set the record straight, with admonitions such as, "The tablets referred to were buried by Thoth. They have since been dug up and are at present in Tibet. Mr. Shaver will never find them."[13] Others offered dark warnings that only added to the appeal. A letter from a reader connected to Doreal's Brotherhood of the White Temple noted that seeking out the caves "would be suicide and one who revealed their location would be a murderer." Another, associated with Meade Layne (founder of Borderlands Sciences Research), commented that tampering with the caves "is probably undesirable and even dangerous. . . . Let the Deros alone. Above all, do not try to reproduce any type of apparatus or machine."[14]

Others seemed curious, if skeptical. In the September 1945 issue of *Amazing*, Betty Yoe, the secretary of the Cleveland Grotto of the National Speleological Society wrote "Mr. Shaver's story in *Amazing Stories* has aroused our deep interest by its reference to large caves, etc. . . . [As] we haven't run into anything such as Mr. Shaver mentioned, we wonder if this was a figment of his imagination . . . [or] if he really had a basis for his claims and had in mind particular caves. . . . We could be grateful for any information you are at liberty to give us."

Astute interpretations also surfaced. In the May 1946 issue, Heinrich Hauser, a German journalist, adventurer, and pulp writer to be, congratulated *Amazing* on the publication of Shaver's stories. He began by quoting Danish author Johannes V. Jensen's statement that "Art results from the nostalgia of captives." He then noted that Shaver must have endured some sort of captivity and created "this amazing world" to preserve his "sanitary." Hauser then attributed Shaver mania to Cold War panic and to a psychological connection between caves and "the mother." "The more calamitous our time becomes, the more we are going to long for return into 'the mother.' With the 'mother complex' being so extraordinarily powerful in matriarchal America, you are certain to hear of more thousands of readers who all seem to 'remember Lemuria.'" This letter was followed in the next issue by Hauser's own story, "Agharti," which was a yarn about the secret building of V-2 rockets in Germany in underground caverns.

The Mystery hurtled on. As Shaver learned his craft, Palmer assigned writers not only to aid Shaver but also to create Shaver-type stories on their own. Shaver and Chester Geier coauthored "Ice City of the Gorgon" and several others. In January 1947, Palmer ran a nonfiction article by Margaret Rogers, "I Have Been in the Caves." A native of Houston, Texas, Rogers described a period of her life when she was a drug addict in Mexico near Cuernavaca. In horrible emotional and physical pain, she was led by a mysterious doctor down into caves and given new health. She learned of the teros' transport ships to other planets, used their flying underground shuttles, and learned to admire their advanced society. In 1947, Palmer put Chester Geier in charge of a Shaver Mystery Club Newsletter jointly funded by Shaver and Ziff-Davis with a separate subscription (two issues for one dollar). The Shaver Mystery also gained its own fan letter section in *Amazing Stories*.

In the June 1946 issue of *Amazing*, Rap added a strange twist that anticipated the plot of Jack Finney's 1955 novel *Invasion of the Body Snatchers*. Palmer asserted that he had been warned there was a plan to kidnap himself and Shaver together with their entire families. "To cover up the kidnapping, trained doubles for all of us were to be substituted and the world would never know . . . [that] the people in our place were dero living a role." Other writers also warned that the dero were "among us." One letter writer, in the October 1946 *Amazing*, even claimed to be a dero himself. He insisted the dero did some good as they have "remained to spur the human race to heights beyond its own imagining." He went on to ask, "Who are Dero? Look about you. Perhaps your neighbor, perhaps your brother, your employer, your business associate, your employee." The Red Scare and the Dero Scare were mirror images.

Plum Pudding and Other Conspiracies

A deep paranoia hovered above the Shaver Mystery. There was more than a whiff of dread to Shaver's assertion that evil green-skinned degenerate beings lurked beneath the earth and all its major cities and that in addition to kidnapping surface women as sex slaves and focusing aug-rays on humans to scramble their thoughts, the dero roasted other humans on spits and feasted on them. Then, for sport, the dero wired lovers into the deadly organ of the opposites.

Many of Shaver's assertions indicate classic symptoms of paranoia. To give but one example, he claimed that while in a charity hospital with a broken leg in Newfoundland, a kind but half-witted maid gave him a covered dish of plum pudding for Christmas. After eating the main course of smoked herring, he uncovered the dish that "contained a big round slice of something covered with brown sauce. I took a big spoonful into my mouth—then it wriggled and before I could spit it out—three lively worms slid down my throat." He claimed the pudding was a slice from a seal's ovary and the worms were baby sea flukes, "A terrible plague of the sea which sometimes in whales gets twenty feet long." The dero, clearly, had arranged the poisoning. He said he did not worry about it until "about a year later after a thing crawled up my back under the skin from my stomach and entered my head. It was two feet long." He appealed to the teros. With their ben-rays they "killed that fluke in my head without hurting me."[15]

Shaver also documented how the dero infiltrated thoughts with their aug-rays, relying on wordplay and puns to disintegrate an individual's sanity. "Thus HOSPITAL—house of piddle, ho, spital, ho spit all."[16] Such punning and splintering of syntax, familiar to readers of James Joyce's *Finnegans Wake*, was a great dero skill as "Everyone is to be provided with needle rays to cut the minds of everyone in range of their rays who displeases them."[17] Shaver offered various examples of his hijacked trains of thought as the deros applied the needle, or as he listened in to their own conversations. The needle would splinter syntax and lead to perverse statements or plain nonsense such as: "Finicule, feenuckle, pragmatic, persimmon frank grab fule gore grind Fort free fool grown grease flick jees flue go hoop." Fighting it off, he arrived back at near sense that once again slipped away, "Dramatic personifications of manifestations underworld. Gramophone frown-etc."[18]

Shaver spun out his curious beliefs on the slenderest of evidence. For example, he indicated that one way the more benevolent cave dwellers advertised themselves on the surface of the earth was through an organization called the "Dogs." He had been invited to join the Dogs. He knew this because they had "left a little china dog on my desk, two of its legs were broken off. This was their talisman." He was carrying the dog a few days later into a greenhouse seeking a job when one of the men "asked me how the two legged dogs were getting along. So I knew it was not a gag by the imps but a real something." He was sent to the boss and told to show the dog to ensure an "in."[19] As a result of evil tamper he decided not to show the dog and wasn't given a job. Shaver said he had a few more similar brushes with the Dogs, always spoiled, and finally gave up on them. He instructed Palmer to put a dog figurine with "brown and white spots, with two legs broken off," on his desk at Ziff-Davis if he wished contact with the Dogs.

Shaver's paranoia was catching. Palmer added his own reports of what Shaver would call tamper. While driving with his daughter, then a toddler, to a printing company on Superior Street to arrange mathematical formulas for an article for the all-Shaver issue planned for 1947, he had a hunch that a driver at a red light was about to zoom out and crash into him. Even though he had the green, he slowed. The other driver ran the light. Rap swerved. The other driver followed. He stopped. The other driver stopped and was laughing like a maniac. Could this be the work of dero?

By the time the all-Shaver issue of *Amazing* hit the newsstands in June 1947, Palmer seemed positively flustered. Rap told his readers that attempting to publish the issue had been fraught with difficulties. "Never in our nine years of editing have such fantastic things happened to make an issue almost impossible." Galleys had disappeared. They were returned full of bizarre errors, the likes of which he'd never seen. Then duplicate galleys were produced with subtle changes. The printers scrambled the mathematic formulas that amateur mathematician and SF writer Rog Phillips had provided to establish "Is There an Ether Drift?" Rap added, "We aren't going to mention the hundred other things that happened to delay everything possible." But he did note one more problem, "The case of nerves we developed which made it impossible to type a single line that wasn't full of typographical errors." This was, in Shaver's idiom, a classic case of tamper.

Individual paranoia becomes conspiracy once adherents agree to the reality of previously unrecognized evildoers. Rather than an individual blaming a mysterious influencing machine, an embattled group posits the existence of a quasi-demonic organization bent on spreading evil in the world. The base organizations might have a public front, such as the Masons, the American Communist Party, the Catholic Church, Proctor & Gamble, or in classic anti-Semitic lore the Jewish people, or the evil group might be entirely secretive and underground, as, for instance, the dero. Onto this enemy are projected forbidden desires. Those privy to a conspiracy know that there are no accidents as they have penetrated to a deeper level of truth. The conspiracy theory is never subject to tests of falsifiability. Just because you don't see a dero doesn't mean it isn't there. That's just part of their deviltry.

As with the positing of an influencing machine, a heroic awareness of a conspiracy inflates a sense of importance and purpose. Announcing a conspiracy offers the opportunity for others to join in the battle. Shaver portrayed himself as an unlikely hero, with the role thrust upon him. In one of his early letters to Palmer, he wrote, "Help me for the sake of all men, I really have a big hunk of the Torch spoken of in the book 'The Torch' and no one capable of the oncarrying. I didn't ask for the job but I had it thrust on me by circumstance, I am trying."[20] First as a lark, more or less on a dare, and then with a dawning awareness of the profound forces that Shaver was grappling with, Palmer provided help.

Palmer and Shaver were ahead of the curve on cultural paranoia and conspiracy theorizing. Wartime America had had its share of panics, including concerns about children being kidnapped or molested, and of course the threat of a Japanese-American fifth column intent on undermining the war effort. The explosion of the atomic bombs over Hiroshima and Nagasaki did nothing to soothe the public's nerves. The ensuing Cold War, however, ushered in a golden age of paranoia as the United States and Soviet Union splintered the world into zones of influence. Reports of Soviet espionage were on the rise as were concerns with loyalty in the United States and possible Communist infiltration of institutions. In 1947, while Rap was prepping the all-Shaver issue, the House Un-American Activities Committee's hearings questioned the loyalty of the screenwriters and directors known as the Hollywood Ten. Similar inquisitions were carried out not only on the federal but the state level and led to shattered careers and boycotts. Soon came additional panics over rock 'n' roll and the link between juvenile delinquency and comic books. As pulp author Hauser had pointed out, who wouldn't want to crawl back into the "Mother" at a time like this?

In the April 1947 issue of *Amazing Stories*, preparing readers for the all-Shaver issue soon to come, Rap said he was fed up with people insisting he was suffering from a hallucination. He mentioned how what appeared to be the lining from a rocket fell to the earth in Oregon. It was not a U.S. rocket. "The papers hinted maybe the Russians did." He wondered out loud why only *Amazing* took such issues seriously. "What if the Shaver Mystery is VITALLY important to our national security?" What if the dero were to begin their invasion of the surface by starting a proxy war? What if they gave some "terrific weapons" to one side of the Cold War divide? "Oh yes, it's all poppycock. Just imagination. Or is it?" He concluded, with wonderful Palmerian logic, that at least Shaver was not an ostrich with his head in the sand. "He might just be fool enough to stumble on the truth."

As best he could, Palmer wanted to have it both ways. He reportedly told several members of the science fiction community, most notably Harlan Ellison, that the Shaver Mystery was all bunk designed to sell magazines. He also repeatedly broadcast to readers, "You don't have to believe the Shaver tales are true—just read them, they are entertaining." But when you read Palmer's correspondence with Shaver, including notes to Shaver indicating that another writer, "Rog Phillips," is "one of us" and add in Rap's fascination with topics such as the Spiritualist bible *Oahspe*, another narrative emerges. Palmer's interest in Shaver wasn't simply opportunistic. Shaver had confirmed Rap's own hunches about the odd workings of the universe. As he wrote in a letter to Shaver in March 1944, "I know the dero have failed with me, because my thinking has been greatly sharpened, and in two months I have been able to entirely revise my concept of the universe, and everything has fallen into order."

Palmer wouldn't be Palmer, however, if he didn't explore both sides and offer evidence that the Shaver Mystery might be either genuine or simply a lark. In February 1946 he remarked, "There is your editor who believes he has a special mission in life connected with the Shaver Mystery." Yet nearly a year later, in January 1947, he reported, the "latest attack on your editor by the dero . . . is the hypnotic ray attack on a group of fans who rapidly proceeded to spread a rumor to the effect that your editor had been committed to an insane asylum. . . . [Their] red faces lose none of their luminosity when encountering your editor—who has never laughed so much in his life!" A lover of paradox, content to be inconsistent, Palmer encouraged dual interpretations, like a sailor tacking into the wind.

Revenge of the Slan

Some readers took the affair with good humor. One wrote, "Sirs, I am just discovering what a freak I am. I don't hear voices, I don't have strange memories, and I am not taking sides as most of your fans are. The only thing I have in common with them is that I like *Amazing Stories*."[21] But there were many true defenders of the faith who were outraged at the direction Palmer was dragging *Amazing*.

In the early months, though, it remained something of a joke to most. SF fans assumed Rap was just kidding and seeking a sensational way to market fairly good stories. Forry Ackerman, in his fanzine *Voice of the Imagi Nation*, printed a letter from a correspondent, Emile E. Greenleaf Jr., with his own parenthetical interjections. "In Fantasy News Palmer (editor,

Amazing Stories) raised the devil (a demonstration, eh?) because the fans didn't read the Shaver stories. I don't know whether or not you've read them, but if you haven't you're missing something. It should be interesting to the scientifically minded among the fans. Got to go now. (This seems to be a common reaction with many fans after reading Shaver.)"[22]

One of the more scientifically minded fans soon did weigh in. Thomas S. Gardner, a medical researcher and serious SF fan, wrote a critique, partially veiled as praise, in the spring 1945 *Fantasy Commentator* titled "Calling All Crackpots: An Analysis of the Lemurian Hoax in *Amazing Stories.*" Gardner's main point was that science fiction publishing was in trouble. Magazines were having difficulty staying afloat, and new audiences simply had to be courted. Various feints had been tried and failed. Palmer, he insisted, had cleverly turned to a new audience. "The crackpots, as they are usually called, number at least a million in the United States. They are, in the main, adults, and have educational levels ranging from near zero to those of PhDs engaged in technical occupations. A great many harbor serious delusions of ancient civilizations superior to ours, believe in pyramidology and the like." With their interest in Lemuria, Mu, and Atlantis, they made a large potential audience if catered to. Gardner wrote, "Frankly, I admire Editor Palmer—up until now, no one in his position has been willing to contact the crackpots. It shows his wisdom in knowing just what to feed readers: exactly what they want, no matter what it is." He also wrote, "I predict this new policy will be an outstanding success, and think the Lemurian hoax will go on for years, possibly becoming a permanent esoteric feature of *Amazing Stories.*" The language of his long analysis of "I Remember Lemuria" made no doubts his own opinion of its merits, as he applied phrases such as "appalling lack of knowledge," "ignorance," "childish," and "fallacious." Gardner, clearly, was going to stick to *Astounding*.

Futurian James Kepner—who decades later would become a leading activist for gay rights—in his fanzine *Toward Tomorrow* stuck in the knife far deeper. He opened issue number 4 of 1945 with a single otherwise blank page with a dedication stamped in the middle:

AMAZING STORIES
R.I.P.

Small type in the lower right corner added, "Dedicated to the fond memory of a good magazine, AMAZING STORIES, dead for twelve years, and buried by Raymond Palmer in March, 1945."

Kepner went on to question Palmer's announcement that science fiction, as Gernsback had proposed it, "is being outstripped in its fiction by fact." Of *Amazing Stories*, he noted, "This magazine had been waning for a decade, and now it is dead. Since we have but small concern with the metaphysical question of an afterlife, we do not care what sort of existence *Amazing Stories* leads from now on. We feel no affinity with cadavers." Kepner went on to affirm his belief in the visionary possibilities of science fiction. "We followers of science fiction are interested in literate attempts to 'pre-construct' the future. The editor of this magazine [Palmer] has renounced his faith. . . . He seems to prefer the more lucrative field of metaphysical 'true' confessions. It is only right then that we should sever all interest in his magazines."

Other fans, at first, were hesitant to go in for the kill. An article in the *Fanews* column "Daugherty's Lights! Cameras! Action!" from July 3, 1945, noted that the Shaver stories, despite the controversy, were fun to read. "I am not taking sides in this fans I REMEMBER LEMURIA feud, but here is one point: I really have to hand it to Shaver (whether he believes the stuff he writes or not). He is a fair writer of run-of-the-mill fiction. HE DOES KNOW HIS MYTHOLOGY. This stunt has very likely run up the circulation of AMAZING for which I should imagine Mr. Shaver is being amply rewarded. . . . For the opportunity of being the lead story in AMAZING every issue along with the cash income that goes with it I'm afraid that I could remember a few things about Lemuria myself." He added "I've read storys [sic] by those whose names are halo'd in Science Fiction halls that aren't half as good in some of their stuff."

This was not a ringing endorsement, but not a demand for the heads of Raymond A. Palmer and Richard S. Shaver. Walter Dunkelberger, editor of *Fanews*, also mounted a defense in that same issue. He noted that Kepner "violently attacks Palmer and I REMEMBER LEMURIA." Dunkelberger, who had visited Palmer in Chicago, and seen the story in advance, commented, "In spite of expressed disbelief by members of his staff he [Palmer] firmly and wholeheartedly BELIEVES THE STORIES TO BE TRUE. That is his privilege." He added, "Whether you agree or disagree with the factual nature of the tales you will agree that they are good reading. Better than Burroughs, we think."

Several months later, Dunkelberger had second thoughts and published an "Open Letter to Rap" demanding he come clean. "As fiction we endorse them. As one who believed that you were sincere and because of this went to bat for you, we ask that you tell the reading public the truth—DO YOU BELIEVE THEM??? Or are you pulling a giant sales stunt?"[23] Soon after came, "Ray Palmer Answers Dunk." The answer: "I do believe that Shaver's stories are true. I do not say that every word is true, because many of them are my words, and they are not true, except by accident: and there were many of those accidental agreements. I know that the stories are true because I have incontestable proof in my files." Palmer went on to insist that Shaver telepathically received information from thought records and that the archaeological record corroborated some of his claims of a past race of giants. He invites Dunk and others to inspect his own files. "But I warn the investigator to be prepared for some mental shocks not to his liking."[24]

The controversy Rap had been courting finally surfaced. Opinion turned against him as the Mystery wore on and the pages of *Amazing Stories* began less and less to resemble those of a science fiction magazine. Actifan Forry Ackerman finally took offense. Forry, of course, went way back with Ray Palmer. He had been "Fan no. 2," back when Palmer had been "Fans no. 1, 3, and 4." In addition to becoming one of the first literary agents for science fiction authors, he was an advocate of "Flantasy Flanguage," as well as Esperanto, and an aficionado of science fiction and horror films.

Ackerman's opinion carried weight in the fan world. His initial amusement over the Shaver affair wore down. According to reports, he circulated a petition demanding that the Shaver Mystery end. He wasn't the only science fiction fan fighting to save the genre from Palmer's foul grip. *Fantasy Times*, a leading fanzine, ran a headline in 1945, "Scram, Mr. Palmer!" Another, *Fantasy Commentator*, was furious at Palmer's effort to become "our own little two-bit dictator . . . who would turn s-f into a plaything for every semi-sane crackpot who ever dreamt he was a Lemurian."[25]

In science fiction club meetings and minutes, the fen charged that Palmer was perverting the genre, confusing addled readers, and pandering to nutcases. To cap their charges, they quoted Palmer's own earlier letter to Hugo Gernsback in which the young author had stated "It is up to the writers of this fiction to include . . . real science and sound reasoning in their stories." The Queens Science Fiction League, begun by Sam Moskowitz and James Taurasi, heavy hitters in early fandom, passed a resolution noting that the Shaver Mystery was a threat to the sanity of readers and forwarded their concerns to the Society for the Suppression of Vice. A fan chapter in Philadelphia considered a petition to have the magazine banned by the post office.[26]

The Mystery Cools Down

It was not just Shaver's fringe pronouncements that disturbed science fiction fans. As the Mystery unfolded, Rap had changed the editorial slant of *Amazing Stories* in a way that ran counter to the founding notion of science fiction—i.e., that it contain some kernel of science. The *Amazing* of the late 1940s indicated Palmer's effort to graft science fiction to studies of "strange mysteries" not only with the Shaver stories, but also in many feature articles. By the late 1940s *Amazing* barely resembled a pulp SF magazine.

In truth, Palmer had been testing this approach well before the Shaver Mystery. Beginning in 1941, Rap's friend L. T. Hansen presented mythological lore and anthropological reports in her column "Scientific Mysteries." Palmer made Hansen into something of an Indiana Jones figure. In one "Observatory," Rap reported that Hansen had to be rescued from quicksand during "his" investigations. Titles of the columns included "Who Were the People of the Dragon?"; "Does the Atlantic Hide a Sunken Land?"; "The Ghost of Pan"; "Was There a Great Flood?"; and "Search for the City of the Seven Caves." The columns often highlighted the mystical beliefs of Native Americans and other preindustrial societies.

After initiating the Shaver Mystery, much of the magazine filled with tales of the caverns or other scientific mysteries. The all-Shaver issue of June 1947, for example, sandwiched the Shaver tales between such nonfiction features as "Visitors from the Void," about mysterious sightings of airships in the skies; "Mystery of the Peruvian Giants"; "A Petrified Stump—or Not?"; "The Magnetic Pendulum," which explained how this device could be used for guidance on decisions and divination, and more to the point, Vincent H. Gaddis's "Notes on Subterranean Shafts." Gaddis informed us, "Throughout the world there are mysterious shafts, caves and tunnels built or inhabited by unknown beings who have vanished into the mists of pre-history." In addition to describing Agartha as an underground city of millions of people who were "devoted to evil," he also told of a great pit in the Ozarks from which "strange sounds, lights, and odors emerge."

Shifting the entire content of *Amazing* to support the Shaver Mystery became tiresome. Shaver's perverse notion that technological progress was an illusion and that moderns could barely imagine the glories of a former golden age did not support the genre's future-oriented agenda. Despite this contradiction, Palmer still liked to position *Amazing Stories*, as had Hugo Gernsback decades earlier, as the midwife of scientific invention. In February 1946, he wrote, *"Amazing Stories* tells science what can be done, and then science does it! . . . The progress of Man towards his mysterious goal has been influenced enormously by this magazine." Logic was on the rack.

Responding to fans' anger, in late 1947 Palmer started a new column, "The Club House," dedicated to fan clubs and other fan news. He put the affable Rog Phillips in charge of the column. ("The Club House" took the fans seriously and was well regarded.) Nevertheless, townspeople with pitchforks, dogs, and torches continued to hound Palmer as he dodged through the mountains. According to many accounts, responding to pressure from fans, Ziff-Davis management finally banned Shaver stories from *Amazing* in 1948, whereupon an outraged Palmer turned in his resignation.

The tale of this ban and resignation, however, is slightly exaggerated.

Palmer with author Rog Phillips (Roger P. Graham) at the Cincinnati science fiction convention, or Cinvention, 1949. *Photo supplied by Forrest J Ackerman; scanned by Andrew Porter*

Howard Browne, although not entirely reliable, insisted in his memoirs that the higher-ups at Ziff-Davis were oblivious to the controversy. Palmer actually stayed on as editor through December 1949. Through much of 1948, he continued to publish the Shaver Mystery stories as authentic tales. It may have been pressure, a demand from Bernard Davis, or boredom, but Shaver's "Daughter of the Night," published in December 1948, was simply labeled "a terrific yarn," and the Shaver stories that ran in 1949 no longer included the racial memory tag. In 1949 Palmer requested reader input on whether to sustain the Mystery and announced that the number of positive letters he had received, 132 "yes," against 6 "no," was still not high enough to do so. It would require about 75,000 "yes" votes. This led to the thrilled announcements of the death of the Shaver Mystery, or as one fanzine put it, "Goodbye to All That."[27]

Thomas Gardner had predicted that the Shaver Mystery might become "a permanent esoteric feature of *Amazing*," but in five years it had run its course. Rather like a lap dissolve in film, as the Shaver Mystery waned, a new craze emerged every bit as beguiling. The flying saucer. And just in time. In the April 1947 issue of *Amazing*, just for fun, Palmer had predicted, "Within a few years, we will be visited from outer space by a ship that will be seen all over the earth as it circles the planet, but such a ship as no one could have imagined even in our pages up to now." Two months later began the near-endless sightings of flying saucers, beginning with those of Kenneth Arnold on June 24, 1947, near Mount Rainier.

Bringing both mysteries into his orbit, the tireless Palmer insisted there was a link. In the October 1947 issue of *Amazing*, Palmer announced with great delight, "A portion of the now world-famous Shaver Mystery has now been proved! On June 25th . . . mysterious supersonic vessels, either space ships or ships from the caves, were sighted in this country! . . . Accordingly we submit: Mr. Shaver has been correct in his insistence that our earth is being visited regularly by ships from outer space; and, that such ships are joined by others, from underground hideouts of an unknown race. . . . Whether they come from space, or from the interior of the earth, is not the present question. . . . If you want to get the straight dope from now on, read *this* magazine. It has guts as well as imagination."

Even equipped with a magnetic pendulum it would have been difficult to predict. The hollow earth served as a giant hangar for flying saucers capable of intergalactic travel.

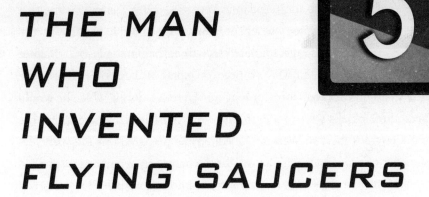

THE MAN WHO INVENTED FLYING SAUCERS

"For God's sake, A.G., what are you doing up there? You're shadow-boxing with yourself!"

"Barney," I said, wonder in my voice, "do you mean to say that there weren't any other pips on your screen the last few minutes?"

There was an instant of cautious silence. "Why? Should there be?"

"There damn well should!" I said.

—Captain A.V.G. (as told to Ray Palmer), "I Flew in a Flying Saucer," *Other Worlds Science Stories*, October 1951

One finds the same remark in old tales—the treasures of the fairies are evanescent—not to be depended on.

—Richard Shaver, letter to Rap, March 18, 1944

For several years, Ray Palmer had led a double life. Married with children; serving as managing editor of a full line of pulp magazines; holding meetings with writers, artists, and production staff to plan issues of *Amazing Stories* and *Fantastic Adventures* was not enough for him. Any good gumshoe quickly would have determined that the problem was not another dame. Yet, as *Amazing Stories* was the first love of his life, the analogy to a kept woman is apt. While the Shaver controversy continued to rage, for nearly two years, beginning in 1947, Palmer had been leaving the Ziff-Davis offices (on North Wabash Avenue as of the mid-1940s) in Chicago's loop for long lunch breaks, during which he would head three blocks west to a drab office on Clark Street. There, using the pseudonym Robert N. Webster, he edited and prepared *Fate* magazine designed for an audience with a taste for the paranormal and unexplained.

With its first issue in 1948, *Fate* also became a centerpiece for the newly forming flying saucer subculture. Unafraid of the tyranny of what he termed the "raised eyebrow," Palmer became the ideal figurehead for the new community of "saucer people." Writer John Keel provided an early sketch of this group, "In the fall of 1948, the first flying saucer convention was held at the Labor Temple on Fourteenth Street in New York City. Attended by about thirty people, most of whom were clutching the latest issue of *Fate*, the meeting quickly dissolved into a shouting match."[1] The telling detail for Palmerites is the copies of Robert N. Webster's *Fate* magazine that participants waved around during this bit of comic opera. From its first issue in the spring of 1948, *Fate*, a digest-sized pulp, served as a guide for the perplexed—particularly for flying saucer aficionados. Revising Gernsback's old motto, Palmer was insisting that "yesterday's extravagant fiction" had become "today's cold fact."

Palmer's publishing partner was Curtis Fuller, the editor of Ziff-Davis's *Flying* magazine. Their alliance began when Ziff-Davis announced it would be moving all its offices from Chicago to New York as of 1950. While continuing on at their jobs, Palmer and Fuller pooled resources and created Clark Publishing Company. Their first effort was *Fate* and then, starting in 1949, *Other Worlds Science Stories*. Palmer and Fuller made an odd couple: the mercurial, outlandish Palmer contrasted with Fuller, a more stolid, thoughtful citizen, who had a masters of science degree from Northwestern University and a background in journalism. While Palmer had a mystic streak and a wide-open imagination, Fuller, although interested in scientific "anomalies," enjoyed calmly leafing through copies of science magazines. Jerome Clark, who later joined *Fate*'s editorial team, recalled, "It was possible to get on Curt's bad side but you had to work at it."[2] A caricature of Fuller, puffing on a pipe and holding a newspaper, accompanied his *Fate* column, "I See By the Papers," in which he offered a digest of startling clippings about science and the paranormal.

Palmer and Fuller's *Fate* served as a *National Geographic* for explorers of the anomalous or weird. It specialized in what historian James Webb has termed "rejected knowledge"—the thought systems and lore associated with the occult.[3] Discussions of abominable snowmen, sea serpents, hauntings, divination, automatic writing, yoga, goddess cults, multiple personality disorder, shrunken heads, as well as diatribes against atomic weapons production and accounts of the effects of visionary drugs such as yage (ayahuasca) and psilocybin mushrooms would all find their way into *Fate* in the 1940s and 1950s.

Decades later, Curt Fuller said he started *Fate* after the first wave of flying saucer sightings in 1947. As editor of Ziff-Davis's *Flying* magazine, he had numerous contacts in the aviation and military worlds. He began to ask questions and concluded military officials were lying to him. He claimed he had been entirely conventional in his thinking until then. It created an epiphany—he realized that, more than likely, "I was being lied to in other areas."[4] In this same period, Palmer was developing an "all flying saucer" issue of *Amazing*. According to Palmer, Ziff-Davis rejected the proposed issue after receiving a visit from a government official.[5] Sharing notes, Fuller and Palmer decided to start a magazine that would question standard assumptions.

Palmer and Fuller purchased a subscription list from Wing Anderson, an occult entrepreneur, reasoning that his subscribers would provide an ideal base readership for their new digest. In a varied career, Anderson had been an electrician, a motion picture projectionist, and the promoter of a positive-thinking system that involved phonograph records that implanted upbeat suggestions in sleepers' minds. Anderson also sold thousands of copies of a Spiritualist tract from 1882 called *Oahspe, A Kosmon Bible in the Words of Jehovih and His Angel Embassadors*; Anderson, as a positive-thinking guru, also formed the Essenes of Kosmon to spread *Oahspe* teachings.

In the 1870s, New York City dentist John Ballou Newbrough, a man "of large stature, with dark, dreamy eyes," after preparing himself via years of fasting and simple meals of nuts and vegetables, had channeled the text of *Oahspe* over the course of a year while sitting at a typewriter each dawn.[6] As he typed, his spirit guides gave him access to knowledge he had requested "about the spirit-world; what the angels did, how they travelled, and the general plan of the universe."[7] The resulting tome, nearly as long as the King James Bible, chronicled a twenty-four-thousand-year history of the cosmos, published complete with star maps tracing the journeys of ancient races through the universe. Palmer became fixated on *Oahspe* after learning of it from Shaver-era *Amazing Stories* readers. He and Marjorie read it to each other at night and discussed it while doing dishes in their home in Evanston. Eventually Palmer decided to publish his own edition of *Oahspe*.

Fate appeared at the dawn of prefabricated suburbs such as Levittown, when families gathered around the television to watch *The Perry Como Show* and when typing out the utterances of angels, listening for rapping noises at séances, or photographing encounters with winged faeries was no longer acceptable behavior. Such interests left one open to ridicule. To decrease stigma, other occult publications such as Eileen Garrett's *Tomorrow*, founded in 1942, took the high road. Garrett, a wealthy Spiritualist medium, followed a humanistic approach in her digest and presented articles from respected scholars of religion and anthropologists. Each issue mixed expert musings on indigenous magic practices with poems, short stories, and reports of investigations by Garrett's Parapsychology Foundation based in New York City. *Time* magazine, nonetheless, took pleasure in ridiculing *Tomorrow* as the work of an eccentric kook, noting Garrett had "two 'controls': 'Uvani,' a 19th Century Arab, and 'Abdul Latif,' a Persian physician who lived at the time of the Crusades."[8] Such claims needed no further comment.

If Palmer and Fuller were tuned in to *Tomorrow*'s problematic reception, the lesson was obvious: there was no need to pander to the Ivy League crowd or solid citizens (that niche, in any event, was already taken). Instead, *Fate* was proudly lowbrow. It made no attempt at courting respectability. With Rap as its early guiding spirit, *Fate* relied on the pulp industry apparatus, including distribution to newsstands and garish covers, many of which featured paintings of scantily clad women, whether an Aztec sacrificial victim, a naked nymph on the shoulders of a satyr, or an image of a kneeling, bikini-clad, multi-armed goddess Kali. Inside were advertisements for the Rosicrucians, the Brotherhood of the White Temple, pulp Westerns such as *Hell's Horseman* or *Dry Gulch Canyon*, as well as Shaver's novel *I Remember Lemuria* and Wing Anderson's edition of *Oahspe*.

To bond *Fate*'s audience, Palmer relied on the model of science fiction fandom, with its chummy editorials, letters, and other features. Just as in the pulps, readers sent in their praise or criticisms of artwork and articles, as well as descriptions of their own paranormal experiences. They often signed letters with their full names and addresses, in an effort to contact others interested in the paranormal, as well as to create discussion groups and clubs. In a typical letter (from the Winter 1949 issue) a reader noted of *Fate*, "It fills the need for circulation of little known fact . . . most people are reluctant to discuss the strange phenomena for fear of public ridicule."

The paranormal was a broad canvas on which to paint, but Palmer decided that for the public of 1948, flying saucers offered something new, startling, and potentially apocalyptic. The first issue of *Fate* had a cover painting of flying saucers stacked in the clouds above a small red airplane, illustrating Kenneth Arnold's "The Truth About the Flying Saucers"—the actual title in the magazine was "I Did See the Flying Disks!" The article was Kenneth Arnold's full report of his by-then famous sighting on

The debut cover of *Fate*. *Used by permission of* Fate *magazine*

June 24, 1947, of nine strange aircraft skimming over the Cascade Mountains near Mount Rainier in Washington State, an event that served as the birth notice for the modern flying saucer craze.

Advent of the Flying Doughnuts

Unlike many who later seized the flying saucer limelight in the United States, Idaho resident Kenneth Arnold wasn't a science fiction fan or an occultist. He had no manuscripts or screenplays tucked away. Arnold was an active, athletic, and fairly unimaginative salesman of fire extinguishers and fire suppressant systems. A former Eagle Scout, college football player, and a skilled "fancy diver" who had attended Olympic trials, he since had become a member of the Idaho Search and Rescue Mercy Flyers and an Acting Deputy Federal United States Marshal.

Arnold began his account "I Did See the Flying Disks!" in Palmer and Fuller's first issue of *Fate* by insisting, "The following story of what I observed over the Cascade mountains, as impossible as it may seem, is positively true. I never asked nor wanted any notoriety. . . . I reported something that I know any pilot would report." The adventure began on June 24, 1947, when he left the Chehalis, Washington, airport at about 2:00 in the afternoon planning to fly to Yakima. En route, he circled Mount Rainier to search for the wreckage of a downed Marine transport plane that had been carrying thirty-two soldiers. There was a reward for its discovery. He was making a sweep of the plateau that surrounded Rainier when a flash of light startled him. He then observed about twenty-five miles away, "a chain of nine peculiar-looking aircraft flying from north to south at a similar elevation." As they approached Mount Rainer, several of them began dipping or changing their course slightly.

Arnold was astonished that he could not see their "tails" and suspected they were some new kind of jet. He likewise had never seen airplanes maneuver so close to mountaintops. They flew directly down the ridge of a mountain range in a formation like geese in a "chain like line as if they were linked together. They seemed to hold a definite direction but swerved in and out of the high mountain peaks." He timed how long they moved between two distinct peaks to later estimate their speed. Before they moved out of range, he opened the window of his airplane to rule out the possibility that they were merely odd reflections on the glass.

At the airport in Yakima he reported his sighting to a friend, who brought in other pilots and flight instructors to hear his story. Arnold was not known as a spinner of yarns. Some suspected he'd seen experimental army aircraft or missiles. They calculated the likely speed of the craft at 1,200 miles per hour. Later that day when Arnold landed in Pendleton, Oregon, a solemn crowd met him, and he spoke with reporters.

Within two days the Associated Press and United Press wire services took up the story. The news spread at a frenzied pace. The sighting, apparently, was not a onetime fluke. There followed an escalating series of flying saucer sightings that peaked in July 1947. Hundreds of people worldwide reported seeing UFOs; witnesses included scientists and military personnel. Among the summer's reports was a June 29 sighting by three scientists of a silvery disk in the sky near White Sands Proving Grounds in New Mexico, as well as numerous separate sightings by airline pilots, military pilots, and others.

On July 8, air force major Jesse Marcel reported the recovery of the wreckage of a crashed saucer at Roswell, New Mexico—an announcement that was retracted the following day with the explanation that the wreckage had been of a high-altitude weather balloon. For several decades the Roswell story was lost among the many other sightings of that summer. The same day Marcel made his misbegotten announcement, a United Press wire story titled "Who Has the Saucer? 40 States Join Game" circulated. The article playfully noted, "The game of spotting flying saucers broadened yesterday to include Massachusetts and Vermont, as stories about the discs continued to swirl fully as rapidly as the objects themselves."

The flying saucer craze did not fade. With sightings reported around the world, military officials began investigating. By January 1948 the Air Force Materiel Command, housed at Wright-Patterson Air Force Base in Ohio, officially set up Project Sign (popularly called Project Saucer), and its successors, Project Grudge and Project Blue Book. J. Allen Hynek, the chief scientist analyzing sightings for the air force, originally categorized the Arnold sighting, or "incident 17," as one in which "evidence offered suggests no explanation." Hynek's main critique was with Arnold's estimate of the crafts' speed. He concluded that the craft would not be visible at the distance Arnold attributed (twenty-five miles away) unless they were enormous; assuming they were closer to Arnold and no more than two hundred feet in length each, Hynek calculated the crafts' real speed at about 400 miles per hour—no longer entirely ruling out conventional craft.[9]

An army intelligence officer who interviewed Arnold several weeks after the sightings reported to his superiors that he found Arnold trustworthy. He concluded, "It is difficult to believe that a man of Mr. Arnold's character and apparent integrity would state that he saw objects and write up a report to the extent that he did if he did not see them. To go further, if Mr. Arnold can write a report, of the character that he did while not having seen the objects that he claimed he saw, it is the opinion of the interviewer that Mr. Arnold is in the wrong business, that he should be writing Buck Rogers fiction."[10] Within a few years, however, the air force rejected this assessment, as well as that of Hynek. The air force concluded that Arnold, who profited from his story when he sold it to *Fate*, must be untrustworthy. In a masterful example of circular reasoning, a new analyst concluded that Arnold's report "cannot bear even superficial examination, therefore, must be disregarded."[11]

Honest, delusional, or both, Arnold started a furor and introduced a new motif to popular culture: the flying saucer. Something about the shape amused people—and aided cartoonists—helping to keep the saucer an object of interest while at the same time barely credible. How the craft became "saucers" or "disks" or "doughnuts" is something of a mystery. In his initial interviews, Arnold used the phrase "saucer-like" as a description of their motion in the sky. Two days after the sighting he described the craft as "flat like a pie-pan and somewhat bat-shaped."[12] In the *Fate* article, written several months after the event, Arnold noted, "They appeared to be completely round" when the sun reflected off them—i.e., when they were tilted. But the sketch he supplied to Palmer indicated a slightly tapering, batwing, or shovel shape.

Palmer and Fuller had access to aeronautics experts through Ziff-Davis. For that same issue, they commissioned John C. Ross's "What Were the Flying Doughnuts?" which compared Arnold's sightings to new aircraft

prototypes. Ross suggested that a batwing-shaped craft would tally with
the "flying wing" that Northrop was experimenting with at that time. The
January 1947 issue of *Popular Science* included illustrations of Northrop's
XB-35, a "flying wing" propeller plane. Ross insisted that Northrop did not
have nearly enough in production to permit nine of these craft to be flying
precision runs and weaving through mountaintops. He also mentioned
another experimental plane, the Vought XF5U-1 (known as the "flying pan-
cake" or "flying flapjack") that looked like "a great flat beetle," but noted
its top speed was 425 mph, well below the 800 to 2,000 mph that Arnold
had attributed to the disks. Ross concluded that if Arnold's observations
were accurate, "I do not believe they were manufactured in the United
States or in the Soviet Union or even on the Planet Earth itself."

Perhaps because they were easier for schoolchildren to doodle in the
margins of their workbooks, the public clearly preferred flying saucers to
shapes with greater complexity. Palmer, who had overseen the artwork of
myriad forms and styles of intergalactic spacecraft during his reign at
Amazing Stories, went with the saucer. In ensuing months, on the covers of
Amazing Stories (in stories such as "Space Ships at Angkor Wat?"), *Fate* magazine, and Palmer's other publications, the saucer shape held dominance.

While followers of the Shaver Mystery numbered in the mere thousands, Kenneth Arnold became a household name, known to millions.
Women fled from diners when they spotted him and preachers urged
him to return to the Lord. Unwittingly, Arnold had initiated a new mystery, and Palmer wanted a crack at it. Like Babe Ruth and a baseball bat, or
H. P. Lovecraft and a chthonic horror, Ray Palmer and the flying saucer
were a perfect match. Rap was persistent, ardent, yet gentle, in his wooing
of the fire extinguisher salesman. Eventually they would become fast
friends, with Arnold visiting Palmer and his family in Wisconsin and giving
the Palmer children impromptu swimming lessons.

Palmer sent his first letter to Arnold in early July. Arnold noted, "At
the time, had I known who he was, I probably wouldn't have answered his

letter. . . . Later I found he was connected with the type of publications that I had not only never read but had always thought a gross waste of time." Nevertheless he was swayed by Palmer's "tone of softness and sincere interest."[13] He received a second letter from Palmer, inviting him to write an article. Arnold declined but sent Palmer a copy of the detailed report and biography he had mailed earlier to the air force at Wright Field in Dayton, Ohio.

Later in July, Arnold received a third letter from Palmer. There had been numerous saucer sightings in the Northwest, including one by United Airlines pilot Emil Smith, whom Arnold had met during a news interview and befriended. More significantly, Palmer had been mailed a cigar box filled with what he was told were "flying saucer fragments" by two men, Harold Dahl and Fred Crisman of Tacoma, Washington. Crisman had previously sent letters to *Amazing* to claim contacts with dero. Palmer wanted Arnold to go to Tacoma and check their story. Arnold balked.

On July 16, two army intelligence officers, Lieutenant Frank M. Brown and Captain William Davidson (both had been investigating Arnold and United Airlines pilot Smith) called on Arnold to discuss his sightings. He had grown accustomed to ridicule, but they treated him courteously—as if he were a colleague—and encouraged him to stay in touch if he learned anything new. Their visit and interest may have emboldened Arnold, as shortly after, he asked Palmer to wire him $200 and went to Tacoma to meet Crisman and Dahl. The misadventure that ensued was briefly described in the first issue of *Fate*, and then more thoroughly treated in a book cowritten by Arnold and Palmer, *The Coming of the Saucers* (1952).

Arnold in Wonderland

Arnold's credibility becomes strained early in the book-length account when he notes that on July 30, while flying over Oregon en route to

Tacoma to meet Dahl and Crisman, he saw what he first took to be a flock of ducks but then concluded were approximately twenty-five brass-colored objects maneuvering in the sky. They were thin, about thirty inches in diameter, flew flat and also wheeled on edge. He took film footage but admitted that of the twenty-five objects only two could be seen and these "only under a jeweler's glass." This new sighting made him what is known in the literature as a "repeater" and possibly less trustworthy. The morphing of "ducks" into "disks" also has a bizarre quality to it that either indicates his honesty about his thought processes or signals a step into a hallucinatory reality.

Much of the ensuing account unveils like a mystery movie stocked with film noir characters and flourishes—including a special appearance of a box of Corn Flakes. Arnold landed at the airstrip in Tacoma. Hotel rooms were tight but after making random calls to hotels, he was told he already had a reservation at the upscale Winthrop. He made the clerk repeat this several times, puzzled over it, wondered if another Kenneth Arnold had made the reservation, but decided it was silly to argue. Soon after, he pulled up in a taxi to the hotel, stepped under its imposing metal canopy advertising the latest swing band, and got his room key in the lobby with its vistas of chandeliers and marble staircases.

After a bath, he thumbed through the phone book and found a listing for Harold Dahl. He dialed the number and Dahl proposed that Arnold simply "go home and forget the whole business." Thirty minutes later Dahl appeared at his room. Arnold was surprised that Dahl, an imposing lumberjack of a man, seemed petrified. Dahl told Arnold he'd been plagued with bad luck ever since he'd observed the saucers (which he referred to as the "doughnuts"): he'd nearly lost his job, his wife had fallen sick, his son was injured, and a valuable boom of logs for his logging salvage business had broken loose and washed away.

According to Dahl, on June 21 he was on his harbor patrol boat with two crewmen, as well as his fifteen-year-old son and his dog, on the eastern

bay of Maury Island, several miles offshore from Tacoma. Dahl then spotted, about two thousand feet above them "six very large doughnut-shaped
craft," which he at first mistook for balloons. Five of them were slowly
circling the center doughnut, which began to lose altitude. The craft had
portholes spaced around the exterior and were of "a shell-like gold and silver color" that shone with brilliance in the sun "like a Buick dashboard."
The ailing craft spewed out a light metal that looked like white shredded
newspapers, and then heavy chunks of dark metal that looked like lava
rock. Dahl snapped several photographs.

Dahl and his men pulled their boat to shore and ran for shelter. His
son's arm was injured and the dog killed by the hot debris that fell. Dahl
also claimed that the following morning, while his partner Crisman was
out investigating, a 1947 black Buick sedan, with its puffed up front and
sharklike radiator grill, pulled up to Dahl's house. A middle-aged gentleman in a dark suit who "looked a lot like an insurance salesman" walked
to his door and invited him to breakfast. Thinking he might make a lumber
sale, Dahl agreed and followed him through town to a small diner. Over
breakfast the man in the dark suit told him he knew about what Dahl had
seen on Maury Island and added, "If he loved his family and didn't want
anything to happen to his general welfare, he would not discuss his experience with anyone."[14]

Arnold was perplexed. One of Arnold's acquaintances from a business
group had vouched for Dahl's honesty. But something seemed wrong.
That same night Dahl drove Arnold to his secretary's house to see the
"fragments." Arnold carefully described the house, noting the design of its
porch, its mahogany door, and its oblong doorknob with a raised relief of
grapes. A producer of the Twilight Zone might have furnished its interior—
it was cluttered with rugs, a radio, and a piano with kewpie dolls you might
"win at a sideshow" on top. While the secretary did some bookkeeping
in the kitchen, Dahl showed him rocks that Arnold dismissed as simply
"lava rock." Dahl shrugged this off and said that samples of the lighter

metal were in Crisman's garage. He also began to tell Arnold of an anonymous letter he had received that proposed the saucers had been on Earth
for thousands of years as protectors of its life-forms.

The next morning, July 31, Dahl appeared with Fred Crisman at Arnold's hotel room. Arnold described Crisman as short and stocky and "bub-
bling over" to tell his story. Crisman confirmed Dahl's account. After
traveling to the island, Crisman had also seen a single doughnut craft that
soon hid in a cumulus cloud. Crisman was even more baffling to Arnold.
He was a cheerful con man whose evidence never quite materialized; in
Arnold's account he appeared a trickster from a nightmare, a cheerful
demon, a mythic swallower of the real. Certain that the men's stories
didn't "ring quite true," but at a loss as to how to proceed, Arnold decided
to call his friend, the airline pilot Smith, to help him investigate. Smith
agreed, and Arnold fetched him later that day from Seattle in his private
plane.

Smith took charge and cross-examined Crisman and Dahl. Smith wanted
rock samples and to visit Maury Island. That night, Smith stayed in Arnold's
hotel room. While they were joking about the day's events, Arnold received
a call from a United Press newsman, Ted Morello, who was based in Tacoma. Morello told them that throughout the day an anonymous caller had
been tipping his office about what was being said in their hotel room. Arnold and Smith searched the hotel room for a "dictaphone" but found nothing. The mysterious caller would continue to phone Morello and *Tacoma
Times* reporter Paul Lantz throughout Arnold's investigation.

The next day, August 1, Crisman brought rock samples to their hotel
room. The darker rock was extremely heavy. Even a hand-sized chunk
was difficult to lift. Crisman proposed that the pieces, which seemed to fit
together, might have been the "lining of a power tube." The white rock
looked to Smith and Arnold like scrap aluminum, although they puzzled
over the unusual rivets in it. Crisman reported that he "couldn't find"
Dahl's photographs.

Hoping to flush out the hoax, Arnold called his contacts in army intelligence, Captain Davidson and Lieutenant Brown. Insisting that the enthusiastic Crisman knew the details of the story, Dahl left for a movie house to pay fifteen cents and trade his current woes for a recent Western or crime film. The two intelligence officers arrived at about 9:00 P.M. and listened to Crisman's story. By midnight they seemed unimpressed. They didn't want rock samples and gave Arnold the impression he'd been caught up in "some silly hoax." As Brown and Davidson left the hotel to get into their car, Crisman pulled up and double-parked in his roadster and opened his trunk; Davidson apparently helped Crisman move a box of Kellogg's Corn Flakes full of rock samples into the trunk of the army car.

Then came a strange turn of events. The next morning, August 2, Arnold read in the newspaper that the plane that Davidson and Brown piloted the previous night had caught fire and crashed twenty minutes after takeoff. There had been four men on the plane. The two others were an army "hitchhiker," Master Sergeant Elmer L. Taff, who wanted a ride to their base in California, and Technician 4th Grade Woodrow T. Mathan. Both, on Brown's urging, had parachuted to the ground after safety equipment failed to put out a fire in one engine. The wing then tore off, along with the tail. Brown and Davidson died in the crash.

According to Arnold, that morning Crisman arrived at the hotel "as excited as Captain Smith and I were upset," over the news. Overwhelmed, and perhaps worn out by Crisman's antics, Arnold noted, "Suddenly I didn't want to play investigator any longer." The weary detective called Palmer in Chicago and offered to return his money. He recalled that "I told him I felt inadequate to investigate the situation. Two lives and a government bomber had been lost."[15] Palmer told him to keep the money but that it might be best to stop for now. Sensing a conspiracy, Rap also advised that neither he nor Smith take any fragments on their planes.

As if trapped in a nightmare, Arnold and Smith couldn't shake loose of Crisman, who continued to tease them and frustrate their hopes of solving the mystery. They went with him to the docks where he showed them a boat that did not appear to be a patrol boat, nor to have been damaged or recently repaired. Arnold asserted it was entirely unseaworthy. A mechanic toiled on the engine, but both Arnold and Smith sensed no work was really being done. Crisman told them he still couldn't "find" Dahl's photographs of the flying doughnuts. He thought they might be in his mountain cabin a few hours' drive away, if they wanted to go. They didn't. He seemed thoroughly unreliable. Crisman promised to call once the boat was ready and Arnold and Smith left the dock. As Arnold noted, "That was the last time I ever saw Fred Crisman."

The amateur investigators returned to the hotel to read further newspaper accounts about the plane crash and the death of the intelligence officers. The August 2 *Tacoma Times*, accepting the tipster's version of events, ran the story "Sabotage Hinted in Crash of Army Bomber at Kelso" with the subhead "Plane May Hold Flying Disk Secrets." Unable to get in touch with Crisman, Arnold and Smith finally reached Dahl, who said that Crisman had "gone off a few days." They didn't know what to think. Crisman seemed a thorough fraud, yet perhaps the crash was not a coincidence? Arnold and Smith continued to blunder on, while national news stories played up their role in the sensational mystery.

They then met with United Press newswire reporter Ted Morello, who told them that the anonymous phone caller had identified the dead officers before their names were officially released. The caller also had told the newsman that army officials were keeping locals away from the crash site. Morello played the tape of an interview with the army hitchhiker Master Sergeant Elmer L. Taff, who stated that on the B-25 the two airmen had a protected cargo in a trunk. Morello added a few other anonymous tips he'd received—the missing Marine transport plane had also been shot out of the sky and Smith would be called to Wright Field to air force headquarters in a few days (both of these tips turned out to be wrong). Another call claimed that one of the two finders of the saucer fragments (i.e., Crisman) had boarded an army plane earlier that day, bound for Alaska. While none of these tips were necessarily true, Morello told them, "Get out of town until whatever it is blows over. . . . I'm concerned with your welfare."[16]

Instead, Smith contacted army intelligence officer Major George Sander, who met with them and assured them the crash was not sabotage, but an accident. Crisman and Dahl were hoaxers. Despite this air of certainty, Sander insisted on collecting all the fragments Crisman had brought to their hotel room, wrapping them in a hotel towel, and saying, "I would like to have them all." Sander then drove the duo to a nearby smelter and showed them slag that closely resembled the dark rocks that Crisman had presented to them. He did not allow them to compare it to the samples wrapped in the towel.

Before leaving town, Arnold and Smith made one last effort to contact Dahl. Arnold remembered Dahl saying he would be at his secretary's house. They drove to the house. Arnold recognized it, with its porch and unusual oblong doorknob. Here Arnold's narrative takes a turn toward the gothic. The house was abandoned. No piano, no kewpie dolls, no radio, no furnishings. Just empty rooms and cobwebs. Arnold feared for his own sanity. Was it the right house? Did he have his bearings any longer? It was as if two clowns, straight out of a surrealist play, had been leading him on a pointless yet terrifying tour. Arnold made several calls to his wife and his mother noting he was concerned for his life.

Like Alice, he had enough of Wonderland and its mad inhabitants. The truth could wait. He flew home. He landed to refuel in Pendleton. On his takeoff the airplane stalled when he was only fifty feet in the air—quite a dangerous moment, as he hadn't gained enough momentum to glide. He put the plane into a dive to build up speed and crash landed. He and the plane survived. He realized that he had shut off the fuel valve. This indicated a suicidal impulse or, as Shaver would insist, that his mind was being tampered with. He had "the realization that my thought or mind in some peculiar way was being controlled or dictated to."

Confidence Games and UFOlklore

A few days after Arnold left town, Crisman appeared unbidden at the FBI office in Tacoma to announce he had no idea what the fuss was all about. Two days later, on August 7, the FBI further questioned Crisman and Dahl. The duo claimed "to be at a loss" as to why anyone thought the fragments could be related to flying saucers. They insisted they had merely found some interesting rocks and sent them to a lab at the University of Chicago. They told the FBI that somehow Ray Palmer had learned about the fragments and kept pestering them until they finally said the metal may have come from flying saucers, as "it appeared that's what he wanted them to say."[17] They signed a statement indicating that the rock fragments had no connection to flying saucers.

The FBI report also noted that another journalist, Ernie Vogel, an Associated Press wireman in Tacoma, had been less gullible than Lantz and Morello. When Crisman had first concocted the story, shortly after the Arnold sighting, Vogel had gone to interview Dahl, who began to recount his story. According to Vogel, Dahl's "wife came into the kitchen and was in a considerable rage, telling Dahl to admit that the entire story was a plain fantasy which he had dreamed up. He . . . admitted that there was nothing whatever to the story and it was an entire hoax." Vogel further asserted, "Dahl was a mental case and that nothing which he reported should be carried as far as a news story."[18] Vogel's wire avoided the story.

The air force's Project Sign report of April 27, 1949, labeled the Maury Island incident a hoax mounted, presumably, for profit or notoriety. Ray Palmer did not let them have the last word. In Palmer and Arnold's *The Coming of the Saucers*, Palmer insisted the air force was erroneous in indicating that Crisman and Dahl were simply trying to puff up a story to sell to *Amazing Stories*. When they sent him the fragments, they had asked for no money. He also wasn't quite sure the whole thing was a hoax. He noted that the FBI had visited his office at *Amazing Stories* to question him and inspect his files and the "saucer" fragments. The next day those files and fragments had been stolen. Palmer also had the University of Michigan run a chemical analysis—apparently on other fragments—with two intriguing results: high amounts of calcium, unusual for a man-made material brought to high temperatures, and titanium, "The only one [metal] suitable to spaceships." To this very thin evidence, he added, "Today neither of these men can be found, having mysteriously disappeared. In the case of Dahl, he left a home, a business, and apparently all his interests unclaimed."

Crisman surfaced long enough to send a letter to *Fate* in January 1950 denying he had perpetrated a hoax or had anything to do with the deaths of the two intelligence officers. After the Maury Island hoax, Crisman continued to pepper conspiracy lore. After some years in personnel at Boeing, then as a high school English teacher, vice principal, and public relations man, he reappeared in 1968 as radio personality Jon Gold, hosting a conspiracy-themed show on radio station KAYE in Tacoma. Following the John F. Kennedy assassination, his testimony before a grand jury placed Crisman in the orbit of Tom Beckham, a shady businessman and purportedly one of the organizers of the Bay of Pigs fiasco, and also presumably an acquaintance of Clay Shaw, one of the figures that Jim Garrison, the New Orleans district attorney, was investigating as part of an assassination scenario. Among the many business fronts that Beckham had placed him in, Crisman was a minister of the Universal Life Church. It is unclear whether Crisman was simply someone who liked to claim behind-the-scenes knowledge, or if he did indeed circulate in the underground world of CIA operatives. Possibly he did both. Palmer saw him as a personal nemesis and later commented, "Fact: Fred Crisman is always present; in the Shaver Mystery, in the flying saucer mystery . . . in the Bay of Pigs, in the assassination of Diem, in the John Kennedy case, and quite often causing Ray Palmer all kinds of hell."[19]

Palmer eventually dropped discussions of titanium and spaceships but refused to drop all thoughts of conspiracy. The deaths of the two intelli-gence officers cried out for a better explanation than mechanical failure. The initial narrative remained open-ended. Was it all an elaborate hoax or a sinister conspiracy? Was the B-25 crash an accident or the result of espio-nage? Were the rock samples smelter slag or flying saucer fragments? Did Arnold really find the right house when he wandered into the room full of cobwebs? Was Dahl really visited by a mysterious man in a black suit? What were Crisman's motives? Who could you trust?

Certainly, you could not trust the mainstream press for news of flying saucers. Palmer had nothing but contempt for journalist Sidney Shalett and his article "What You Can Believe About Flying Saucers," printed in two installments in April and May 1949 in the *Saturday Evening Post*. In these pieces Shalett insisted that all sightings of UFOs involved false rumors, misinterpretations, vertigo, and mirages. Shalett concluded, "If there is a scrap of bona fide evidence to support the notion that our inventive ge-niuses or any potential enemy, on this or any other planet, is spewing sau-cers over America, the Air Force has been unable to locate it."

Shalett also ridiculed Arnold for having written an article that had ap-peared in *Fate*, the self-described "cosmic reporter," alongside articles such as "Invisible Beings Walk the Earth." He described *Fate* as a publication that "beat the drum for the interplanetary-spaceship theory." Shalett's articles, which relied on the air force's resources, were timed to the pruning of personnel in Project Sign who gave any credence to the "extra-terrestrial hypothesis" and signaled a rejection of Project Sign's January 1949 assess-ment that there was "something" to the sightings and its recommendation that UFO units be assigned to every air force base.[20] Simultaneously, inci-dent 17, or the Arnold sighting, was downgraded from "unexplained" to "mirage."[21]

Regarding Shalett's reporting skills, Palmer noted that he spoke with Stuart Rose, an editor at the *Post*, who admitted that air force personnel were parked all over his office, shaped Shalett's story, and set its tone.

Wasn't this simply government whitewash? Palmer's faith in journalism was restored when Donald Keyhoe published his article "Flying Saucers Are Real" in the January 1950 edition of the mass-circulation magazine *True*. Keyhoe insisted the sightings were not delusional and indicated visitors from other planets.

Keyhoe, who developed the article into a book that sold more than five hundred thousand copies, had an approving audience. He was a retired Marine captain who had dabbled in pulp writing and aviation journalism and had numerous contacts in the military. On assignment with *True*, he spent several months researching the flying saucer phenomena and attempting to interview military personnel. Like Curtis Fuller, he sensed an intense secrecy that amounted to a cover-up. After discussing numerous mysterious cases, and approaching the cover-up as the hero of a detective novel might, Keyhoe concluded, "The American people have proved their

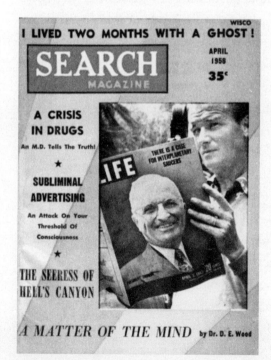

In *Search*, Palmer hailed a 1952 edition of *Life* magazine that presented flying saucers as worthy of serious study. *Department of Special Collections, Davidson Library, University of California, Santa Barbara*

ability to take incredible things. We have survived the stunning impact of the Atomic Age. We should be able to take the Interplanetary Age, when it comes, without hysteria."[22]

Palmer praised Keyhoe's piece and his premise that the military was hiding the truth. However, Palmer once again insisted that he did not know if the saucers were indeed "from another solar system, or even another planet." In *Amazing Stories* he had already proposed that the saucers might be coming from the inner earth, or underground bases. Palmer offered a tongue-in-cheek conclusion in the May 1950 *Fate*: "We don't know what flying saucers are. As for Army Intelligence, we suggest they read Buck Rogers with great care, and then at least they'll know as much about space ships as the average American Boy. . . . He's the lad who's going to Mars, when Americans go there, not the 'guys' who write this 'inspired' poppycock we see in newspapers and magazines these days."

Palmer, as always, was hard to pin down. How serious was he? Where was he taking *Fate*—and his subsequent publications? *Fate*'s mission was to examine "unexplained mysteries," often based in old folklore and "rejected knowledge." But at the same time it was helping create the new folklore of the space age. Lore—a dignified term for a body of knowledge that is capable of bearing truth, nonsense, or notions in between—was Ray Palmer's ultimate realm. The new lore centered on the elusive, flirtatious saucer. It also soon encompassed tales of alien contact and rumors of conspiracies and disinformation. It included, as well, figures such as the "man in black" that appeared, courtesy of Crisman and Dahl, in Palmer and Arnold's *The Coming of the Saucers*. Crisman and Dahl's man in black, who drove a black car and issued subtle threats over breakfast sausage, was only the first of many to appear in UFO lore.

UFO lore developed and veered about as unpredictably as a doughnut, with many authors contributing to shaping the narrative. Was there a center to this shifting topography? As in a Venn diagram, Palmer's desk on Clark Street represented the overlap of three circles: science fiction, the

occult underground, and the flying saucer crowd. His typewriter and printing press and his correspondents' grab bag of ideas helped place the flying
saucer at the center of a mystery. John Keel, in a 1983 article, declared that
Rap was "The Man Who Invented Flying Saucers," noting that Palmer had
been there at the beginning and nursed the saucer mystery through its dark
ages in numerous publications, such as *Amazing, Fate,* and later in *Flying
Saucers from Other Worlds.* While he cannot take full credit, Rap helped
shape perceptions of the many sightings and to sustain interest when the
military began its debunking campaign. In UFOlklore, Palmer had found
his métier. With a fragment of the material retrieved from Tacoma as a
paperweight on his desk, he set up shop as a purveyor of rejected knowledge and the folklore of the interplanetary age.

TRAPPED IN THE HOLLOW EARTH

June 30th, '54

Dear Sir,

In the August 1954 issue of "Mystic" magazine there was a fantastic story by Paul M. Vest entitled "Venusians Walk Our Streets!" published as a "true" story. The author claims that the F.B.I. has a "heavy plate of the hardest alloyed steel" which a man from space marked with a half inch streak by simply, and without effort, passing his fingernail over it. . . . All I want to know, is did the F.B.I. receive such a plate? (And of course anything else that can be reveiled [*sic*] at this time.)

Sincerely,
xxxx [name redacted]

July 8, 1954

Dear xxxx,

Your letter of June 30, 1954, has been received and the thought prompting your writing me is appreciated.

For your information, the FBI has never received a steel plate such as the one to which you make reference.

Sincerely yours,
John Edgar Hoover, Director

I n 1949, as the break with Ziff-Davis approached, Ray and Marjorie bought a 124-acre farm in Wisconsin. The spread included a mill-pond, a trout stream, and a refurbished ten-room farmhouse. Ray planned the move with his wife and three young children as a triumphal return to the state that he regarded as "heaven on earth." The Palmers, however, had no intention of farming, as Marjorie had had enough of that as a child. Rap was taking a big chance—he would attempt to run Clark Publishing and its magazines, *Fate* and *Other Worlds Science Stories*, from his rural retreat.

Moving to a new home can be traumatic and this move to Wisconsin had its share of ambiguity; for instance, Palmer, recently out of the hospital, was no longer certain if *he was alive*. Marjorie Palmer's version of how Rap injured himself in June of 1950: while attempting to repair the plumbing in the basement of the house in Evanston, "Ray tripped and fell." Palmer's version was more elaborate: he insisted that several of Shaver's dero flung him up in the air until he neared the ceiling, then smashed him down on his back where he lay in a cold puddle on the concrete for hours, unable to move.

The accident was serious. His back was again broken. As he later put it, "I lay totally paralyzed, with death creeping slowly upward from toes to heart." He struggled to stay alive. He had visions of beautiful dancing women who reminded him he must breathe, no matter how painful. Hours passed, then ambulance attendants carried him out on a stretcher with a blanket over his face. He was in critical condition. At the hospital, he hallucinated that the long-dead doctor who had operated on him as a child, Dr. Herman Gaenslen, was once again preparing to perform surgery. While the earlier operation had not been successful, Gaenslen, an expert on bone grafts, had returned to "make good." The doctor's hands felt around inside his body. While the "real" surgeons questioned him, Gaenslen gave his assessment: "I can repair some of the damage."

Palmer recalled that during the ensuing operation, he was in a "great open space, nothing visible but darkness," with a circle of nearly one hundred people around him, including Gaenslen and an assistant who worked a machine that looked like a combination of an old-fashioned radio and an organ. Afterward, as excruciating pain set in, Gaenslen told him, "You will walk if you want to. But you will always have pain."[1] This entire episode, which he admitted could have been inspired by the morphine administered to him, inspired Palmer's eerie later essay "How Do I Know I Am Alive?"[2] As in a *Twilight Zone* episode, he reasoned that he might well have died that day and was in some afterlife, unaware that he had not survived.

When he regained the ability to walk again, several months later, his doctors at St. Francis Hospital in Evanston were astounded. But he was never again fully able-bodied. His bowling days were over. In early November 1950, a still shaky Palmer, along with his wife and three young children, finally moved to Wisconsin. After settling in, Rap got down to work. He handed off the magazine *Imagination: Stories of Science and Fantasy* to his friend William Hamling (Palmer had fronted the magazine, which was really Hamling's, while Hamling remained at Ziff-Davis). Rap's plans were ambitious. In addition to publishing the magazines *Fate* and *Other Worlds Science Stories*, Palmer began a book publishing company; his office, which was stuffed with manuscripts, galleys, and address plates, was an upstairs room of the farmhouse. (Several years later, when he hired Helga Onan, a local woman, to provide clerical support, she remembered reporting to a chicken coop where he'd moved his office, and seeing typewriter ribbon from an electric typewriter strewn over the floor. Her kindergarten-aged son, who came with her, later said, "Mr. Palmer leaves his stuff in chicken nests.")[3]

The Palmers' closest neighbors in Wisconsin were Richard and Dottie Shaver, who had moved to the area a year earlier. This was no accident. The families were close. Even prior to the publication of "I Remember Lemuria," Shaver had proposed moving to Chicago. Slowly, Palmer warmed to the idea. In June 1945, Palmer wrote to Shaver, "When the war is over and we can drive, you'll see much of us, family and all. Maybe by then you can move somewhere near here. There are lots of nice little towns near Chicago, and places where you can be situated as we are now, with a place to raise things if you care to—or not, as you wish. I'd like to have you near, as I think a place like a small town would be free from dero as much as any other small town. I believe the big cities are the place of most dero control."[4]

As a result of Rap's encouragement, the Shavers had left Pennsylvania in 1946 and moved to Lily Lake, Illinois, a small town forty miles west of Chicago. Shaver and members of the Shaver Mystery Club set up a printing press there to supply the two thousand subscribers of the *Shaver Mystery Magazine* with copies, but zoning laws stopped the presses. By 1948, with the Shaver Mystery on the wane, and plagued with ulcers and what he believed was tamper, Shaver and his wife decided to move to the farm in Wisconsin, where they kept two goats, a Jersey bull calf, a pony, a horse, three dozen laying hens, roosters, as well as rabbits, dogs, and a cat. Shaver made no progress on his planned history of the Elder Races, for which subscribers had already paid. He was haunted by the recent death of a friend. John Carson Buford had stayed with the Shavers off and on in Illinois to help with farm tasks. One afternoon, after talking with Rap at Ziff-Davis about Shaver Mystery matters, such as the reality of dero, Buford had jumped off the Dearborn Street Bridge and drowned in the Chicago River. Buford's suicide left Shaver in a depression. Hard work was impossible.

The Palmers' arrival was a relief, socially. When Shaver Mystery Club members from Chicago came up to visit, they could chat with the "master," Shaver, and then walk over to the farm of the "Boss," Palmer. If it was Saturday, Palmer would cook everyone his potato pancakes, a tradition learned from his German-American grandmother. Rap also purchased a tractor. Shaver, capable with machinery, took to driving the tractor for farming tasks.

Palmer liked the country life in Wisconsin. He also, evidently, liked having Shaver near. Perhaps in his mind, their nearby farms approximated the forming of a utopian colony à la *Oahspe*. In his off hours, after a hard day at the typewriter or printing press, Palmer fished for trout in the stream that ran near his house. He and Shaver played chess. Often Shaver would babysit the Palmers' children. Palmer regarded growing lima beans as among his supreme challenges. Following Shaver's advice, Palmer would go out in his garden and sing "The Battle Hymn of the Republic" as loud as he could to gain the attention of Shaver's tero to send rain for his vegetables.

Wisconsin was proving to be a lively place for an editor of the paranormal. One night, while driving home, Rap said he slowed to let a rabbit cross the road. It stopped and looked at him. He then realized it was a little man who ran off with a humping movement. Rap also informed readers that he had spied a UFO on his Wisconsin farm on February 3, 1952, at about 6:00 P.M. "The author was facing the row of windows which give a view of Spring Creek which flows directly past his home. Across the creek, some 300 feet from the house, along a private roadway which runs east and north, an orange globe, emitting blue flashes, sped past at approximately 180 mph—approximately the size of a basketball."[5]

Rap began a study of the geology of the area and believed he had mapped out an ancient lakebed and the remnants of a large settlement that had been there long ago. Through his own studies and talks with his friend L. T. Hansen, Rap fancied himself an anthropologist. The title page of *The Coming of the Saucers* identified him as "Editor and Publisher; Owner Clark Publishing Company, Publishers of Fate Magazine and Other Worlds Science Stories; Author and Traveler; Amateur Archeologist and Ethnologist." While Palmer explored the terrain seeking Native American artifacts and possible village remains ranging back to the time of the mound builders, the intense but clear-eyed Shaver took walks with Palmer's son, Raymond B. (Bradley) Palmer, searching the potato fields for mysterious rocks that

Shaver dubbed "elder stones" that he was certain held glimpses of lost worlds.

According to Palmer, for miles around he and Shaver were known as "nuts." This reputation bothered Marjorie, who was engaged in fundraising for schools and in a sewing club and homemaker's club she helped organize. Although a school board member and a member of the Lions Club, Palmer had no time for such worries. He simply said, "They could all jump in the lake." Every Fourth of July and New Year's Eve, Ray and Marjorie threw big parties, inviting neighbors, employees, friends from social clubs as well as members of the Chicago science fiction community and Shaver followers.

After dropping his children at school, Rap liked to mingle with neighbors at the Fleming Diner, certain that his conversation added spice to the usual proceedings. (Later he would bemoan how "freakish" he was regarded in the town of six hundred people when he spoke out against the Vietnam War or offered other unorthodox opinions.) When he ran errands in Amherst, small children pointed out the "funny man" to their mothers. He would approach them and say, "When I was your age, I ran out into the street without looking both ways, that's why I look like this

Ray Palmer reveals that he is "Robert N. Webster," publisher of *Other Worlds Science Stories*, at Cinvention, 1949. *Cushing Memorial Library and Archives, Texas A&M University. Estate of Sam Moskowitz*

now." They would nod solemnly. On other occasions he would simply say, "I'm from Mars."

Curiously, now that Shaver and Palmer lived close together, their professional collaboration was on the wane. The Shaver Mystery had become stale, and Palmer was busy with flying saucer publishing, *Fate* magazine, and *Other Worlds Science Stories*. As Robert N. Webster, Rap had published one Richard Shaver story in the first issue of *Other Worlds* in 1949, "The Fall of Lemuria" (a title which might have summed up the current state of the Mystery). Webster told readers, "Mr. Shaver, as some of you well know, puts a certain verisimilitude into his writing, and in all sincerity claims it is not entirely fiction. We don't take any stand on that."

In 1949, shortly after leaving the hospital, Rap also had appeared at the 7th World Science Fiction Convention in Cincinnati (or "Cinvention") and surprised the two hundred attendees by announcing the real identity of Webster. Yes, he, Rap, the archenemy of fandom, purveyor of the Shaver Mystery, and admirer of hack literature, was Webster, the editor of not only *Fate* but also *Other Worlds Science Stories*. After the gasps of horror subsided he declared that he intended to make it a brilliant magazine, along the lines of *Astounding*. He also gave conference organizers the cover art for the first *Other Worlds* to auction off—Malcolm H. Smith's depiction of Shaver's shimmering Snake Woman. Of his surprise visit, a British fanzine noted, he "departed, to the accompaniment of every indication from his audience that he wasn't, in their estimation, such a flop after all."[6] Most important, he met the young Cleveland SF fan Bea Mahaffey and hired her on the spot to assist at Clark Publications, then based in Evanston.

Mahaffey became a huge hit—possibly the ultimate It Girl for the fen. Elaine, Rap's secretary at Ziff-Davis, had been a good sport and perfect as a Mac Girl but Mahaffey had a classical, graceful presence and intellect and humor to spare. The young men of SF fandom loved her—no, they worshipped her. Fans flocked to the Clark Publishing offices to get a glimpse of or try out witticisms on her. Rap, who had difficulty traveling after his accident, sent her to conventions where SF fans in England, Ireland, and Los Angeles pined for her, penned cartoon fantasies of their encounters with her, reported Bea sightings, appeared in the hotel corridors chanting "Bea, Bea, glorious Bea!" at 3:00 A.M., and met her at airports and docks with odd tributes, such as a Liverpool fan group's published volume *Sex and Sadism*. One fan bragged of giving her a ride sidesaddle on his bicycle in London in 1953. In Liverpool, fans placed notes under her hotel door telling her where to find them. She announced the next day that the notes would provide Shaver with "material for at least a dozen novels." One over-wrought writer to a letters page insisted that Bea was not simply smart, graceful, and gorgeous, but more glorious than any of the temple dancers of Isis in days of yore. Bea ran the Evanston office and also knew how to cultivate writers and secure high-quality fiction. Eventually she became coeditor and is often credited with making *Other Worlds Science Stories* one of the better SF magazines of the early 1950s.

Long derided for having publishing cliché-ridden space operas in *Amazing Stories*, Rap was determined to reclaim his reputation as a science fiction editor. With the help of Mahaffey, Rap took risks and won over many readers with *Other Worlds Science Stories* (in the 1950s he also published *Universe* but soon merged it with a revamped *Other Worlds*). Wilkie Connor wrote in the fanzine *Spacewarp* that the early issues of *Other Worlds* were impressive. "Seems like Palmer is going to give out with fresh yarns, written from the point of view of an adult. Maybe he will assist Campbell and Merwin in their efforts to raise the standards of stf from the Buck Rogers level to something on the level of a modern 'light-heavy' novel . . . it is a refreshing mag now and I am for it 100%."[7]

Now that he no longer served others, Palmer followed his impulse never to turn down a dare. For example, in July 1950 Palmer published Ray Bradbury's "Way in the Middle of the Air," which describes a group of African-Americans who choose to escape Southern racism by colonizing Mars. Earlier that year, in May, he also published Eric Frank Russell's "Dear

Devil." The devil of this story is the hideous-looking Martian, Fandor, capable of communication through telepathic tentacles (as a BEM, or "bug-eyed monster," it had quite a few other tentacles). Fandor, is actually a thoughtful artist left behind on Earth who, as a last resort, kidnaps terrified children on the post-apocalyptic planet in order to befriend them and help them adapt to their radioactive world. The story is a plea for looking beyond the surface of people, a message that surely resonated with Palmer with his disabilities and daily brushes with "gapers." As the Martian Fandor says, "I cannot help my shape any more than you can help yours."

Bea Mahaffey between meetings at Midwest Con 2 in Cincinnati, 1951. *Photo courtesy Margaret Ford Kiefer*

Several years later, in June 1953, Palmer also published the first science fiction story sympathetic to homosexuality—Theodore Sturgeon's "The World Well Lost." John W. Campbell, custodian of SF standards at *Astounding*, loathed the story and had urged other editors not to print it. Supposedly, one of these editors, "out of sheer spite very nearly bought the story but finally decided against it, the temper of the times being what it was."[8] Palmer, who enjoyed taking risks, bought Sturgeon's story and printed it in the first issue of *Universe*. Rap was finally turning out a quality SF magazine.

Bea Mahaffey and members of the Cincinnati fan group in 1949.
Photo courtesy Margaret Ford Kiefer

From Esperanto to Solex-Mal

Yet Palmer was hedging his bets—and pushing many of his chips away from science fiction and over to flying saucers and occult phenomena, both of which he highlighted in his new book publishing enterprise.

In 1951, Rap inaugurated his Amherst Press with the reprint of Sir Hubert Wilkins and Harold M. Sherman's *Thoughts Through Space: A Remarkable Adventure in the Realm of Mind.* Sherman had written two popular novellas for *Amazing,* "The Green Man," published in 1946, and "The Green Man Returns" in 1947. Light in tone, Sherman's stories were early examples of the Psi-Fi that Palmer had begun to favor. The Green Man stories explored the repercussions when a highly evolved being, Numar from the planet Talamaya, lands his spacecraft on Earth, speaks before the United Nations, and is interviewed on television. The first installment concludes with Numar the Awakener informing a crowd at Chicago's Soldier Field that lights in the sky would soon indicate a new age's arrival. In the second tale Numar and other space beings save mankind from nuclear armageddon.

Sherman and coauthor Wilkins were both devotees of the occult, linked by their interest in the *Urantia* papers, then a recent entry in the channeled texts genre. Sherman also hosted a radio show called *Your Key to Happiness* that encouraged positive thinking principles and aired three times a week on Chicago's WGN. The book *Thoughts Through Space* was based on telepathy experiments Sherman and Arctic adventurer Sir Hubert Wilkins conducted. Before leaving on a trip to attempt to rescue Russian airmen who had crashed in the region of the North Pole, Wilkins and Sherman agreed that Wilkins would send thoughts daily at a set time; the book reports that Sherman tended to be 70 percent accurate in his telepathic notes.

Following *Thoughts Through Space*, Amherst Press began to specialize in flying saucer phenomena and helped to usher in what some have called the Golden Age of UFO religions. In the 1950s, as sightings continued, "contactees" came forward to tell of their meetings with highly evolved extra-terrestrials. According to these contactees, the saucers carried "Space Brothers" prepared to aid humanity at a critical moment. Although the contactees presented themselves as bearers of new mystic truths, their tales relied heavily on popular culture and did not appear until after Hollywood took up the question of such contact.

The science fiction movie most influential in shaping early ideas about extra-terrestrial contact was *The Day the Earth Stood Still* (1951). Directed by Robert Wise, the film was loosely based on former *Astounding Science Fiction* editor Harry Bates's "Farewell to the Master," first published in *Astounding* in 1940. In the movie, a flying saucer lands in Washington, D.C. The noble Klaatu, clad in a seamless jumpsuit, emerges from the ship to deliver a message to the leaders of nations, warning that other galactic inhabitants will not permit humans to progress to the point where they might build rocket ships stocked with nuclear weapons. As the world's leaders cannot agree on a meeting, Klaatu appeals to the world's scientists, and to prove his power, stops all machinery on Earth for a period of thirty minutes. Later, soldiers shoot down Klaatu. Gort, a robot who protects Klaatu, carries the body of the heavenly messenger into the mysterious, womblike interior of the flying saucer and resurrects him with the help of a mysterious machine that emits pulsing sounds. Healed and whole, though perhaps only temporarily, Klaatu once again steps from the saucer to pronounce judgment on the earthlings: "Your choice is simple: join us and live in peace, or pursue your present course and face obliteration."

The Day the Earth Stood Still offered a fully realized image of flying saucers to the world and created numerous genre standards, much of these related to its art direction, including its depiction of the spaceship with mysterious exterior doors that appear and disappear from seamless metal, since referred to as fluid metal, which has become the norm for flying saucer door mechanics. Likewise, Klaatu's tight jumpsuit became standard garb for humanoid aliens or humans of the future.[9]

The Day the Earth Stood Still's optimistic view that the occupants of flying saucers represent a more advanced civilization with a message of unity for the schizoid era of the Cold War world was similar to that provided by Harold Sherman's stern yet bemused Numar in his Green Man series. As with "The Green Man," the film *The Day the Earth Stood Still* indicated that although nuclear warfare threatened, heavenly aid was en route; when the New Age arrived, we would all be able to enjoy the wonders of fluid metal, seamless fabric, and pulsing sound therapy.

Twentieth-century occultists had long heralded the arrival of the New Age. The concept borrowed the general outline of Christian millennialism, in which one thousand years of peace would follow the final defeat of evil at Armageddon. The occultists also added dashes of astrology and science fiction. Astrologers assert that their discipline tracks roughly twenty-five-thousand-year cycles, in which the Earth's axis shifts its orientation to new constellations of the zodiac; the Aquarian Age, beginning somewhere between 1900 and 2400, marked the end of twenty-five thousand years of the Piscean Age. The New Age of the astrologers was here. So were the awakeners—in flying saucers.

In 1951, Klaatu appeared on movie theater screens; in 1952, there was a fresh wave of sightings in the skies, and on April 7, 1952, Robert E. Ginna and H. B. Darrach Jr. published an article in *Life* magazine called "Have We Visitors from Outer Space?"—an article that thrilled flying saucer enthusiasts. It rejected the debunking mentality and noted that the many sightings pointed to objects that "cannot be explained by present science as natural phenomena—but solely as artificial devices created and operated by a high intelligence." The journalists concluded with a series of questions: "Who, or what, is aboard? Where do they come from? Why are they here? What are the intentions of the beings who control them?"

Proposing to have answers to Ginna and Darrach's queries, the contactees stepped forward. In books, pamphlets, and radio and newspaper interviews, they began to "top" each other in their accounts of encounters with Klaatu-like humanoids on heavenly missions. The first contactee celebrity, George Adamski, was the suitably colorful coauthor of *Flying Saucers Have Landed* (1953). Adamski was a Polish immigrant who had been a member of the U.S. Cavalry's K-Troop that patrolled the border during the Mexican revolution. In the 1930s, Adamski founded the Royal Order of Tibet in Laguna Beach. In 1940, Adamski moved his commune to the mountains of California near Mount Palomar where he purchased a twenty-acre tract of land and operated a diner. A science fiction devotee, Adamski wrote and self-published *Pioneers of Space, a Trip to the Moon, Mars, and Venus* (1949), a narrative that mixed spirit voyage literature and science fiction. (He had apparently once sent *Amazing* a story about Jesus in a flying saucer that Palmer had rejected.)

Prior to his contactee adventure, Adamski distributed photographs of saucers that many insisted were obvious frauds—one was identified as part of a Hoover vacuum cleaner. One of his first venues for these photographs was *Fate* magazine. Sandwiched between discussions of "Masks—

the Oldest Form of Magic" and "The Art of Dowsing," the September 1950 *Fate* included an Adamski photograph of a blurred spaceship. The July 1951 *Fate* ran an article by Adamski explaining how he made his photographs of space vessels. Rap added the subhead "Astronomer-philosopher in private Palomar Gardens Observatory reports incredible observations of the Heavens."

In *Flying Saucers Have Landed*, coauthored by British Theosophist Desmond Leslie, Adamski reported that in 1952 he witnessed a landing in the California desert, not far from the boundaries of Joshua Tree National Park. From a great cigar-shaped mother ship came a bell-shaped flying saucer that was "translucent and of exquisite color," flashing with rainbow hues in the sunlight. Adamski left friends in his car and hurried on foot to the landing area. The spaceman that emerged, Orthon, had long yellow hair and was clad in seamless fabric. Adamski said that as he neared Orthon, "Suddenly, as though a veil was removed from my mind, the feeling of caution left me so completely that I was no longer aware of my friends." Adamski was moved to great emotion and felt "like a little child in the presence of one with great wisdom and much love."[10] Orthon assured Adamski that earthlings must give up their warlike ways as nuclear fallout could spread damage throughout the solar system. Adamski described the meeting as one might describe a meeting with an angel. Orthon was the first "Space Brother."

After his account gained notoriety, Adamski was joined by other contactees, including George Van Tassel, who in 1954 began hosting a yearly UFO conference in his home at Giant Rock in Yucca Valley, California, north of Palm Springs. Another early contactee, Truman Bethurum, wrote *Aboard a Flying Saucer* (1954), an account of his meeting with beings from planet Clarion, who took him for a flight on their saucer. He met their gorgeous female captain Aura and was told, once again, that earthlings should prevent atomic warfare. Previous occultist narratives of encounters with

Contactees at the Second Interplanetary Spacecraft
Convention at Giant Rock, California, in 1955.
Courtesy J. Allen Hynek Center for UFO Studies

enlightened Lemurian or Atlantean sages in underground realms were
shifting to such outer space scenarios.

In media coverage, colorful contactees quickly trumped serious UFO
investigators—who term themselves "ufologists." Long John Nebel's all-
night talk show on WOR in New York, dedicated to discussions of voodoo,
beatniks, perpetual motion, the paranormal, and the otherwise bizarre,
often featured conversations with Adamski, Van Tassel, and Bethurum. (In
1956 Ray Palmer and Richard Shaver were invited on Nebel's show to discuss deros.) Steve Allen, host of the nationally syndicated television show
Tonight also featured contactees in the 1950s, as did other radio and television programs. Over 150 contactee-oriented flying saucer clubs were

started by the mid-1950s in the United States, vying with more mainstream groups seeking to review flying saucer sightings. Many of these groups morphed into flying saucer religions with contactees as their prophets of hope, and Palmer's magazines and book publishing company became conduits of their work.

Catching up with the contactee movement, Palmer followed up his printing of Kenneth Arnold's *The Coming of the Saucers* with George Hunt Williamson's *Other Tongues—Other Flesh* (1953). Williamson was an associate of Adamski and claimed to have been a witness to the landing of Orthon's flying saucer. In *Other Tongues* Williamson discussed his part in the Adamski affair—he was one of Adamski's associates left behind in the car in the desert. While acknowledging he did not meet Orthon, Williamson insisted he had made plaster casts of the Venusian's footprints in the desert sand. These footprints, apparently, were not merely saintly relics, but information enriched.

Williamson reproduced the pictographs etched into the footprints and interpreted them at length, his analysis laden with obscure references. The left foot's markings indicated the visitor was from Venus, gave clues as to the type of propulsion the craft depended on, and reflected Orthon's belief that mankind was divided into three spiritual categories ranging from highly materialist to the spiritually leaning and to those with true faith in the "All Creator." The right footprint included a swastika that represented the four primal sources of energy, as well as the sun or primal fire. As a whole, the footprint, he announced, represented the emergence of the Aquarian Age. Williamson referred the curious reader to his previous article, "A Preliminary Report on Analysis of Symbols from Footprints Left by a Man from Outer Space—November 20, 1952."

As it sounds, this was all insane drivel. Although Williamson had some training in anthropology, and pursued what would later be called the "ancient astronauts" theme that Erich von Däniken successfully popularized in the 1960s (i.e., the earth has been visited many times by extra-terrestrials who wrought marvels recorded in architecture and legend), he also had fascist leanings. Williamson had been loosely associated with the Ballard's "I AM" movement, a Theosophy offshoot with connections to William Dudley Pelley's Silver Legion of the 1930s. Pelley, an admirer of Hitler, led mass rallies with supporters dressed in uniforms emblazoned with red Ls. Pelley also printed an anti-Semitic pamphlet in 1939 titled "The 45 Questions Asked Most Frequently about the Jews with the Answers by Pelley." In the late 1940s, Pelley's organization was shut down and its leader imprisoned. After his release he began the organization Soulcraft, which offered mystic teachings. In the early 1950s, Williamson moved to Noblesville, Indiana, to write for Pelley's magazine, *Valor*.

Pelley's book *Star Guests* (1950)—not published by Palmer—provided a cosmic history based on information he channeled from extra-terrestrials and served as a model to Williamson. In the book Pelley argued that intelligent extra-terrestrials from Sirius had come to Earth millions of years ago and interbred with Earth's apelike humanoid species, hastening the "Fall." Following the biblical Flood, another wave of highly evolved "Christ people" or "Goodly People of the Avatar" came from the stars to redeem the earth with its mix of Sirians and ape people. Pelley's account went on to further entwine into the cosmic order his racist, anti-Semitic, and anti-Communist notions.[11]

Following Pelley's teachings, in *Other Tongues* Williamson insisted that space beings had been continuously visiting Earth. Among his new discoveries was a primordial language, Solex-mal, that was universal to space beings. Williamson was pleased at the spread of Esperanto as a global language, but asserted that a language that could be used throughout the universe was even better. Overlooking Shaver's Mantong, he insisted of Solex-mal, "This language was the original tongue once spoken on Earth by all people and is still used by the inhabitants of other worlds in outer space. It is a symbolic, pictographic language." Williamson noted the language had similarities to the "scroll writing of the Atlanteans." Catharine Adair Robinson had contributed the article "Scroll Writing of Atlantis" to the August 1951 *Fate* magazine, and Williamson's system was nearly interchangeable with hers. Both, however, drew from James Churchward's *Ancient Symbols of Mu* (1933), which deciphered the sacred symbols of "Naacal," a language Churchward found inscribed on tablets in India. As to how he came upon the symbols of Solex-mal, instead of ascribing them to emerald plates in some exotic locale, Williamson vaguely noted, "The following symbolic writing was received by our research group in northern Arizona in 1952."

While Williamson was pleased to announce that the space visitors included the star people that came from the Pleiades who would lead "mankind thereby into a New Age as the vibrations of Aquarius," he warned of hidden dangers. In addition to Space Brothers, or, as he called them, the Wanderers, there were "Intruders" from Orion. His description of Orion-influenced humans reflected anti-Semitic stereotypes. They were often "small in stature with strange, oriental type eyes. Their faces are thin. . . . They prey on the unsuspecting. . . . They astound intellects with their words of magnificence. While their wisdom may have merit, it is materialistic. . . . They are the Universal parasites. . . . They are a stubborn race."[12]

Palmer's decision to publish George Hunt Williamson's *Other Tongues—Other Flesh* was among the most morally dubious of his entire career. It is possible that in his hurry to get a book out that could serve as a matching set with that of Adamski, Palmer published it without spotting the dark currents floating beneath its impenetrable prose. But that's unlikely. While Palmer frequently aired progressive views, this, sadly, would not be the last time his "way out" ideas connected with America's far right. Coincidentally, it came at a time when he was making a break with the Fullers, his partners at Clark Publishing.

Carl Jung's Favorite Venusian

After Curtis Fuller's wife, Mary, recovered from tuberculosis, Palmer's formerly silent partners began to insist on more editorial control of *Fate*. The Fullers were more hard-nosed and practical than Palmer. Jerome Clark, later hired as an editor at *Fate*, has noted that Mary Fuller's simple criteria for articles was "We don't have to believe it ourselves, but it must be capable of belief."[13] In her eyes, the Shaver Mystery and many of Palmer's ideas did not make the cut.

Starting in 1952, Curtis Fuller's "I See by the Papers" began to replace Robert N. Webster's editorials in *Fate*. Fuller's first column, in April 1952, after detailing various mysterious doings, concluded with, "Some of the foregoing incidents are undoubtedly easily explained. But for others we have not the slightest idea concerning their cause. We have been criticized by some of our readers for not offering more 'theories' about unknown phenomena. But to do that, we believe, would be unwise and presumptuous." Fuller offered a far more moderate point of view than Palmer. In December 1952, Fuller's article "Let's Get Straight About the Saucers" offered more damage control, noting that while something was going on with the saucer sightings, no one really knew what it was. The extraterrestrial hypothesis was seductive but not backed by solid evidence. The Fullers had no patience with material such as Solex-mal or the contactee subculture. While the Palmers and Fullers maintained a somewhat strained friendship, the business partnership soon dissolved.

By late 1953, Palmer had ceased to participate in *Fate* magazine, selling his share to the Fullers. Relying on Bea Mahaffey for editorial support, he began the rival magazine *Mystic*. He wanted to inaugurate it with a bang. While *Fate*'s first issue, in 1948, had heralded the era of flying saucer sightings, *Mystic*'s first issue, in 1953, jumped aboard the contactee movement, relying on Orfeo Angelucci's article "I Traveled in a Flying Saucer." This opening issue helped Rap build up a credible circulation, that remained at 20,000 as late as 1960. In the meantime, under Curtis Fuller's skilled management, *Fate* grew to a circulation of 120,000 or more and became a slightly damped down version of the magazine Palmer had started.

For issue one of *Mystic*, Rap had found a superb vehicle in Orfeo Angelucci. Angelucci's brand of mysticism avoided Williamson's pseudo-scholarly discussions of myth, symbol, and numerology and instead offered a solid narrative with an authentic voice. Angelucci had no interest in discussing Aryans and swastikas and sought, as had Swedenborg centuries earlier, to ground his mystic vision in a Christian cosmos. His writings set the high-water mark for 1950s' contactee texts. Angelucci continued his narrative with installments in *Mystic* in 1953 and 1954, with the further titles "I Meet the Flying Saucer Man," and "My Awakening on Another Planet." Each of these also gave Los Angeles journalist Paul M. Vest, a frequent contributor to *Fate* and *Mystic*, an "as told to" credit. (Angelucci admitted his own writing was rambling and only partially coherent.)

As an Italian-American, Angelucci was singled out by bigoted readers, and the occult community, which included people like Pelley and his followers, had its share. The irate J. R. Latham wrote to *Mystic* in October 1954, complaining that "Venusians Walk Our Streets," written by Paul Vest, was "a lie and a hoax as also is the story referred to of the man with the 'Dago' name who says 'I rode in a flying saucer.'" Latham evoked the authority of the Very Reverend Floyd M. Gurley, commonly known as the "White Thunder God," as the only person who actually had been to Venus. Gurley insisted the Venusians have greenish skin and could not simply walk the streets of the earth's cities. Latham also added that they are not little but average fourteen feet tall. Further, they were hermaphrodites and nudists, traits which would make it hard for them to mingle with Earth's population.

Palmer responded, "We always say, a letter that's worth writing is worth being printed. So, yours is printed. Next, we don't know Mr. Angelucci's ancestry, but we do know he's an American, and not a 'Dago.' However, that is beside the point. We have many 'Dago' friends, and we always call them 'Mr.'"

Two years later, Palmer collected the Angelucci articles together in a single volume with a pale blue cover titled *The Secret of the Saucers* (1955). A copy of the book made its way to Carl Jung in Switzerland. The elderly psychologist found it oddly compelling. In his own work, *Flying Saucers: A Modern Myth of Things Seen in the Skies* (1959), Jung singled out Angelucci's account—direct from Palmer's press—as having the authentic ring of visionary experience.

Jung's essay rested on the analysis of the dreams of patients in which flying saucers appeared, as well as the artwork of patients and artists that featured saucers. Through such media, as well as contactee tales and rumors, Jung believed a new myth was emerging. The saucer had become a symbol of "wholeness" appearing above a disturbed, even schizophrenic, planet. On the microcosmic scale, more than ever, modern man was alienated from his true being, and in need of "individuation"—union with his or her buried self. On the macrocosmic scale, the Cold War between the United States and Soviet Union had divided the planet. The shape of the saucer was like that of the alchemist's rotundum, a symbol of wholeness or the union of opposites. Significantly, Jung believed that the saucer offered the hope of individuation—or self-realization—to those to whom it appeared. The saucers, he wrote, "Bid each of us remember his own soul and his own wholeness." A wholeness that "we have lost in the midst of our civilized, conscious existence."[14]

Jung granted that the saucer may or may not be physically real and further that they tended to act in a "weightless" manner that would suggest they were not physical objects, but more like thoughts. They had, however, a "psychic" heft. But that did not mean he accepted equally all witnesses to this visionary experience. Jung commented of George Adamski, "There are 'eyewitnesses' like Mr. Adamski, who relates that he has flown in a UFO and made a round trip of the moon in a few hours. He brings us the astonishing news that the side of the moon faced away from us contains atmosphere, water, forests, and settlements without being in the least perturbed by the moon's skittishness in turning just her inhospitable side towards the earth. This physical monstrosity of a story was actually swallowed."[15] In contrast, Jung regarded Angelucci's narrative as a credible example of what he deemed the UFO encounter as visionary experience. Angelucci, in the psychiatrist's words, was "naïve, and—if appearances do not deceive us—serious and idealistic." In his work the "individuation process . . . is plainly depicted."[16]

The original volume of *The Secret of the Saucers* places Angelucci's name on its pale blue cover (making it his own project blue book), but the title page only includes the note "Edited by Ray Palmer." In addition to Paul Vest, who coauthored the three chapters already published in *Mystic*, Rap undoubtedly had a large role in shaping its prose into the form that gained the attention of the eminent Swiss psychoanalyst. In this sense, we can see that Ray Palmer, whom many dismissed as a mere carnival barker, had placed himself in the center of this new visionary rumor—the flying saucer's command to humanity to undertake a journey of self-discovery.

Angelucci had a sickly youth in rural New Jersey. He was beset with migraines and other sensitivities. Thunderstorms in particular upset and pained him. He married in 1936, but soon after had a physical breakdown and required hospitalization. As he recovered, he read widely and became convinced that he had important medical insights involving the use of vitamins to treat polio. He also began to experiment with the effects of high altitudes on fungus. During one launch of balloons with fungi samples into the atmosphere, he, his friends, his family, and a reporter were staring in the skies when they all spotted a flying saucer. Soon after, he agreed to move to California, in part because there would be fewer thunderstorms to affect his delicate constitution. Before leaving New Jersey, he self-published his own far-ranging scientific and cosmic speculations in a work titled *The Nature of Infinite Entities*. Such entities were to figure in his later contactee reports.

In Los Angeles, Angelucci became a Lockheed factory worker and as a hobby composed a screenplay about a trip to the moon. In May 1952, while driving home from his night shift, feeling ill and nervous and as if he "might die at any moment," he saw a red glowing oval object that kept growing in brightness. He began to follow it. His physical discomfort increased. He pulled to the side of the road on a hill and watched as the red disk accelerated and disappeared. Then two "eerie green balls of fire" appeared and hovered near his car. A voice told him not to be afraid and to step out of the car. He stared at the green fireballs.

The voice instructed him, "Drink from the crystal cup you will find on the fender of your car."[17] He did so. It was delicious. All his physical symptoms of pain and foreboding left him. A "screen" then formed between the two green fireballs and he could see a female entity and a male entity smiling at him. They spoke with him telepathically, condensing an hours-long conversation into only minutes, and then faded.

From these ethereal entities Angelucci learned he had been chosen. They were from another world but wished to help humanity. The flying disks that people had begun to see in the skies collected information for mother ships. Although "etheric entities," these beings could materialize in visible forms. He was to let other people know that the star visitors meant no harm. They told him, "We are Earth's older brothers and thus we will aid Earth's people insofar as they, through free will, will permit us to do so."[18]

This was his first initiation. Angelucci underwent a more intense ordeal several months later, in July 1952. After leaving a café only a few blocks from his apartment, he felt the tingling in his arms and body again. Ahead he saw a dome appearing, like "an igloo." An etheric flying saucer materialized, its shell glowing with iridescent mother-of-pearl hues. He stepped inside and rested in a reclining chair. The entrance disappeared. Engines hummed. He was in a semi-dream state as the saucer zipped off into the heavens. His favorite song, "Fools Rush In," began to play, reassuring him. He looked out at a planet and a voice told him that it was Earth, and encouraged him to weep for his planet and its many problems, adding, "For all of its apparent beauty Earth is a purgatorial world among the planets evolving intelligent life. Hate, selfishness and cruelty rise from many parts of it like a dark mist."[19] He was also told that Jesus was "an infinite entity of the Sun." After weeping, Angelucci felt a God-like presence and peace.

Next he was ushered into a giant sky ship where green flames instructed him further. "Tonight you, an entity of Earth, have come close to the Infinite Entities. For the present you are our emissary, Orfeo, and you must act! Even though people of Earth laugh derisively and mock you as a lunatic, tell them about us!" Angelucci promised he would, although he first asked if they could improve his health. He was told that was not possible and that it was because of his illness and sensitivity that they were able to reach him. He was preached to about his mission and the need to follow a true teaching of love. Then came the voice, "Beloved friend of Earth, we baptize you now in the true light of the worlds eternal." A white beam of light flashed down and he lost consciousness. Then "everything expanded into a great shimmering white light. I seemed to be projected beyond Time and Space and was conscious only of light, Light, LIGHT!"

Angelucci underwent a conversion experience: he felt that he died and was reborn. "I am dying. . . . I have been through this death before in other earthly lives. This is death! Only now I am in ETERNITY, WITHOUT BEGINNING AND WITHOUT END."[20] He "drifted in a timeless sea of bliss" and came to awareness again in an empty lot near his home. He apparently had a burn mark, or stigmata, shaped like a hydrogen atom, on his chest, to remind him of the reality of this searing initiation.

This narrative conformed to the outlines of a spiritual initiation—or what Jung called the process of "individuation," that is, the discovery of one's own soul and its terrain. As Jung commented, "In religious experience man comes face to face with a psychically overwhelming Other."[21] (As in many conversion experiences, the initiate receives the "call," which he or she often tries to evade, but ultimately undergoes a death and resurrection and becomes imbued with a new perspective.) As with a prospective shaman, Angelucci's physical infirmities and "differentness" are established from the outset. Flying saucer travel doesn't appear simply as some space-age bachelor pad in the sky or wish fulfillment fantasy, as in Adamski's later writings. We get the sense that Orfeo in some ways did not welcome the advances of the Space Brothers, rather as Jonah tried to avoid his duty to preach to the sinners of Nineveh. Nevertheless, the tale's basic outlines, which include compassionate Space Brothers trying to warn earthlings and help them reach a higher consciousness, helped confirm the standard contactee narrative.

The "Long View" from Wisconsin

To the extent that Palmer had influenced Angelucci's account, the Wisconsin editor was also working through his own emotions about shifting from science fiction to the paranormal. One of the book's later chapters describes Angelucci's efforts to set up a flying saucer conference in Los Angeles, with the help of psychic Jerome "The Amazing" Criswell, and Max B. Miller, president of Flying Saucers International. Contactees, science fiction authors, and the curious attended. Angelucci was appalled at the hostility emanating from the science fiction authors. Rap had encountered some of that hostility during a staged 1952 debate on UFOs with rocketry expert Willy Ley at a science fiction convention in Chicago. To begin the debate, Ley asked, "How do flying saucers fly?" While Rap prepared to reply, Ley took a china saucer, tossed it in the air, watched it smash, and said, "That's how saucers fly!" The crowd roared its approval and Rap retreated to an ironic pose in which he offered only the inanities the crowd would expect of a flying saucer nut.

Serving as a proxy for Rap, Angelucci remarked, "As I looked about that busy room I thought that it was small wonder that the concoctors of science-fiction horror diets had declared the saucers 'taboo.' Far too much beautiful reality was on the side of the saucers. Harmony and beauty are much too tame for the horror boys. . . . But the joke is on them, for reality has slipped quietly past them and established new frontiers of its own. . . . The actual flying saucer phenomena and the extra-terrestrials were left to the inexperienced but honest handling of rank amateurs."[22]

Although Palmer had maintained his passion for science fiction, by the early 1950s, while contactees roamed the galaxy and the talk-show circuit, the pulp industry was crumbling. No wonder its writers had become horror boys. As early as April 1949, one of the leading pulp publishers, Street and Smith, stopped publication of nearly all its pulps, a line that included *Doc Savage* and *The Shadow* (although its *Astounding* survived). Most pulps were no longer profitable. As of 1955, American News Company, the main pulp distributor, began a downward spiral that culminated in its collapse in 1957. With this calamity, science fiction became an endangered species—so much so that in 1960, fanzine editor Earl Kemp asked numerous science fiction luminaries, "Who Killed Science Fiction?" Several expert witnesses, still outraged by the Shaver Mystery and Palmer's defection, attributed part of the blame to Palmer. However, most of the contributors, who included Palmer, pointed to competition from mass circulation paperbacks, comic books, and television.

Rap commented on the imminent demise of pulps, noting, "Did you know that you, as a science fiction fan, have a problem? . . . Your favorite kind of reading matter is threatened with extinction." Soon after, Bea Mahaffey lost her job and returned to Ohio. In 1957, Rap threw in the towel. *Other Worlds Science Stories* became *Flying Saucers from Other Worlds*. Briefly, all-fiction issues alternated with "nonfiction" issues; however, in 1959, he jettisoned the science fiction altogether and renamed the magazine *Flying Saucers* and added the subtitle "The Magazine of Space Conquest." Several years later the tagline morphed into the more comely "Mysteries of the Space Age."

In a familiar process of grafting, Rap attempted to replicate the structure of the SF fan community in the flying saucer world—as he already had done for the more general field of the paranormal. In the first issue of *Flying Saucers from Other Worlds*, he noted, "If you are a member of a flying saucer club, you will find a section of this magazine devoted to such clubs, and news about them. You will find competent reviews of books published about flying saucers. You will find readers' letters printed, giving free voice to expression."[23]

He had left science fiction behind, but rallied around him other refugees from the pulps to bolster his enterprises. In 1950 the very highbrow British SF writer Olaf Stapledon appeared in *Fate* with an essay on "Interplanetary Man." Forry Ackerman briefly wrote a column on "Scientifilms" for *Flying Saucers*. Hannes Bok, one of the leading science fiction pulp cover artists, whose work had first appeared in 1939 in *Weird Tales*, also contributed articles to Palmer's *Mystic* about astrology and about mandalas, a topic dear to the heart of Jung who saw them as symbols of integration.

Flying Saucers, nonetheless, was a homey affair that included advertisements for Kenneth Arnold's new uranium prospecting business and for "Turn-ers" a dandruff cure endorsed by Kenneth Arnold and Ray Palmer, as well as a chili seasoning that Palmer was distributing. (In another sign of his shoestring budget, in 1955 Palmer published a notice in *Mystic* indicating that he would no longer pay contributors. He claimed this would improve the content as he would get less fraudulent work from professionals, but he admitted that relying on unpaid submissions added to his editing load.)

Even Palmer, who stressed the homemade aspects of his publications, at times craved respectability. In 1963, Palmer purchased *Space World*, a magazine dedicated to news of astronomy and of the U.S. and Soviet space programs, from SF and comic book author Otto Binder. It served as a counterpoint to the lore-based *Flying Saucers*. As Rap put it, "Now in *Space World*, you will be able to get the latest developments in space matters, while in *Flying Saucers* you will continue to get the world's only complete coverage of space mysteries."[24]

While Rap was getting comfortable on his new beat, the "Mysteries of the Space Age," his neighbor, the irrepressible Mr. Shaver, insisted that mysteries resided much closer to home. Indeed, they were underfoot and easy to trip on. After toiling for nearly a decade on his unfinished history of the Elder World, Shaver showed up at the Palmer house with an enormous manuscript pile—and yet another challenge to the commonsense view of the world. As he pondered the mass of papers, Palmer was once again drawn into the vortex of Shaver's bizarre imagination.

PALMER AND SHAVER INC.

People so ignorant they ignore the rock library and our greatest and best books while they read penny dreadfuls and fashion magazines may not be precisely the kind of population most likely to survive under the best conditions.

—Richard S. Shaver, "The Ancient Earth, Its Story in Stone" (1975)

There was but one course left, therefore—to try the whole thing anew upon a better plan, and to commence a total reconstruction of sciences, arts, and all human knowledge, raised upon the proper foundations.

—Francis Bacon, *Great Instauration* (1620)

A traveler in the dairy and farming land of central Wisconsin in the late 1950s might have seen a reassuring sight: a man, accompanied by a boy about ten years old, walking along fields, and hillsides, enthusiastically searching for stones. They favored potato fields, where farmers were glad to have stones removed, and often left them in piles to the sides. This was not an outing of the Boy Scouts, but a slightly more eccentric expedition. The man was Richard S. Shaver and the boy was Rap's son, Raymond B. Palmer. Shaver put special significance in certain stones.

As they searched, Shaver would show the boy the rocks he deemed important. Ray B. Palmer confessed years later, "He could see things in rocks. But I couldn't." Then, with characteristic Palmer generosity, added, "But then again, it's a matter of knowing what you're looking for." He got the feeling Shaver was looking at the stones as at a book of optical illusion puzzles, each with a hidden pattern. Shaver saw the pattern, but Palmer didn't. They looked. They weren't afraid to get their hands dirty. Shaver found treasures.

Shaver's fascination with rocks began shortly after he and his wife, Dottie, moved to Wisconsin in 1949. His wife was putting together a sub-sistence farm and Shaver was either writing or feeling "goofy as a bed bug"—if he'd been hit by a dero ray. The suicide of his friend John Carson Buford in Chicago had depressed him. He was certain the dero had hounded Buford to death via ray tamper. The dwindling of the Mystery in *Amazing Stories* and Shaver's inability to complete issues of the *Shaver Mystery Club* magazine were troubling as well. He had subscribers to his planned history of the Elder Races but his progress was uncertain.

Perhaps his wife was just trying to cheer him up. He recalled, "Dottie kept coming in with colored pebbles. She insisted I look at them. . . . She put the pretty rocks around the flower beds, in the paths, on the tables . . . so it had to happen. One day I really looked at one. My hair rose when I saw engraving."[1] Cutting into the rocks and at times relying on a magnify-ing lens, he became certain that the rocks contained images and informa-tion. Some of these were very clear representations of scenes, indicating a weird blend of nature and artifice; such "accidentals" had fascinated con-noisseurs for centuries and had been exhibited in the wonder cabinets of the Renaissance. Others—well, he could see the patterns, anyway, and their amazing depictions of the Elder Races.

With the rocks as his guide, Shaver began to shift from his role as a pulp writer to an artist, daubing strange canvases, inspired by the images he found trapped in the mineral realm. Although distracted by flying saucers, his neighbor, friend, and publisher, Ray Palmer gave Shaver a hand in pro-moting his new discoveries. He no longer relied on the Shaver Mystery as his mainstay, as he had in *Amazing*, nevertheless, after leaving *Fate* magazine, information about the Shaver Mystery, the Elder Races, and Shaver's rocks began to appear in a series of articles in *Mystic* and then *Search*—the same magazine after a 1956 name change.

As he began to dedicate himself to the study of rocks, in 1960, Shaver brought to Palmer's farmhouse an enormous stuffed folder and said, "Ray, you finish this book—it has me licked." In his office, Palmer studied the sprawling, disorganized portfolio, which contained ten years of Shaver's notes about the Elder World. Rap was delighted but baffled. He wrote that, in truth, it "had me licked" also. Palmer decided to publish Shaver's writings with related materials in a loosely structured twelve-volume paperback series to be called the *Hidden World* that appeared from 1961 to 1964. It eventually grew to sixteen volumes. Advertised in *Search* with its 19,000 readers, the first four volumes of *Hidden World* had about 5,000 subscribers; the next four volumes, 3,000, which then dwindled to 1,700 and a rather pitiful 900 for the final four volumes. No one was getting wealthy from this operation.

Shaver's discoveries in stone were only one aspect of *Hidden World*, but this new source of information clearly obsessed Shaver, and it was an obsession to which Palmer slowly warmed. In 1961, when Shaver first began to hand Palmer stones along with cross-sections and photographs and to spin out his tale about the images encoded in them, Palmer said he could see some "resemblances" to faces and representations but thought these were "just freaks of nature." Palmer hedged on the rock books. They weren't, after all, telonion plates. Yet he felt obligated to present them to readers as Shaver had a way of coming up with outlandish ideas that later gained credibility. A few years later, in the September 1969 *Search*, Palmer still commented that geologists referred to such found images in rocks as accidentals, but added, "Shaver, who now spends his whole time in his hobby of collecting picture stones, does not accept the accident theory. . . . One thing is sure—the pictures are there, no matter how." Throughout the

1960s, Rap shifted position on the rocks. At times he supported Shaver, noting that his favorite source of wisdom, *Oahspe*, made references to such stones and "even to the specific location of Wisconsin!" As always, he would let his readers judge for themselves.

Shaver, meanwhile, was on a crusade. The February 1962 *Search* had an ad in the inside cover for "Prediluvian Wonder Stones." Shaver promised to send to clients "Five slices of these stones at no cost." He said if his customers could see the pictures in the sample stones, he wanted them returned with one dollar and he would send five more. "If you DECIDE TO KEEP THE STONES, you can buy them by arrangement, as these miniature works of art must be individually priced to be fair. . . . My only interest in this is to save this immense library in silica of the prediluvian world from loss." By the end of the year, however, Shaver's crusade was officially a commercial enterprise. He was advertising "Pre-Deluge Art Stones" that were "Rare . . . Voluptuous . . . Exciting." He requested $25 for "large cubical cuts for patio or mantle," $15 for bookend cuts, $10 for wall plaques, and $1 for a sample box. He also offered a money-back guarantee.

Glimpses of the Hidden World

Most people, confronted with a friend who held rocks and insisted they contained secret messages, would simply shut the door. Palmer did not. Over the years, he had begun to accept that Shaver had glimpsed a "hidden world," and he wanted in. Shaver was not deluded but inspired. Having once warmed to the idea of a hidden world, Palmer set off on a long journey that combined creativity and pathology with discovery. Such is the result when you create an entirely new set of rules for the universe.

Their friendship began with the letters they wrote each other in the 1940s. Both were intelligent men with working-class backgrounds and high school educations, united in their curiosity about the universe. Both had harsh memories of state-run institutions—for Palmer it was the sanatorium, while Shaver's "education" included stays in jails and mental wards, as well as a stint in art school. While Palmer had been largely content to live among science fiction buffs with their hopes pinned on the wonders of the future, he was fascinated with Shaver's subversive narrative—one of grand decline from a golden age of the past—and also by Shaver's sweeping explanation of the cosmos and attempted renovation of the sciences to fit his vision. The truth was being hidden away. Much of the received wisdom was a sham. People, simply, didn't know beans.

This attitude placed Shaver in the Gnostic tradition later more successfully embraced by fellow paranoid and science fiction visionary Philip K. Dick. Like another fellow pulpster, L. Ron Hubbard, Shaver was more or less poised to establish a new religion, but didn't have the sales skills or ruthlessness required for the job. At one point Shaver wondered if he might not start an "organization" dedicated to redeem the cavern world and free people from dis, noting that Hitler, with far less material, had come out of nowhere and moved millions to his ends. This goal of creating an organization was just one of many projects he considered and tossed aside. In a way, his mental turbulence (in addition to his innate decency) kept him honest.

While Palmer hedged on some of Shaver's ideas, the two of them were firmly united in the view that organized religion was little more than "wool"—as in "wool pulled over one's eyes." Palmer had rejected the Catholic teachings of his childhood and genuinely disliked doctrinaire approaches to religion. He preferred questions to pat answers. To this end, Rap frequently would scold readers who bragged of "born again" experiences and asked if their peace of mind had been bought at the expense of the closing of their minds. Since organized religion was a sham, Palmer turned to Shaver for knowledge of the Hidden World. That world's workings were so complete in Shaver's mind that even when he went about

tasks such as driving a tractor on a farm or picking up rocks in a potato field, he was living in an alternative universe. How did that universe
operate?

Shaver held firm to his basic insight, formerly expressed by Mutan Mion
on telonion plates, that the universe consists of the never-ending inter-
action of integrant and disintegrant forces. From this insight sprang his
new sciences. All matter, he declared, eventually succumbs to disintegrant
forces and becomes *exd*—or ex-disintegrance. The ashes of disintegrance
"fill all space and we call that filled space ether."[2] The mystery then deep-
ens, as Shaver posited that ultimately this exd once again returns to matter; that is, integrates. Entropy, it seems, is not a one-way street; systems
can return to complexity; as alchemists had once presumed, the universe
contains the seeds of immortality. By a mechanism not entirely clear, the
exd-based ether "begins to whirl." As the ether whirls and condenses, it
draws in even more exd. In such a fashion matter emerges, beginning,
perhaps, with the simplest of atoms, hydrogen, until increasing mass and
pressure cause the "creation of new suns, and of planets." Gravity, in fact,
is a product of the inrush of exd as planets, such as Earth, are born and
sustained. When you jump in the air, inrushing exd pushes you back down
as you are caught in its spiraling flow into the earth.

In their letters in the mid-1940s, Palmer encouraged Shaver to flesh out
the new sciences prompted by his awareness of cosmic forces such as *de*
and *te* and exd. Shaver had trouble realigning chemistry and physics in
their entirety with "de and te" theory. At first, he boldly rejected atomic theory. He insisted that matter be thought of as elastic bubbles of condensed
exd that adhered "just as soap bubbles" might. Solids, more tightly bonded,
had less dis. The expansion of gases and properties of liquids suggested
that films of dis coated molecules. Molecular motion actually relied on dis,
which added a "slippery" property to atoms and molecules. (He later posited that dis might relate to "heat," as heat loosens molecules up and allows
for motion.) Finally, perhaps weary of constructing a consistent narrative,

Shaver admitted that some atomic theory might be necessary to explain chemical interactions and properties. "Disintegrant matter may seem to contain and may actually contain particles in orbital motion."[3]

Shaver, whose ultimate goal was to defeat dis and elevate humanity to a more godlike state, had an easier time with biology. He informed Rap that the creation of stars and the life of a plant both depend on the inrushing of exd. He wrote to Palmer in 1944, "A plant is a small flame of integration, as long as the plant exists, it grows and spreads the life flame, its growth condenses exd by a vacuum effect." All species of animals and plants rely on exd, as they "condense and integrate it into their patterns which their life processes are formed around."

Men could be gods if they learned the secrets of the Elder Races. The Elder Races' mastery of the de and te dynamic had allowed them to create machines that beamed ben or stim rays that slowed down disintegrance, intensifying this natural process. Shaver remarked, "Life, when supplied with a greater supply of exd—becomes a mighty god-like thing."[4] True progress, enhanced health, and perhaps even immortality could be attained if humans could unravel the secrets of the mech the Elder Races had abandoned in the caverns when fleeing our poisonous sun.

At times, Shaver would recommend a bold assault on the cave world to wrest the secrets of the ancient technology. A great man must lead such an expedition. He suggested that Palmer in his publications "plant this idea—the trip to the polar regions where the caves can be entered" and humanity might finally succeed.[5] However, as it was most likely that we could not wrest the secrets of the Elder World from the caverns' cruel inhabitants, we would have to work on humanity's redemption through such clues as he'd already gathered. With Rap, Shaver puzzled over a variety of questions: How could we slow the ageing process? Gain immortality?

For a while, perhaps influenced by *Oahspe*, Palmer had tried a vegetarian diet. Shaver was unimpressed. He had his own ideas for a life-enhancing diet. Rejecting vegetarianism, Shaver informed Palmer that he must eat only "young" things that had minimal exposure to dis—food sources shielded either by a mother's womb, eggshell, or plant. To Palmer, Shaver recommended a diet of milk; meat from young animals such as suckling pigs, newborn lambs, and fruit and vegetables—but not celery, which grew unshielded. "Meat of an old animal is particularly stupid fare. . . . Watch the principle—an egg is good—a hen is not."[6] (Prior to dispensing this advice, Shaver had attempted to incur longevity in mice. He fed them only milk, corn, and wheat, and shielded them in other ways from dis, but, as he notes, his experiment was inconclusive, as his mice froze to death when he was out of town.) Shaver also thought houses could be redesigned to minimize dis by installing distilling apparatus for water and fluids, as well as centrifuges and walls that would somehow filter out dis. He had some idea of charging the air to minimize dis as well.

Adam, Eve, and the Ape-Bats

All of Shaver's glorious theories of the 1940s led the two friends nowhere. The no-celery diet did not evoke miracles. They were still getting old. No one had recovered the ancient mech. Palmer was reeling from the crumbling of the pulp industry. Shaver couldn't finish his history of the Elder Races and satisfy his subscribers. All their plans and theories, instead, had been overrun by dis. Then Shaver stumbled upon a new source of hope, a source that most people avoided or walked around. Rocks.

When Shaver listened, the rocks whispered to him information about the lives of the "Merm," an Atlantean race of mermaids of myriad shapes, as well as others beings, including a small black race, bearers of great secrets, who may have come from the depths of space. These surface rocks were invaluable "libraries of the past." Shaver wrote in 1964, "After writing about the prediluvian world so many years, as my fans know, you can imagine how excited I have been late months scouring the stone rows and fields for miles around, tracing down foundations and carved stones . . . and trying to keep my elation from blowing my top clear off!"[7]

Shaver had been immersed in this discovery when he brought to Rap's door the thousands of pages of manuscript in 1960. From this orphaned manuscript, with other additions, came the sixteen volumes of the *Hidden World*, published from 1961 to 1964. But it wasn't until Rap published their final book, *Secret World*, over a decade later, that humanity had a full picture of Shaver's ideas about rocks. The *Secret World* is a "dual autobiography." The first half, titled "Martian Diary," is Palmer's life story—although much of it describes his meeting with Shaver and their mutual discovery of a hidden world. The second half, "The Ancient Earth, Its Story in Stone," is Shaver's explanation of his adventures in the rock realms and includes dozens of color plates of his paintings, or "rokfogos." Shaver died in 1975, the year it was published. Palmer lived on another two years.

"The Ancient Earth" served as Shaver's last testament. Fittingly, he informed readers that the rock books proved that the Bible was largely wool. Quite simply, Shaver wrote, "All of the real picture of the past was obliterated from the Bible long ago and substitute writings inserted."[8] The original, ungarbled tale of Adam and Eve described the process by which life became enmeshed in matter, with te (the apple) inexorably leading to de. The original story of Exodus was actually an account of the evacuation of Earth as the Elder Races fled to the stars. Once again, Shaver pointed out that the supernatural realm needed to be stripped from the universe. The Christian hell was a prime example. The dero were a living, breathing species and should not be placed outside the natural realm. If humanity followed its true path we could all become like the gods—that is, remarkably healthy organisms free of dis.

"The Ancient Earth" also explained Shaver's technique for unlocking the images from the mineral realm that inspired his rokfogos. He split open "elder stones," sawed off thin slices, and then used "back lighting" to project them "like a slide" onto a canvas or piece of cardboard treated with light-sensitive material. (If details on the surface of the rock or on a thick slice interested him, he would instead use an opaque projector.) He would treat the canvas with photosensitive chemicals, or simply with glue or wet varnish or even water, then sift dry glue on top. He says the treated surface reacted to the light rays, capturing the stone's patterning. He then enhanced the pattern by spraying the surface again with water, or brushing with a thinned paint. He also used soap powder and dye powder. After distributing this on the canvas, he would then spray the surface with wax spray (either Tone or Pledge) and then with water vapor. "Presto the dye takes hold where the wax was held back by the soap."[9]

As with the Surrealists, who had experimented with random techniques such as automatic writing for evoking art, John Cage's use of the *I Ching* in musical composition, or William S. Burroughs's use of "cut ups" from newspapers to create new texts, Shaver's technique opened his imagination to forms he would not have come up with on his own. From the mineral world, he uncovered images of giants, little people, and horrifying warfare. He saw massings of naked females in many of the stones and found it curious they tended to take on a *Playboy* magazine ideal with their out-thrust breasts. Perhaps, he thought, it simply had to do with water's buoyancy. He also speculated that the ancient earth might have been simply a vacation destination for all these races, a place where they could experience delight for a few weeks or months. Shaver said, "The men of this ancient Earth were space men, kings of space as well as sea kings in their own seas."[10] He also suspected they were at war with a serpent race.

The post-pulp Shaver daubed numerous hallucinogenic paintings, often violent and erotic. Some of the canvases had a quasi-Mayan look, such as *Amazons Defending Against the Attack of the Ape Bats* and *Adam and Eve in Space*. Of the "ape-bats" he noted, "the flying ape-bat was a fearsome fact of early life on earth, and a deadly one, dropping from the tremendous forest trees in swarms like flying squirrels, but man-size and ferocious."[11] As for the Amazon, "Her uniform consists of little else than head-dress, sword and dagger and shield—and in time of battle, a scale armor that I suspect was sometimes fashioned from serpent hide."[12] His canvas shows a fanged ape-bat locked in combat with an Amazon, the ape-bat attempting to push aside a short sword aimed at its open mouth. In other paintings, a naked giantess, a kind of Eve, held cavorting little people on her hands before an assembly of other giants.

A Shaver rokfogo showing giants and little people juxtaposed in a hallucinatory manner. *Photo courtesy Brian Emrich*

His painting *Adam and Eve in Space* offered a further twist on the biblical tale. Adam's face is doubled. The inner face wears a fish helmet, but around it, as if a larger space helmet, is a black face. Demons surround him. Thrust near him is an apple in the mouth of a "serpent"—which actually looks more like an ape-bat. Shaver said that the painting, recovered from a stone record, represents a "false Adam"—a cavern person "dressed up in a black beast suit of hair." The apple the serpent was offering was poison. It was not the real te-charged apple that was "the ancient symbol for the antidote to age poison."[13] No, this one had a de charge. This "God" was an imposter, using the apple to turn people into dero. This particular dero, in control once the Elder Races fled, had a simple goal, to "fool the Other Nuts left behind into behaving and into obeying HIM."[14] And so the real Adam and Eve, two of the many abanderos, rather than receiving immortality, were poisoned and made thoroughly mortal. This truth became obvious to anyone who penetrated the wool.

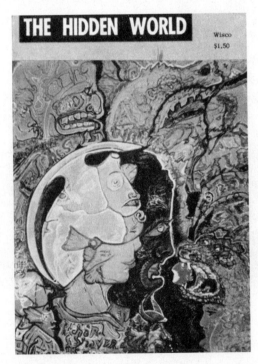

This 1962 *Hidden World* featured Richard Shaver's "Adam and Eve in Space." The figure with multiple masks to the left has already taken a bite from the apple held in the serpent's mouth. *Department of Special Collections, Davidson Library, University of California, Santa Barbara*

Shaver was convinced not only that many stones bore the chronicles of these early races, but that each of these individual "rock books" had once been shaped to fit together to create larger sculptural forms that added further layers of meaning. Apparently very little of the earth's material was random or meaningless. One of his oddest claims: many of the stones he found were not books but in fact "foot casts" or "lasts" used in shoe making. He indexed his photographs of these objects, with simple notes such as "we think of women8s [*sic*] boots as modern, actually the thigh high boot for women was high style in the Amazon empire. . . . Here is a photo of an Amazon boot, which had a flap for riding out brush . . . much as chaps do today."

He sent photos of foot-casts and other rocks along with notes to scientists who failed to share his interest. Shaver was astonished. How could others overlook the importance of his findings? As Shaver noted, "When I first found the rock books I had no intention of doing anything like work on them. I thought all I had to do was tell about them. . . . It was then I found that present-day American science was not receptive to being informed of the presence of rock books in the farmer's rock piles." Once again, the wool was too thick. If scientists were blind, he would have to do the work himself. As he modestly noted, "This is a new field, a new science. I started it. There are few quotes because there are no others to quote."

With or without support, Shaver saw his task as urgent. Cataclysm was imminent. Denizens of outer space were referring to Earth as the "Old Tomb," a toxic place to briefly visit, plunder, then quickly flee. Our planet was in critical condition. In addition to concerns over nuclear holocaust, environmental disaster, dero manipulation, and a poisoned sun, in the rocks Shaver found evidence supporting Immanuel Velikovsky's cataclysm theory of the cosmos, and this theorist's notion that Earth had been bumped into its present orbit. Shaver suspected the Atlans had only lived on Earth before it had wandered into its present orbit around the sun.

Velikovsky, who had a background as a psychoanalyst, had been publishing his theories since the 1950s and had many fierce defenders well into the 1970s. His books, which include *Worlds in Collision* (1950), *Earth in Upheaval* (1956), and *Mankind in Amnesia* (1982) argued that the myths and legends of the past, as well as the geologic record, showed the earth had had close, cataclysmic brushes with other planets or celestial bodies. Paleontologist and evolutionist Stephen Jay Gould remarked, "Velikovsky is neither crank nor charlatan—although to state my opinion and to quote one of my colleagues, he is at least gloriously wrong."[15]

Glory is all in pulp and art. Wrong has nothing to do with it. Shaver adopted many of Velikovsky's ideas. The main concern of this Wisconsin resident and discoverer of the former Amazon presence in the dairy state was "moon falls." According to Shaver, the moon had crashed into the earth on more than one occasion, causing great tidal waves and floods. The Elder Races had learned how to sidestep such cataclysms. They had a template for survival and for escape. Since the earth was a "dying mother" people would do well to heed their advice. After all, "The plans and the space charts lie waiting . . . in their own scattered rock books." But Shaver was somewhat resigned, noting, "To the ignorant, nothing matters, I guess. To a population that sits ignorantly under a surely falling moon, I would wish a better fate than to be doomed to ignoring the escape hatch underfoot."[16]

Given the crisis, Shaver was appalled that scientists chose to ignore him. In his mind, archaeologists and paleontologists had spent decades piecing together an absurd and rather dull narrative—that modern humanity had emerged from more primitive species. This story, Shaver argued, "skips along the path of progress, as we quaintly call our present precarious position beneath an enigmatic moon and the threat of atomic war."[17] He countered evolution with a tale of devolution. We were a blind, ignorant, doomed people. Well before the advent of the environmental movement or the descent of postmodernists onto college faculties, he was declaring progress an illusion.

Shaver's thoughts tended to develop from tentative statements to dire conclusions. That is, from intriguing if odd insights in to wild rants. And so, he first gently chided scientists and then latched on to a conspiracy notion. It was an "old conspiracy, to keep the technology of the past civilizations in the heads of a few. . . . It is no accident we have not had rock books translated and the needed information in them made available. . . . It may be that our repressors are already boarding the 'secret' UFO on their way to greener pastures than those of Earth." In full rant mode, he declared that present-day research was "a science without honor and without value."

Shaver in his studio, circa 1970s. "Attack of the Ape-Bats" is in the background upper left. *Photo Courtesy Brian Emrich*

That not even one learned person would listen to him galled Shaver immensely. He felt martyred in the task of uncovering the truth. "Out of my poverty I must weave miracles of rejuvenation over the lovely fabric of the real past of man. . . . Am I to do it all by myself, without one helping hand from all those mortar boards I have looked up to all my life, until I found they had never dirtied their soft hands with even one lowly stone?" And yet he felt that he had risen to the task and found redemption from his torments. He heard the happy voices of the Merm; he heard their singing, and communed with their playful, wise civilizations. He was in touch with a golden age when the "air was quite invigorating, and life was long and happy and filled with a sense of accomplishment and rightness that is no longer present."[18] This particular Hidden World was not full of tormentors. We had much to learn from these records. The Elder Races had democratically distributed their knowledge in the world's rocks; if the warning had been inscribed on telonion, the solution could be found in common minerals.

The agitated artist drew some comfort in the fact that his neighbor and friend Ray Palmer was listening to him and making his work available to the public. However, other agents of disruption were at work.

Shaver in the Smut Underground

In 1964, the year that the sixteenth and final volume of *Hidden World* was published, Shaver and his wife left Wisconsin and moved to Summit, Arkansas. Palmer's son, Ray B. Palmer, believes it was because Shaver feared prosecution for the allegedly pornographic publishing he was aiding and abetting for William Hamling, who had served as an associate editor to Palmer at *Amazing Stories*. In a very small way, both Shaver and Palmer were involved in the science fiction community's move toward the soft-core magazine and sleaze paperback industry boom of the 1950s and 1960s.

Curiously, Ziff-Davis's decision to abandon Chicago for New York encouraged this shift from science fiction to sleaze publications. Hamling, a Rap protégé at *Amazing*, was central to this development. The science fiction market was in freefall at the same time that Ziff-Davis marooned numerous writers, editors, and artists in the Midwest. In addition to the science fiction magazines *Imagination* and *Imaginative Tales*, Hamling, in 1955, started up *Rogue* magazine, a girlie magazine similar to *Playboy*, which it followed by a year. (Hamling and his wife, Frances Yerxa, Marjorie Palmer's close childhood friend, edited his first magazines from the basement of their Evanston home.) Hamling and Hugh Hefner were, for a time, friends. According to the lore, they had either met while working as editors at Ziff-Davis or at Publisher's Development Corporation, which put out *Modern Sunbathing & Hygiene Magazine*. Hefner, Hamling, and others were willing to risk legal challenges for profit.

On the prompting of science fiction writers Robert Silverberg and Harlan Ellison, in 1959, Hamling also began publishing sleaze paperback books, following the model of Bedside Books, which had begun printing earlier in that year in New York. To this saga, Palmer and Shaver entered as minor characters, akin to Rosencrantz and Guildenstern in *Hamlet*. Shaver and Palmer agreed to help Hamling incorporate Freedom Publishing Company in Wisconsin, with Nightstand as one of its first imprints, followed by Midnight Reader, Bedside Books (which Hamling purchased), Greenleaf Classics, and others. In addition to setting up Freedom Publishing in Wisconsin, Hamling purchased the stock of a defunct corporation, Blake Pharmaceutical, in Evanston, Illinois, and used it as another shield for his publishing efforts.

Much of the staff at the Evanston offices of *Rogue* and Freedom Publishing was from the science fiction community. Likewise, most Nightstand authors were recruited from the ranks of science fiction and crime writers, usually with the help of literary agent Scott Meredith (a former science fiction fan named Sidney Feldman). These authors included Harlan Ellison, the first editorial director of the line; Marion Zimmer Bradley; Donald Westlake; Robert Silverberg; and Lawrence Block. When Nightstand began, two books per month were published, many set in a beatnik milieu. Among the dozens of books published included *Campus Tramp* ("One Passion-Soaked Night Turned Her into the Campus Tramp—Illicit Passions gave Linda a Scarlet Reputation") and *Pads Are for Passion* ("Anita Was a Virgin—Till the Hipsters Got Hold of Her"). Even Ed Wood Jr. got in on the act and contributed—without bothering with a pen name—*Orgy of the Dead*. Wood's writing was as bad as his filmmaking; 4E Ackerman, who represented SF authors, jokingly called himself Wood's "illiterary agent." Wood turned *Orgy* into a 1965 movie that largely depicts a striptease act in a graveyard with a cast that included the Amazing Criswell, who had contributed an astrology column to *Fate*.

Nightstand was also a pioneer in publishing lesbian and gay erotica, such as *Sin Girls* ("A Shocking Novel of Lesbian Love," "Tormented Passions of Woman for Woman"). Published in 1960, it was written by science fiction writer Robert Silverberg under the pen name Marlene Longman (he could write as many as three such novels a month while also writing science fiction). Marion Zimmer Bradley reportedly became Longman for "her" second title *Lesbian Love*. Other lesbian titles followed, including *Butch* and *Three of a Kind*. In the 1960s, Nightstand offered *Why Not?* the first of the Hamling books to feature male homosexuality, which led to many others, including *Good Bye My Lover* ("Their Life Was a Sad Song") and the less apologetic *Song of the Loon*, which featured a frontiersman and Indian companion involved in an erotic relationship, as well as the spy send-up *The Man from C.A.M.P.* (1966) and the celebrative *The Beefcake Boys* (1967).

Many of the titles and covers in the late 1960s began to reflect Hamling's and editor Earl Kemp's origins in the science fiction community, including *Nautipuss* (1965), *Those Sexy Saucer People* (1967), *The Day the Universe Came* (1968), *Fantasex* (1969), and *Starship Intercourse* (1971).[19] Pulp artist Harold W. McCauley, who had long adorned the covers of *Amazing Stories* with Mac Girls, and who also went on to work for *Rogue*, did most of the covers for the early Nightstand sleaze paperbacks through the early 1960s. When McCauley moved from Chicago to Florida, Robert Bonfils became the main artist in residence.

According to Kemp, who took over editing Nightstand in the 1960s, Shaver did not write any of the books. Nevertheless, Palmer and Shaver's association with big-city porn publisher William Hamling proved difficult in small-town Wisconsin. A series of articles ran in 1963 in both the *Milwaukee Journal* and the *Milwaukee Sentinel*—including one front-page story that detailed Shaver's and Palmer's connections to Freedom Publishing Company, which became notorious after it was named the "worst of the worst" of the new smut publishers in an article in the *Saturday Evening Post*. The first of these local news articles, from April 4, 1963, indicated that

Richard Shaver was listed as president and Ray Palmer as a director of Freedom Publishing, then under investigation for distributing pornography in Illinois.

The *Milwaukee Journal*'s bemused reporter noted that "Wisconsin had a literary mystery on its hands, complete with a ghostly publishing house and a cast of intriguing characters." He found Palmer "in the back room of the Amherst post office, where he is a star customer, having given it enough business in recent years to raise it from third class to second class status." Palmer cheerfully denied any role in publishing racy material. He described the magazines and books he published and said that he employed local farm wives "who certainly wouldn't stand for anything out of line." He insisted that he had signed the incorporation papers for Freedom as a favor to Shaver. Shaver, less comfortable during his interview, eventually said he was simply a "figurehead" and added, "I don't know too much about it." The reporter concluded that Shaver had "allowed 'friends' to use his name, in return for which he is paid."[20] In this era of "naming names" neither Shaver nor Palmer mentioned Hamling.

While Palmer seemed amused by the whole affair, clearly they were being targeted—and not only by newspaper reporters. The lawyer who had incorporated Freedom Publishing was currently at work for the governor of Wisconsin, adding a mild scent of scandal to the affair, and the newspapers continued to report on it through the summer. Even in July, the district attorney in Portage County, Wisconsin, continued to insist he was "investigating," which suggests official visits to Shaver's and Palmer's remote farmhouses in 1963. Sensitive to the otherworldly persecution of the dero, Shaver might well have been troubled by the questioning of real-life investigators. In 1964 he made his move to Arkansas.

That pulpsters, eking out a living in fringe publishing, should be attracted to smut is no shock. By the mid-1950s, concomitant with the collapse of the huge magazine distributor American News Company, many of the science fiction magazines faded from the scene, leaving writers with few markets. The men's adventure magazines that continued to thrive after 1950, such as *Man's Life*, *Adventure Life*, *Gusto*, *Peril*, *True Men*, *Wildcat Adventures*, *Modern Man*, and *South Sea Tales* were watered down pornography, featuring manly adventures among headhunters, exotic natives, and lascivious local dancers. "Death Orgy of the Leopard Woman," "Bride of the Anaconda," "Blood Revenge of the Gilded Glamazons from Yongdong-Po," or Frank Zappa's favorite, "Weasels Ripped My Flesh" (published in *Man's Life*, September 1956), were typical articles from these magazines, many of which flourished into the 1960s.

While only tangentially involved in Hamling's publications, neither Shaver nor Palmer was a prude. Shaver was outraged when another author Rap was cultivating, Roger Phillips Graham, described Shaver's mind as a "cesspool." Shaver declared, "One reason for sex in my story is my desire to relate the idea of sex reward with scientific effort as a spur to scientific effort in the young mind that might go to dance hall and booze road else— it is a lot of lure to a young student who must pass up these flesh delights to get anywhere as a student. I want to put that lure in the science effort where it was really put by the ancients—and they got results."[21] Regarding the erotic pursuits of the ancients, Shaver noted, "Their love-life was beautiful beyond our beauty, and soft with sentiment beyond our concept of undying love. They had . . . a vitality that demanded a much deeper indulgence of love gratification than our own."[22]

Shaver seemed to draw the line at the sadistic antics of the dero, commenting that, unlike the Elder Races they came from, the dero were essentially dead. They had no inner life and needed mechanical stimulus. He had much the same feeling toward moral crusaders against smut. These were "the same types of men who close our burlesque shows and go to honky-tonks or smokers in their clubs and holler 'take it off' and get it taken off for them. Who squall about juvenile delinquency and contribute to it themselves . . . who never give a sucker a break . . . who ban good books from publication on moral grounds and themselves do not understand morality or give a damn."[23] These sorts of men were hounding him. District attorneys and J. Edgar Hoover's clean-cut G-Men.

Shaver wasn't the only one to hit the road. Despite Hamling's successes, it had been getting expensive to pay off local police and politicians in the Chicago area. (Palmer alludes to this same fact when he discussed how, hypothetically, he could make a fortune publishing pornography in Wisconsin—and whom he would have to bribe.) Hamling decided to move from Illinois to California, slowly closing down what many of the former pulp writers had called the "Porno Factory" in Evanston and shifting the operation to the West Coast, where in 1965 Freedom Publishing was reorganized as Phenix Publications, Ltd., with Greenleaf Classics as a subsidiary. Greenleaf's first title after the move, Terry Southern's *Candy*, sold close to one million copies.

As his fortune grew, Hamling's legal challenges increased. He fought two cases to the U.S. Supreme Court and received positive rulings, allowing subscription mailings of *Rogue* in 1957 and a rejection of a Kansas district attorney's 1961 decision to impound *Rogue* from newsstands. In July 1966, a two-month trial against Hamling began in Houston on a twenty-five-count federal indictment based on the prohibition of the interstate transportation of obscene materials.

Shaver was called to testify. According to Earl Kemp, the SF editor who worked for Hamling, in the Houston courtroom Shaver, "formerly of Wisconsin and Lemuria . . . under oath. . . . testified that he was 'President' of Hamling's Freedom Publishing Company . . . did not know anything about the books and had nothing to do with the company, and that he was paid regularly by check."[24] The defense brought in witnesses including an expert from the Kinsey Institute, a journalism professor, an editor at *Playboy*, and a young married couple who were swingers to testify to the authenticity of the books. A literature professor, who read from *Temple of Shame*, broke up the courtroom and testified to its value as literature. Ultimately it was ruled a mistrial, and all charges were dropped. The prosecutor was named

Susman, so Hamling ordered his writers and editors to name all the evil characters in their books Susman for the next few years.

Both Kemp and Hamling were later sentenced in California as the anti-smut forces closed a stronger case based on racy advertising mailers for Hamling's publication of the U.S. government's *The Illustrated Presidential Report of the Commission on Obscenity and Pornography* (1971). As a result of this prank on the government, Kemp and Hamling spent three months and one day in federal prison in California. Palmer, who had apparently helped only arrange the incorporation of Hamling's Freedom Publishing, was never subpoenaed.[25]

Less footloose than Shaver, and more firmly grounded on the soil of Wisconsin, Rap was not going to let smut investigations run him away from his vision of heaven.

Friendship Under a Poisoned Sun

Although Shaver was likely as close a friend as Palmer ever had, Rap never let that friendship get in the way of business. As early as 1945, after the Shaver Mystery broke, Palmer began cultivating other "wild men" hoping to turn up another Shaver. His main effort involved Roger Phillips Graham. According to Palmer, his introduction to Graham was a letter from him that said, "Send me $500 so that I can come to Chicago to kill you. You know too much about the caves!" (The only problem with this anecdote is that Graham's first published story, "Let Freedom Ring," appeared in *Amazing Stories* in January 1945, several months before the publication of "I Remember Lemuria." Graham's second story, in the February 1946 issue of Ziff-Davis's *Fantastic Adventures*, however, had the evocative title "Vacation in Shasta.") Whatever the circumstances, Palmer decided to bring Graham out and make him part of the Ziff-Davis stable.

If the January 1945 "Meet the Authors" column in *Amazing Stories* can be trusted, the tall and husky Graham was yet another welder turned genius. He had been working in a shipyard in Kirkland, Washington, when he first contacted Rap. Graham was a mathematical wizard, or could at least pass himself off as one, as well as a science fiction fan, an inventor, and apprentice writer. He also had very malleable views about the nature of reality. Turning Graham into a character straight out of Sherwood Anderson's *Winesburg, Ohio*, the *Amazing Stories'* biography noted, "While he worked, he scribbled on odd bits of paper, and the scribbling was always numbers. He says the answers he got confirmed his suspicion that knowledge is just something that seems to fit the most known circumstances at any particular time."

Graham was apparently a very sunny presence but also a font of crank ideas and subject to frequent psychic experiences. He informed anyone who asked that he had arrived on Earth from Halley's Comet and that he had a mission to save earthlings from the atom bomb. He jokingly wrote a memoir of his life in science fiction titled "Christ, an Autobiography."[26] Just as Shaver had created an entire new science from his isolation of de and te as the primal forces, Graham had worked out a new math that explained the universe. He was happy to discourse on these matters with Palmer in the letters they fired back and forth. Graham became one of the correspondents with whom Palmer also discussed Shaver's de and te theory. Palmer sent him money and Graham left the West Coast. He also began writing fiction. As Palmer tells the story, as with Shaver's, Graham's fledgling writing efforts required extensive rewrites, but eventually he was contributing stories that Palmer printed. Unlike Shaver, he went on to write stories good enough for other markets.

Among Graham's early published efforts was an article in the February 1946 *Amazing* that began as a praise song to the Shaver Mystery but ended up, instead, touting the value of *Oahspe*, which Graham had first read on the train from the West Coast to Chicago. At times, Graham's taste for paradox also seemed downright Palmeresque. He began his take on the

Shaver Mystery by discussing his own childhood. "My oldest and most persistent conviction of childhood and adolescence was that I was not the child of my professed parents. This conviction . . . was strong enough to cause me to look up my birth record. . . . I was left with incontrovertible proof that I actually am the child of my professed parents, and also the still persistent conviction that I am not." Graham's article went on to insist that "I Remember Lemuria," Shaver and Palmer's composite story, was serving as a trigger to the larger drama of humanity leaving adolescence for adulthood. Man, thanks to the Shaver Mystery, "is about to take his place in the community of the universe as an adult, with his eyes finally open, a true knowledge of the workings of the universe around him, and his own nature."

In his science fiction, Graham took the not very disguised pen name of Rog Phillips, as well as many of the pseudonyms available to Ziff-Davis writers of that era. He published as many as 150 stories in the 1940s and 1950s not only in *Amazing* and *Fantastic Adventures*, but also in *Astounding* and other pulps. Many of his stories were also republished in anthologies, indicating their staying power. His novelette "Rat in the Skull" was nominated for a Hugo Award in 1959. His stories' titles place him firmly alongside Philip K. Dick as a chief proponent of Psi-Fi. Examples include, "The Cube Root of Conquest," "Step Out of Your Body, Please," "Prophecy, Inc.," and "You'll Die Yesterday."

Graham had an affable and confident nature, and Palmer relied on him to go to conventions and talk to angry fans about *Amazing*, the Shaver Mystery, and *Amazing*'s interest in helping fans. Graham served as a goodwill ambassador at a time when the Shaver controversy raged. From 1947 until several years after Rap left Ziff-Davis, Graham wrote the "Club House" column for *Amazing* and later for Palmer's *Universe Science Fiction* and *Other Worlds*. His columns were a premium source for fan news.

Before both had moved to the Chicago area, Palmer attempted to forge a friendship between his two wild mystics. But, as Palmer recalled, they

simply hated each other. Graham believed there was "something" to the
Shaver Mystery though. He recalled getting an early letter from Shaver: "I
brought my mail into the kitchen and laid it down on the drain board.
Pepper was standing there wagging his tail, looking up at me. I opened
Dick's letter. *Something* seemed to jump out of it. Pepper backed up, and
then ran into the front room like the devil was after him."[27] Graham couldn't
pinpoint exactly what "it" was but after about an hour "it" left and his dog
calmed down. Although they shared a belief in the Hidden World, when-
ever the two authors met, they clashed. Shaver resented what he perceived
as Graham's one-upmanship, opportunism, ability to command attention,
and his charm.

As he couldn't get them to collaborate, Palmer, the grand manipulator,
sought out drama. Palmer gave Graham his entire file of letters from
Shaver explaining his theories of the dero, the caverns, the Elder Races, and
de and te. Graham read the file and decided that Shaver had it all wrong.
Much of what he blamed on the dero fit much easier into the categories
of spirit disturbances and activities on the astral plane. To further stir up
trouble, Palmer handed Graham's critical letters to Shaver.

Shaver's response was a howl. First, like Houdini, he had little use for
spirits. He preferred the simplest explanation: "living agents." He said
Oahspe might have some truth to it, but it was unlikely there was a cosmic
"plan" or that spirits guided everyone's destiny. A sampling of his response
to Palmer included, "Darn you, I write my own stories, and no 'spirit' does
any more than help me out in the same way you help me out. . . . Rap, I
am hurt."[28] He also denounced Graham as a hypocrite and flatterer who
would say anything he thought Palmer might want to hear. Shaver then
noted that although he had left Pennsylvania to be near Palmer in Chicago,
he felt abandoned. "I am as much a recluse out here as I was before, though
I had hoped differently. I want to play poker with the boys and with the
bowling to bowl and all—but I can't make it out here."[29] He then under-
lined why he referred to Rap, however jokingly, as "the Boss." "Most work-

ing men so too, depend on one string to their bow—one boss's whims—and so do I—so don't think I want to fly off the handle at you."

In response to Shaver's anguished letter, Palmer penned a response that was a classic of diplomacy, emanating sincerity and warmth. Palmer said he was struggling to process Shaver's ideas. He insisted that before Shaver's letter had arrived he had a fairly conventional worldview. "I had never heard a voice, never knew there was such a thing as a cave, didn't know any philosophy, hadn't read any books on mysterious things, not even [Charles] Fort."[30] He added that he didn't have "the slightest knowledge that there might be any truth in science fiction outside of the fact that it did forecast certain gadgets such as the atomic bomb."

Rap went on to say that Shaver had told him many incredible things and he had to find out the truth. Even though he heard "voices" at Shaver's house in Barto, "How could I say definitely it was not you who spoke, even if you didn't realize it, while in some sort of a 'trance.'" His attempt to find the truth made him turn his attention to "mediums, to spiritualists, to Oahspe, to the book of Mormon, to Indian legends, to voodooism, to anything occult. I learned, and listened." He claimed he was trying to determine the path down which to take *Amazing*. "I change my concept of the whole thing every day." He added that Roger Phillips Graham had not fooled him or his wife. Of Graham, he said, "We know he is bombastic, we know he likes to be a big shot, we know he lies. . . . But I must listen to every theory, to every 'evidence' and weigh it in my mind."[31] He added that he had, in truth, subjected Shaver to many tests. "Most you passed. Some you did not. Now I have subjected you to another, a very big one. I have found you to be a man."

He added that unlike Shaver, he, Rap, had a good poker face. "Do I get both sides of the story if I stick my nose into just one hole in the ground?" He added that "Occult literature has all been one sided. I intend to present both sides. You . . . are to present the cave side." On a personal note he said, "You should have no fear of losing my friendship. My friendships aren't based on will-o-the-wisps, and withdrawn in anger the minute they are not handled with kid gloves." He urged Shaver to join him to play poker. He added that Hamling, another poker player, could be very annoying, and he was sorry if he had bothered Dot. "He likes to drink and I do not. . . . When Margy has had the baby, maybe the four of us can get in some bowling just between us. Believe me, we have found the social company of the Shavers very pleasant. . . . We have not been to the Brownes in a year, nor to the Hamlings. But we call on you regularly."[32]

While this argument took place behind the scenes, Shaver and Palmer had a very public dispute two decades later, following the publication of the sixteen-volume *Hidden World*. As such, it is unclear if this marked a "clearing of the air" after Shaver's departure for Arkansas, or if it was more in the nature of a put-on to pique the interest of readers. In any case the November 1966 *Search* reprinted the article "Shaver Versus Palmer" that had earlier appeared in the small fanzine *Searchlight*.

Shaver's main contention was that Palmer had not created him, nor had Palmer had any creative role in any of his stories. Regarding his first story, "I Remember Lemuria," Shaver noted, "He often says he wrote three quarters of it, or gives that impression, the truth is he did not write anything in it but a few paragraphs that managed to change the whole story from one of strict actual background to one of misty psychic remembering which was not my intention at all. NO Palmer does not now, nor did he ever, write any of my stories." Shaver then went on to say Palmer had not "made" him. "I was raised as a writer. . . . My brother was well known as a writer in Boys Life. . . . My Mother was a well known poet in many slick magazines. . . . I was a writer and a good one before I ever ran into Palmer."

Palmer's response was to insist they were the best of friends before revealing his claws. "[That] Ray Palmer liked Richard Shaver is also true. There never lived a more gentle gentleman than Richard Shaver. . . . Friends? You can be sure of that." He then went on to explain that he had taken the ten-thousand-word "A Warning to Future Man," written as a sort of a tract, and turned it into a thirty-thousand-word story with characters and dialogue. As for changing the story to reflect "misty psychic remembering," if he had not made the changes, Bernard Davis would never have allowed it to be published as "true," and "no one would ever have heard of it."

Then Palmer slashed at Shaver. While some of Shaver's stories were well written, and required little editing, "Others were—well never mind." He added that he knew Shaver had sent many of his stories to numerous science fiction editors in New York and collected rejections on them before they came to *Amazing*. "The other editors told me about it often, over a cup of coffee in Greenwich Village on my frequent trips to New York." He said they would ask, "How can you accept manuscripts in such unrevised form and pay your regular rates?" He concluded, somewhat diplomatically, "No I did not 'make' Shaver . . . but I did make the Mystery!"

While Palmer and Shaver continued some sort of friendship after this published exchange, clearly Shaver—by then living in Arkansas—wasn't dropping by for potato pancakes every Saturday. The Shaver Mystery Club's members, a small coterie, began to see Palmer as the devil, or as dero controlled. Shaver had left. Not quite for the dark recesses of outer space, far from the poisoned sun, but to his painting studio in the Ozarks, a land of caverns. Shaver's band of followers continued to hound him for clues, for ways to enter the caves. For their own good, he gave them garbled directions. His main interest, however, was in his rokfogos.

Palmer cast around, but soon discovered that there were no other Shavers to be found. Rog Phillips had turned into an excellent science fiction writer, but no Phillips Mystery emerged. Surveying the landscape of the 1950s, Palmer concluded that outside the occult pulp and flying saucer world, the only other alluring frontier was that of the soft-porn magazines such as *Playboy* and *Rogue*. Money was to be had in that hustle, but ultimately, he valued his freedom. Despite offers, he did not want to return to the "hectic scramble that the big city is" to work with Hamling. As he put it, "We prefer our life on our 124-acre farm with our trout stream, and our six dogs and two cats and our three husky and healthy children who can look out their window and see a blue heron stalking fish in the shallows, or a deer coming to drink."[33] Instead, he kept riding the flying saucer as it zigzagged about in its "weightless" manner, while playing to his loyal but shrinking audience.

ESP, OR THE ELDER STATESMAN OF PULP

What I meant was that a man with two heads would be shunned by his fellow man, be considered a freak, and would be very lonely as a result. Your editor, because of his "out of the ordinary" interests, thoughts, activities, is shunned in this manner, considered a freak, and as a result, he has very few friends, and very few people he can talk to.

—RAY PALMER, *FORUM*, NOVEMBER 1, 1966

Dear Ray, Sorry I can't renew Search Magazine. But I have found the truth and joined "The Beatnik Holyness Church of Christ in the World." Therefore I can't search for truth anymore since I have found it, can I?

—RON AMOS, *SEARCH*, JULY 1969

I n 1960, Ray Palmer turned fifty years old, and, as his thoughts ran toward mortality, he grudgingly accepted that he had become a superhero. That year, the DC comic book hero the Atom appeared in *Justice League of America* and in the spin-off comic book *The Atom*. The Atom was a miniscule superhero who did daring deeds in a tasteful skin-tight red and blue uniform with an atom symbol on his mask and on his belt. In the comic book's panels, Atom morphed back and forth between his tiny superhero form and his everyday persona of "Ray Palmer," a brilliant Ivy Town scientist who had unleashed the properties of the matter from a "white dwarf star."

The originators of this revamped Atom, DC Comics editor Julius Schwartz and writer Gardner Fox, were both veterans of the pulps. Fox had written for *Weird Tales*, *Planet Stories*, and the Palmer-era *Amazing Stories*. Julius Schwartz, before entering the comic book industry, had been a fanzine editor alongside Palmer at the *Time Traveller*, *Science Fiction Digest*, and *Fantasy*, as well as one of the founders of Solar Sales Service, the first literary agency for science fiction authors. His clients included Stanley Weinbaum, Robert Bloch, and others who worked with Palmer. Placed in charge of the All-American Comics line (later officially renamed DC—short for Detective Comics) in the 1950s, Julius Schwartz began reworking old heroes introduced in the 1940s such as the Flash, the Green Lantern, and Hawkman.

Ray Palmer, scientist, transformed into hard-punching
comic book superhero the Atom.

Schwartz recalled that when he got to "the Atom, I gave him a thorough revamp, as well. The original Atom was Al Pratt, a small, regular person who was exceptionally strong, and I changed him into a hero who could shrink his size down to atomic size (his normal height as a hero would be six inches). . . . I called up Ray and asked his permission to appropriate his name for the civilian identity of the new Atom, and he graciously assented. (An added bonus of the call was that it inspired me to come up with one of the Atom's unique powers, where he could travel from place to place along the phone line as if he was one of the transmitted sound particles.)"[1]

Schwartz and Fox gave playful Palmeresque twists to some of the Atom's adventures and traits. The superhero's origins occur when the brilliant Ray Palmer is leading his fiancée and young members of a nature club on an expedition through an underground cave system. No deros appear, but the hikers are trapped by a rockfall. Palmer deftly utilizes a lens he had earlier fashioned from dwarf star material retrieved from a meteor; with it he focuses the sun's ultraviolet light, creating a ray that shrinks him to about six inches tall. In his tiny form, he finds and improves an escape route, and he then returns to normal size via the mysterious lens to lead everyone to safety. Delighting in his new powers, Ray Palmer develops a special belt that turns him into the Atom at will. He carefully hides his superhero identity from everyone, including his feisty fiancée, law student Jean Loring (the pair eventually marry then divorce).

The real Ray Palmer was not likely amused by all of the Atom's adventures. In addition to riding in tiny flying saucers, the Atom often was involved in slapstick situations, such as being trapped on flypaper, made a member of a flea circus, placed in a slingshot, half-eaten by a Venus flytrap, locked in a "Lethal Lightbulb" by "Doctor Light," flattened by an iron on an ironing board, nearly drowned in a bathroom sink when the plug is pulled, and other indignities. His power was always subject to reversals. Likewise, the tiny Atom was associated with dwarfishness.

Nevertheless, as the 1960s progressed and the world was catching up with Rap in celebrating weirdness, the comic book remained a genuine tribute to Palmer and his interests. The second issue of *Atom* featured scientist Palmer's meeting with Oscar D. Dollar, aka "Mr. Odd," a seemingly ordinary fellow who claims his lucky silver dollar triggered spontaneous fires, earthquakes, and other fantastic events.

The Atom also was part of the Justice League of America, and like his superhero counterpart, Palmer also crusaded for truth and justice. In his memoirs, Rap offered his own "superhero origins tale," noting that at an early age, as a result of his mother's sadness, "coupled with the accident that crippled me, made me a hunchback, I became a lone-wolf, a bitterly determined, stubborn man dedicated to defying injustice and meanness wherever I found it."[2]

His efforts to provide a forum for people with an interest in the paranormal—or for that matter, flying saucers—were central to this crusade on behalf of the marginalized, yet did not tell the entire story. The causes he took up landed him all over the political map. His unorthodox musings often provoked the wrath of anti-Communists who were certain he was a "Red." At times, however, he fell prey to conspiracy theories (regarding enemies planning world domination) straight out of a right-wing comic book. Was he a superhero or villain? Patriot or subversive? Hipster or square? Paranoid nut or well-informed provocateur? To simplify, he began to call himself a Martian.

A Brief History of Rap's Crusades

While Palmer took up many causes over the years, one of his first efforts to right an injustice began in 1948, when his friend L. T. Hansen reported that starvation was rampant on the Navajo lands. Rap immediately began a pulp-based crusade to raise food and money to aid the tribe. He published editorials in the Ziff-Davis pulps *Mammoth Western*, *Amazing Stories*, and *Fantastic Adventures* and also in *Fate* describing the Navajo Indians' desperate need for food. Palmer encouraged readers to donate nonperishable food to an aid group in Los Angeles. Pulp westerns and dime novels for years had featured wily, bloodthirsty (and occasionally noble) Indians, but now through that medium genuine Native Americans were being acknowledged and helped. Donations poured in, and trucking companies arranged convoys. The aid helped many Navajo. A year later, however, hunger had returned. As he would in the decade that followed, Palmer reported on the situation in *Fate*, noting, "We are certainly a just nation. We never seem to have any trouble raising money for guns or for grafters or for international crooks. But for the hungry . . . our impotency is complete and final. . . . Well, after all, what's a few hundred thousand Indians more or less? . . . America, land of the free and the brave . . . and the stinkingly selfish."[3]

In another of his early crusades, Rap published a series of articles in the 1950s stressing the danger of pesticides such as DDT and other chemicals in the food chain. This was five years before Rachel Carson published *Silent Spring* (1962), a book on the same topic that launched the modern environmental movement. In one of his smaller crusades, in June 1957, Palmer made an earnest appeal to readers of *Search* to help the Lions Club fund a summer camp for blind children in Wisconsin. Punning on the usual paranormal language, he titled his request "Second Sight in Action." He noted that everyone in the next thirty days would plan to spend a few nickels on something they didn't need. "Close your eyes and imagine that you are a boy who will never open them again! Now do you know what to do with that nickel?" His readers were convinced and helped fund the camp where sightless children could enjoy summer's pleasures.

Palmer's most outspoken campaign of the 1950s, however, was his opposition to atomic weapons tests. He began to raise the alarm in the late 1940s when he questioned military expenditures and the wisdom of the belief that "The only way to insure peace is to prepare for war with such a gigantic war machine that nobody would dare attack us."[4] The deadly effects of fallout from a 1954 hydrogen bomb test on the crew of the Japanese fishing ship *Lucky Dragon* in the Pacific revitalized the issue (and also inspired Japanese filmmakers to create *Godzilla*). In the February 1955 *Mystic*, Palmer editorialized, "The radioactivity we loose today will infect our descendants systems for unknown centuries. It will change the genes of the body cells. It will create human monsters. And every person, be he president or peasant, who denies this known fact is either innocently or willfully ignorant." The next issue of *Mystic* featured the twenty-five-page cover story "Atomic Power—Will It Murder the Human Race?" Palmer again insisted that the true dangers of atomic fallout were constantly being downplayed, and that government agencies were lying to the public. Two years later, in 1957, for example, the Atomic Energy Commission distributed pamphlets to people that lived near the atomic test site in Nevada assuring them that "your best action is not to be worried about fallout."[5]

Palmer's criticism of militarization left him vulnerable to the era's Communist hunters. In March 1955, the *Los Angeles Examiner* ran Jack Lotto's article, "On Your Guard: Reds Launch 'Scare Drive' Against U.S. Atomic Tests." The article suggested that critics such as Palmer were part of "a big communist 'fear' campaign to force Washington to stop all American atomic-hydrogen bomb tests [that] erupted this week." In August 1955 Palmer responded. Intentionally misnaming "Lotto" as "Jack Blotto" (i.e., a drunk), he added, "Let it be said, the chips falling where they may, that the editor is crusading, and not only that, he is crusading mad! . . . Mad enough not to overlook an opening in the other guy's guard, through which he can smash his ugly nose flat against his skull-bone!"

Accused of spreading Communist propaganda, Rap's response was to present himself as a super-patriot sounding an alarm. "Paul Reveres aren't too welcome . . . they tend to disturb our sleep and get us out of bed." He marveled that the argument was even being disseminated that radiation from fallout might "improve the race through mutation," or the equally foolish notion that "maybe it's all part of God's plan." He said he felt like a disobedient child being scolded and told to shush. He added, "Nothing to be proud of, disobeying your parents—unless, of course, they are wrong, and need to be corrected. Then you just ignore 'em, or if that doesn't work, spit in their faces."[6] Rap also ran an editorial that began by supporting the decision to add the phrase "Under God" to the Pledge of Allegiance, but went on to ask, why, if we were so godly, were we dedicated to H-bomb production?

This wasn't the first time his nonconformist thought gained the attention of anti-Communists. In 1952, celebrity columnist and FBI informant Walter Winchell passed on to his friend J. Edgar Hoover a letter denouncing Palmer. The tipster noted of the just published January 1953 issue of *Amazing Stories*—this was several years after Palmer had left—"if the two stories, 'Frontiers Beyond the Sun,' and 'Death Beyond the Veil' are not the rawest Commie propaganda I ever saw, I'm totally blind." Possibly a fan of the now-absent Shaver stories, the writer added, "For some time the magazine has been losing quality in its fiction. Apparently it is being sacrificed to the 'red' message." The letter included the postscript, "Ray Palmer, Editor of Other Worlds has been putting out some 'peace at any price' editorials that taste phony." An FBI agent paged through back issues of *Other Worlds* and reported he couldn't find any "peace at any price" message or praise of Communism or the Soviet Union. The FBI ran checks of Rap's other employees, including Bea Mahaffey and cover artist Malcolm H. Smith, but found nothing subversive to report.[7]

Two years later, Hoover received a copy of a letter from Vee Terrys Perlman, a member of the then new blacklist group AWARE, Inc., which, as Perlman wrote, was "combating Communism in the entertainment fields." Perlman, a female journalist, believed that an editorial of Palmer's in *Mystic* reeked of anti-Americanism. After preparing a reply for *Mystic*, Perlman noted to Hoover, "I was about to mail the original to Mr. Palmer when it occurred to me that it might be better to withhold same until I learned from you whether I would be spoiling anything by thus putting him on notice." Hoover responded diplomatically, "I would like to point out that it is not possible for me to advise you whether or not to send the letter in question to the editor of the magazine you mentioned."[8] His response suggested, however, that Palmer was not number one on the anti-Communist hit parade in 1954.

In the editorial that Perlman objected to so strongly, Rap had insisted that people's lives were controlled by propaganda that constricted freedom of thought and of experience. The daily news was "processed," filtered into predetermined categories. The sorts of unusual "facts" Rap was interested in, if ever considered in the mainstream news, were presented as the "oddity of the day"—that is, made into a laugh line. People had been conditioned to accept this thought control. Elsewhere, Rap had noted that he had nothing but contempt for advertising and "the hypnotic propaganda machine dinned at unwary, inexperienced minds to bilk them of their cash." But in this editorial he was distinguishing what he believed a far more dangerous version of thought control. Propaganda was not only to be found in the Soviet Union but here in the United States. Dipping into conspiracy thought, he suggested the real enemies were not only leaders such as Stalin, but also secret "power groups" behind the scenes. Although "darkness rules the world today," Rap wanted "to peer into the darkness and penetrate the fog of 'propaganda,' 'conditioning' and hypnotism that surrounds us."[9]

Perlman's letter accused Palmer of equating Western democracies with totalitarian regimes. In so doing, he was guilty of "evil propaganda." If he tried to print a similar magazine in the Soviet Union he would be sent to a prison camp. Perlman suggested Rap was a typical Red of the 1950s, apologetic about Stalin but not about Communism itself. Perlman concluded, "There is nothing mystic about what you are up to. It needs to be exposed."

In the February 1955 *Mystic*, Rap published Perlman's letter verbatim in the letters page, "The Séance Circle—Letters from the Undead." His response was long and eerily calm. He noted that as Perlman had slandered him, he felt "automatically released from any charity in our reply." He went on to insist that the "people of the world" should be distinguished from any particular regime or "ism." He had no praise for the Soviets. The people of Russia were "oppressed." He went on to wonder what Perlman intended by "exposing" him. Did the journalist wish to ruin him financially? Have him ostracized? Shot? He added that Perlman should look up the word "communism" in the dictionary. "Perhaps it isn't a way of doing things we Americans would go for, but it IS a way of doing things, and it isn't so horrible as you seem to think. I, myself would NOT like to do things that way!" He concluded by suggesting that Perlman was deluded; "the monster (propaganda) has eaten your brain. Your thinking is predigested for you by the 'power group.'"

Yet even in this period of Red hunting, for many of Rap's readers, creeping Communism was low on the list of priorities. During the warm months, hundreds of visitors came to Wisconsin unannounced—he noted, for example, that 405 visitors dropped by in July of 1961. They came to say hello or talk up their crank projects or to ask Rap to explain, in a hundred words or less, the Shaver Mystery. Some didn't want to leave his farmhouse or office until they had persuaded him they were right on issues such as the reality of reincarnation. (Rap rejected reincarnation as being "too repetitive.")

They could get nasty. One visitor, he claimed, had the "hobby" of climbing up in trees and brandishing a hatchet. Rap was hesitant to call the police, as he disliked dependency on government. But like Robert Bloch's imaginary editor, even Palmer began to tire of cranks. In a surprising move for an editor of journals that depended on an interest in psychic phenomena, he denounced most psychics as "subconscious and conscious frauds." He announced that he loathed reading through long manuscripts of channeled material that proclaimed the vapid truth that "universal love" was the answer, then to get visits from furious authors when he refused to publish their platitudes or who accused him of stealing their fortunes when he did publish their tomes and no sales followed.

Some "fans" were just outright insane. In 1964, Rap received a subscription renewal envelope for *Space World* that had odd annotations such as "Use no hooks—beware of mouse" and "If anyone opens this letter is going to be shoot!!!" The message inside: "I don't fool around with (obscene) like you. Get that (obscene) off the market or I will kill you deader a door nail. I want five hundred dollars by May 1964."[10] The sender, who obviously did not want to renew his subscription, added the address to which Rap should send $500. The threat led Rap to contact the FBI, whose reports do not disclose the identity of the letter writer or his fate.

Stress—whether a result of pressure from crazed fans, government investigators, disgust at the war in Vietnam, or overwork—began to take its toll. Then, in the early 1960s, around the same time that the Milwaukee papers were reporting his and Shaver's connection to Freedom Publishing's smut paperbacks, serious illness slowed Palmer and delayed his own publications. In 1963, he shifted his employee Helga Onan (who had begun working for him as a typesetter in the renovated chicken coop) to serve as associate editor of both *Search* and *Flying Saucers*. Rap's illness served as a wake-up call. Julius Schwartz had given him a taste of pulp immortality by naming the comic book hero Atom after him, but now Rap wanted to shape his own legacy.

Diary of a Martian

In April 1963, Rap informed readers that his illness had brought on the "realization that time is short. This editor is 52, and he has so very much to tell you! He had better be about it! Helga will take the load off our shoulders, and let us do it." He had two projects in mind, a book about Moses (never again mentioned), and one that would detail "the story of Ray Palmer himself, at least of his enormous file of notes and the unknown nature of the world and of life, and of the psychic, mystic, mysteries, etc." For the autobiography, he settled on the title "Martian Diary."

The title did not appear from nowhere. The notion that Palmer was a "Man from Mars" began when a woman hypnotized her daughter in order to contact Palmer through extrasensory methods. The daughter, who knew nothing of Palmer, provided an accurate description of his looks and whereabouts. The girl also told her mother that Rap was "not really an Earthman, but a Martian!" This announcement amused Palmer and confirmed his sense that he was a man apart. The women in the office began to call Rap "The Martian."[11] The Man from Mars gag was also a way to smooth over his physical handicaps. He put at ease visiting journalists, goggling at him without meaning to, by saying, "As you can see, I really am from Mars."

Rap began to work on a book in which he was a Martian come to Earth to report home on its civilization. Palmer soon concluded that many SF writers had already produced better versions of this clichéd plot. Instead he would write his life story, offering his perspective as an outsider, cued by the same title, "Martian Diary." He was again unsatisfied with the results and sought another direction. By 1970, after seven years of struggle, he believed he had found his way. He ran ads in his publications announcing: "Ray Palmer's Done It! He's Written His First Book! Not just any book, The BOOK! Martian Diary—Book I."

The advertisement insisted that in his sixty years on Earth he'd gained special knowledge that made him "feel like some sort of outcast, some sort of alien. . . . The more I learn, the fewer people I find to talk to about what I've learned without having them cut the conversation off and walk over to the other side of the street. . . . That's why I call it 'Martian.' . . . I feel rather like a Martian who has been transported to Earth, and abandoned." He explained his method. "What I have done is taken my diary and done to it exactly what I've done to so many readers' letters, taken it apart and blown it full of holes, and replaced it with the thinking that I never even doped to put down in my diary."[12] He planned to print it in a lavish volume for his sixtieth birthday in 1970 and included a $10 subscription form in his magazines.

The response was underwhelming. Readers were not ready to pay $10 to subscribe. They suggested he put it out in paperback instead. They queried whether he would really offer up the secret knowledge he kept promising. They were content to read his editorials. Rap was shocked and hurt. He wondered if perhaps he had been too full of himself, planning to print "Martian Diary" on the highest quality paper with the best bindings and full color illustrations. The rejection stunned him. In a rambling editorial, he informed readers, "The diary will be cast aside as a triviality to the majority, and will be cast aside also by the minority who will not want to be reminded of their cruel position. . . . As a report back to Mars, the diary can only be a negative report that says 'Earth is incompatible to Martians. It is advisable to remain where you are, and shun the planet.'"[13]

Grumbling, bitter, Palmer tabled the project. He saw it as the worst failure of his career and noted his "despair and despondency." Meanwhile, that same year, Palmer announced his plans to publish Richard Shaver's work on rokfogos, *Ancient History in Stone*. Rap finally concluded that he was a superhero who needed a sidekick. In 1975 he published *The Secret World*, which bundled together Ray Palmer's "Martian Diary, Book 1" with Richard Shaver's *Ancient History in Stone*. Although he had originally planned numerous volumes of "Martian Diary," he admitted there would probably only be the one. It was to prove to be their final joint statement to the world—Richard Shaver died in November, prompting a eulogy from Palmer which began, "He took us into a strange and mysterious world" and concluded with "For a brief lifetime there was a Titan among us!"[14]

"Martian Diary" is disappointing to a reader hoping for a standard coming-of-age narrative or insights into Palmer's career. As he noted, that sort of book had been blown to pieces and he had substituted a more open form. As with Shaver's rokfogo technique, he felt that chance promptings enhanced creativity. In his introduction, Palmer elaborated, "Planning a book like this is impossible—it insists upon writing itself; and it is amorphous in form because, like life, it just 'happens.'" He believed the guide for this process was a "Deliberate Manipulator—some super Intelligence beyond normal comprehension." Not a standard autobiographical narrative, "Martian Diary" detailed Rap's dawning awareness that there was a "Secret World" and his developing abilities related to enhanced memory, imagination, and psychic travel.

His long hospital stays and isolation as a child taught him to let his mind roam freely. For example, as a child strapped facedown on a Bradford frame to allow his back to mend, he developed his sense of memory until he could recall details such as the "brilliantly redbreasted bluebirds, fat and saucy, perched among intertwined vines and leaves" painted on a long-vanished cradle. He also remembered nursing on his mother's bosom and believed it might be possible to retrieve memories from the womb or even back to the moment of conception.

"Martian Diary" described Palmer's many psychic travels, including an encounter with his brother, Dave, shortly after he had died of wounds sustained in the Battle of the Bulge. In an altered state, Rap was led to his brother, who was outside a small schoolhouse in a heavenly setting. Dave wanted "to play tag." From his brother, Rap learned the previously unknown details of Dave's death (his leg had been blown off), and that his father had taken money that Dave had wanted to leave to his fiancée (both these facts were later confirmed). Rap also insisted that his own writing was psychically charged, as he often borrowed scenes and images from his lavish dreams. He detailed numerous incidents, including an astral projection dream in which he saw the details of a disastrous U.S. naval battle with the Japanese near Savo Island in the Pacific, and so was able to predict the precise details of the battle long before they were released. In another, he described writing a short story for Shade's *True Gang Life* about the sinking of the car ferry *City of Milwaukee* on Lake Michigan because it was over-loaded with bootleg alcohol. His source was a dream. It turned out to be true and gangsters frightened his editor into ending the fictional series. Palmer also detailed his ability at controlling his thoughts to aid the healing of his spinal column.

"Martian Diary" has the "Palmer touch," a sense of intimacy and good-heartedness, but as in so much of his work, Palmer also mixes in self-serving advertisements. How many of these uncanny experiences and miracles should we believe? Readers had to decide for themselves. As in all his writing, the book's passages tend to drift toward endorsements of the importance of the Spiritualist bible *Oahspe* (which Amherst Press printed and distributed) or the writings and ideas of Richard Shaver—to learn more, readers need only purchase sixteen issues of *Hidden World*.

Aquarian Wisconsin

If history was predictable, the 1960s would have been the time when Ray Palmer would seize the stage, become a full-blown guru like Timothy Leary or Buckminster Fuller. That's not the way it worked. He had been "Rap" too long to reinvent himself as a genius on the college circuit. He remained busy at work as usual in Wisconsin, but the strangeness of the times splintered his world. It was as if a mad scientist had zapped him with a beam that created duplicates. At least three Ray Palmers were slugging it out (four, if you include the brilliant Ivy Town nuclear scientist who doubled as the Atom).

The first was a wise elder statesman, helping his readers chart a course through the psychic storm of the 1960s. This Palmer could primarily be found in the pages of *Forum*, which he began publishing in 1966. The second emerged as a bitter right-wing crank, a supporter of Barry Goldwater, George Wallace, and Richard Nixon, convinced that these men could thwart a worldwide conspiracy to destroy personal liberties. This Palmer showed up most frequently in *Search* magazine. The third Palmer was the old provocateur, offering up hoaxes and playing Zen master pranks—the Palmer most frequently found in *Flying Saucers* magazine, where he promoted mind-blowing theories about the origins of flying saucers and the possibility that there was an entrance to the hollow earth at the North Pole.

True to one aspect of the 1960s ethos, Rap "let it all hang out." Always, Rap's goal was to be open and personal with his readers, or "one of the gang" as he had put it in *Amazing Stories*. He wrote with pity of the typical editor and his typical column—the product of an "organization man." "Behind every word we see a man sitting at a desk, earning a salary, being careful with every word he writes lest he step on somebody's toes, and he be fired. . . . Because of his stilted approach, not one word of sincere humanity in what he says. No real friendship, no true contact with the minds of his reader, no real get-togetherness."[15]

To provide the ideal medium for "get-togetherness," from 1966 to the end of his life, in addition to *Search* magazine (*Mystic*'s successor) and *Flying Saucers*, Palmer published the small, biweekly (eventually monthly) *Ray Palmer's Forum*, or simply, *Forum*. He explained it as follows, "All through the years the two things you have liked best are my editorials and my answers to your letters." Each issue of *Forum* would be thirty-two pages printed in a small format, newsletter style, and would only contain an editorial and letters. "It won't be anything fancy, except that it will be published on good stock (for permanence). No frills, just facts. No hanging back, everything out in the open, blunt and unconcealed."[16]

In its format, then, *Forum* was the anti-pulp. In addition to high-quality paper, the cover, rather than offering a lurid rendering of a female in peril, simply sported a black-and-white etching of the Roman Forum. Later, he substituted an image of Auguste Rodin's *The Thinker*. *Forum* offered the simple exchange of ideas. He noted on the cover, "It was in this place

Portrait of Palmer in his later years.
Photo courtesy William Lampkin's
Pulpster

that any man could speak his mind. Here was born the concept of free speech. . . . This magazine is, in its small way, the spirit of that ancient forum."[17]

In *Forum*, Palmer served as the resident sage for a small community of subscribers (perhaps three thousand initially), as it navigated the 1960s and early 1970s. He often took an optimistic approach, insisting that despite critical events and dangers he and his readers could, "guide our own lives through them to accomplishment, not disaster."[18]

He was fascinated by the hippies and began to go out among the flower children in his Man from Mars guise, interviewing them, trying to determine what made these kids different. He briefly hired a teenage girl from the *Search* typesetting and proofreading staff to bring a youthful perspective to his publications as Teen Editor. Sharon Schuster wrote one giddy column in which she insisted the dero did not exist and dared them to kill her. She then joked that her boss might not be able to protect her because of his diminutive size. It was her last column. Other teen contributors lasted longer in *Search*, writing about why they wore long hair, why they protested, and the rewards and dangers of illicit drugs. Rap's readers argued the merits of the hippie philosophy, with most concluding that the youthful philosophy was appealing but evaded responsibility.

Like many of the kids, Palmer opposed the Vietnam War. He was especially determined to keep his teenage son off the battlefield. He noted, "I emphatically do not want him to be shipped off to some stinking swamp and shot into fragments of human hamburger."[19] While fretting over the war, Rap came up with a novel solution to the "youth problem." In October 1972, he wrote that overpopulation and discontent could be solved by colonizing outer space. "Space provides the answer the young people are demanding. It is out in space these youngsters want to go. . . . They are adventurers, visionaries." The young people were not interested in a spiritually deadening "ant-like existence." His proposal, "Let's keep on with our 'rockets' and our 'astronauts.' Let them go out and find a place in the sun. . . . If our beautiful, talented, forward-looking young people must die, let them die in spaceships rather than in a stinking Vietnam swamp."[20]

Similar proposals began to gain adherents. Advocates for the utopian possibilities of space colonies included Stewart Brand, publisher of the *Whole Earth Catalog*, and California's young governor Jerry Brown, elected in 1974. In 1977, Brand published the earnest yet offbeat *Space Colonies*, which offered commentary on Gerard O'Neill's 1975 congressional testimony on the viability of space colonies. It also included a vintage Edward S. Curtis photo of two elderly Blackfoot Indians in front of a horse and travois gazing off into the sky, with the word balloon above the elderly man, "Good Bye. Good luck," while the woman's thought bubble added, "Good riddance."

Rap appreciated the spirituality percolating through the 1960s and 1970s. He was an admirer of the musical *Hair* and noted that while some of his readers might think it a "dirty" play because of its nudity, the lyrics of the song "Age of Aquarius" offered "today's most hopeful and promising and bright message to the fearful people of a world gone mad with gadgets and some barren with spiritual values."[21] He was also intrigued by the period's sexual revolution, wrote editorials that explored the "war between the sexes," and even noted that in his mind homosexuality was not a disease, adding, "I doubt very much if there is anything either wrong or harmful in homosexuality."[22]

What he liked most about the hippies, however, was not their free love philosophy but their optimism, which he traced back to earlier occultists. In a September 1971 *Search* column he mused over a visit from some "bright and earnest youngsters who call themselves the 'new people.' . . . Astrologically speaking, they also call themselves 'Aquarians.'" He described the Aquarians' creed of self-growth and love and then concluded it wasn't very new at all. "For all of his life, this editor," he wrote, "has been a 'new person.'" In his early science fiction he had "pictured a new world in which vast changes, vast improvements were made. It was a sort of prophecy." And what about the counterculture's awareness of mysticism? It was because he and other "old people" had "lavished our love upon the world, leavening the whole mass of people with new concepts of VALUE. . . . We fired the world with imagination. . . . We often bore the ridicule of the 'crackpot' and 'impractical' labels. But we loved what we were doing, and did it because we loved it."

But Rap would not completely tumble into the rabbit hole of the counterculture. He was critical of the new taste for mind-altering drugs. When readers offered laudatory letters about LSD and its ability to open the door to another world, or to cure alcoholism, he debated them. He viewed acts such as consuming LSD and consulting psychics or oracles as creating dependency. (He noted that he had not taken LSD but inadvertently had been given a drug that triggered hallucinations during one hospital stay.) When the Beatles began to put out albums with psychedelic covers, Rap emphasized that LSD might provide glimpses of heaven, but also could open for users the unwelcome vistas of hell. It was not all just "Strawberry Fields Forever."

He affirmed, "The time has come for us to become aware of the 'area' that exists beyond our five senses, but I do not think that area should be entered as a common practice." He was concerned that there was, in psychological terms, a death wish involved in attempting to open such doors. He confessed that the "LSD user doesn't live a hellish life, but he can live a perfectly useless one. . . . I know people who . . . spend hours each day trying to 'raise their vibrations' (while the dishes go unwashed). This is something I don't want to be responsible for." People, he said, "consult handwriting experts, they consult seers, they consult the spirits . . . and they never consult THEMSELVES."[23]

To Palmer's mind, the era's Jesus movement, also gathering young adherents, was as dangerous as LSD—just another way to lose one's independence and free will. Rap frequently jousted with readers who had found Jesus and no longer wanted part of the "Search." These converts warned him he was headed for hell and that flying saucers were a lure of the devil. (One reader, announcing she wished to cancel her subscription to *Flying Saucers*, concluded with the plea, "Please, brother Palmer, is it what you want to be thrown into the lake of fire? Yours in Christ.") His response to a similar letter: "Even if Jesus Christ appears before you, and commands you to kneel to him, first insist that he prove that he is indeed Jesus Christ— and should he be able to do this to your own satisfaction, recognize that you are no less an individual than he is. . . . Only you have the right to dictate your destiny. You are your only master."[24]

While Palmer can be depicted as a heroic nonconformist or as a voice of reason, neither would be particularly accurate. The social chaos of the 1960s stirred his own pathology—specifically, a panic over lessening freedom—that led him down another rabbit hole: the world of right-wing conspiracy theory. By the late 1960s, Palmer did not have a positive vision of the social upheaval. The chaos, whether cosmic or social, was threatening the American Dream, and more specifically Ray Palmer's Wisconsin Dream. The symptoms included "flying saucers, the war in Vietnam, the

student unrest and riots, and black revolution and burning of cities, the
pollution of our planet, the collapse of churches, the madness that evi-
dences itself in such wild and senseless killings as the murder of eight
nurses, the shooting of dozens of people by a supposedly model student."[25]

He blamed the disorder on Lyndon Johnson's big-spending liberalism
and a variety of evil conspirators. He sarcastically noted, "It is called 'The
Great Society'! It is Social Security, Federal Aid, Civil Rights, Equal Pay for
Equal Work, The Right to This and the Right to That, it is One Man One
Vote, it is the Liberal Left and the Conservative Right. . . . They all add up
to one thing: DEPENDENCE." Liberty was on the wane. The American
Dream was endangered. More particularly, Palmer's comfortable farm in
Wisconsin was under threat. "I have worked all my life to gain this happiness (the nice home on the lake where I live, the publishing business that I
created, and in which I employ 15 people at better wages that I earn myself). But Karl Marx says I have no 'right' to my happiness nor to my liberty
nor my clean lake, which I converted from a stinking, fishless sucker-filled
swamp, by good conservation practices over 20 years and the expenditure
of thousands of dollars."[26]

New environmental regulations were threatening his homestead. In
1969, he complained that local government had forced him to provide public access to his privately owned lake and had enacted new zoning laws that
would make it illegal for him to rebuild should his home burn down. When
he drained his lake to repair a century-old dam on his property, a coalition
of neighbors began a lawsuit over the silt that flowed downstream. They
were joined by enforcement agencies, including the Department of Natural Resources. Palmer spent $5,000 in court to defend his right to repair his
dam. He complained that "Public servants, so-called, became plotters and
planners to involve me in endless entanglements, indulging in such persecution and harassment that I could not sleep, made my wife want to sell
out and move away from our beautiful home, and our happiness totally
wrecked."[27]

His musings grew more pathological. He began to suspect an evil conspiracy based in the Department of Natural Resources. He wrote in 1973 that some twenty-five years earlier, in South America, there had been a "conference of nations" to discuss the world's natural resources. The sinister purpose of the conference was to force all independent landowners into subservience. He argued, "[The] total goal they are aiming at—world socialization under one world government under the control of the 'secret hidden government' that causes such belly laughs when it is mentioned to the 'free' citizen." If the Department of Natural Resources had its way, private property would be abolished and centralized control established. An elite minority would become "the owners of our very souls, the masters of our freedom."[28]

To be paranoid is not necessarily to be wrong; nevertheless, Rap began to see conspiracies everywhere: Nixon's secret bombing campaign in Cambodia had been designed not to hamper Viet Cong supply lines on the Ho Chi Minh Trail but to protect a secret UFO observation base at Lop Buri in Cambodia. He floated less wild notions, such as that the CIA was behind or involved in the killings of Ngo Dinh Diem (the first president of South Vietnam), John F. Kennedy, Martin Luther King Jr., and Bobby Kennedy. He added the odd notion that the Watergate break-in had been designed by the CIA's G. Gordon Liddy to discredit Nixon, who "sacrificed himself to protect our country from world disgrace." Aware of some of the mind control techniques fostered during the Cold War by the CIA and military, he predicted that once Big Brother took over the country, "this editor" would be "marched to a firing squad, or more likely, to a mental institution for observation, where he will be rendered either a mindless robot, under the influence of drugs, or an actual madman by techniques already perfected."[29]

Scholars of conspiracy theory have noted that such theory takes particularly well among people dedicated to ideals of self-reliance and liberty. Palmer's political beliefs and interest in unorthodox thought made him a prime candidate. Michael Barkun also has noted that "the villains who populate conspiracy theories tend to multiply," so that many conspiracy theories, even if not anti-Semitic in origin, eventually will drift in that direction.[30]

Drift happens. Palmer began to be particularly alarmed over the evil intentions of "one-worlders." Toward the end of World War Two, when the charter of the United Nations was being drafted, even Ray Palmer seemed enthusiastic for the one-world idea and published several editorials speculating on its possibilities. In the immediate postwar period, atomic scientists' concerns over nuclear annihilation led them also to urge a single world government. Such idealism fizzled once the Soviets developed nuclear weapons, and calls to world unity became, to some, treasonous. In 1958, wealthy backers founded the reactionary John Birch Society to oppose what they termed the "one world government" movement, and its purported instigators, which included socialists and "international bankers" (a code word for Jews since the late nineteenth century).

Even before the Department of Natural Resources began to torment him, Palmer was on high alert for one-worlders. In 1968, he fretted over a newspaper article titled "World Governing Body Planned" that announced one hundred delegates from thirty-three countries would meet in Wolfach, Germany. The delegates planned to select a world language, a world capital, unit standard, calendar, and money system. Should they be simply ignored as cranks or was there something more sinister going on? Palmer believed a secret government was already in power.

About six months later, a letter writer, Russell O. Shadel accused Rap of going "off the deep end." Shadel insisted the one-worlders who met in Wolfach sought an end to world war and nuclear weapons, both admirable goals. Rap fired off the reply, "If America ever gives up its arms to this Zionist World Government, it is true we will have no more war, nor will we be anything but slaves and cattle ruled by total despots. It must NEVER happen!" He went on to insist he had once worked for a Zionist with political ambition; they stood together at the window of his office on the twenty-second floor of a building in Chicago and, according to Palmer, this would-be politician looked down at the "teeming humanity below, and uttered one word: 'SCUM!' with such sincerity that it was unbelievable."[31]

Palmer was almost undoubtedly referring to publisher William B. Ziff—the Ziff-Davis editorial offices were on the twenty-second floor of the Transportation Building in Chicago, and Ziff wrote the book *The Rape of (Jewish) Palestine* in 1937, which argued against British rule of the area. It is possible that Ziff, an ardent Zionist, was misanthropic, or that Palmer distorted the incident. Assuming the event occurred as Palmer reported, to spring from one such anecdote to a belief in a world conspiracy indicates a loss of balance. Three months later, another letter writer noted, "I was astonished at the anti-Semitic sentiment you expressed in your answer to Russell Shadel's letter. What evidence do you have to support your claim that there is a Zionist plot to dominate the world?"

Rap backpedaled. "I am not anti-Semitic. . . . It is unfortunate that I must describe the secret rulers as 'Zionists,'—actually they are not Jews, Israelites, or even 'Zionists'; but the meaning of the word Zion is 'mountain,' and I want to make clear that it is the inhabitants of that mysterious 'mount' that I refer to. . . . It is inhabited not only by 'Zionists' but by the peoples of all Earthly races. . . . Perhaps I should call them a coined name, such as the 'Zunks'?"[32] While his response to the charge of anti-Semitism rings slightly hollow, it does show how his own concerns for "rugged individualism" made him susceptible to the far right's agenda.

To the end of his life, Palmer feared a takeover of the United States, leading him in October 1975 to disclose details of a plan for "The Internal Capture of the United States." He believed the Potomac River Basin Compact that involved dividing the United States into twenty-two river basin systems was evidence of a foreign takeover, as "none of the compacts require the commissioners to be citizens of the State, or the basin, or of the United States." Because of this devious plan, a wolf wrapped in the sheep's clothing of environmentalism, America, very soon, "will be a colony of another country." This conspiracy theory originated in the late 1960s, when a group of farmers became convinced that the purpose behind government cloud-seeding projects in the Potomac Valley was to create floods to destroy their livelihood.[33]

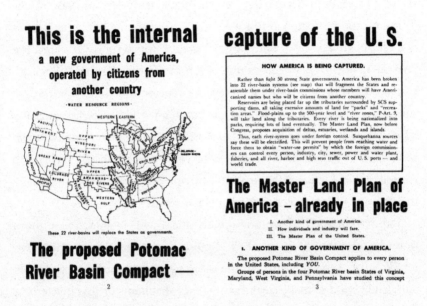

In the October 1975 *Search*, Palmer announced that water resource policy was a cover for a plot to take over the United States. *Department of Special Collections, Davidson Library, University of California, Santa Barbara*

A few months after disclosing the Potomac River conspiracy, Rap wrote that Nelson Rockefeller, hell-bent on ruling America, would soon gain the role of vice president and then move on to the presidency, and ultimately bring in a mock constitution that would destroy the foundation of American liberty. Rap's guest editor and debate partner, Peter Kor, gently suggested that Palmer was suffering from "conspiracy syndrome."

The Rap of these later years seems unhinged—a veteran baseball player having trouble with his vision and swinging wildly at the plate. The lack of readers' interest in his proposed "Martian Diary" stung, as did his neighbors' lawsuits and the hearings held by the Department of Natural Resources during which he felt vilified. The "long view" of science fiction was eluding him. Some of his wild swings, though, connected. For example, he was accurate about the CIA's and military's use of sinister "mind control" techniques, and prescient about the erosion of privacy accompanying the rise of digital and electronic media that could be used for surveillance.

In the same 1975 article in which he depicted Nelson Rockefeller as the devil, he offered a vision of a near future in which money would be obsolete, and the number of a "world credit card" would be emblazoned on a person's hand. "The police will have scanners that they can aim at you as you walk down the street, or pick you out of a crowd; they will read your number, which will be fed into a computer terminal in their car. Within an instant the TV screen in the patrol car will begin to pour out data about you. . . . No doubt you think such things cannot happen."[34]

Heading off his critics, he also confessed he might simply be paranoid and suffering from a "persecution complex." With mock humility, he commented, "I only put out a lot of paranoid baloney, and I have a suspicion that's exactly what it is. But in my mind it passes for reasoning and logic—and I kinda like it. I have a fertile imagination."[35]

George Wallace on Mars

Rap may have admired the Aquarians and their philosophy of love, but everywhere he looked, he detected rising tyranny. As a result, he veered to the far right, which shared his concerns. Palmer voted for Barry Goldwater in his bid for the presidency against Lyndon Johnson and bemoaned the "Great Society" that ensued after LBJ's victory. In the 1968 Republican primary, Palmer voted for George Wallace, whom he believed would defend personal liberties. Palmer continued his support, even after Wallace lost the nomination.

Then came the dream. In 1969 Palmer dreamed George Washington was looking down at an American flag on the ground. Washington's face was grief stricken. He tried to stoop down to pick up the flag, but each time he tried, his body faded, "leaving only his face floating against an ebony background and eerily lighted by flames that somehow we knew came from distant burning cities. Above the Founding Father's head appeared the letters 'GW.'" Suddenly George Washington's face faded out and George Wallace's face faded in. He was full of triumph. "George Wallace picked up the flag and held it over head. As he did so, a shot rang out, so loud that your editor awakened with a terrible start. . . . And the thing that we 'knew' was the conviction that with one pistol shot, liberty in America was dead."[36]

Rap's dream now appears prescient of Wallace's later shooting by an assailant dressed in red, white, and blue in 1972. But at the time he saw it as a ringing endorsement for Wallace as a politician. "Our vote goes to any man who will pick up the flag—even in a dream." He announced he had voted for Wallace in the primary, but acknowledged that Wallace, famous for fighting against desegregation, was unlikely to be a favorite with most of his readers. For unclear reasons, Rap insisted that Wallace should not be written off as a racist or bigot. He admired Wallace as a proponent of small government. While he had shown more fervor supporting Native Americans than the struggle of blacks in America, Palmer had never published racist articles in any of his magazines. (Science fiction luminary Alfred Bester, appearing under the byline Craig Browning, offered a fairly liberal vision of the race issue in the Palmer-edited May 1949 *Fate*. His article "The Negro in Tomorrow's America" noted that through racial mixing "technically Americans are going to be a race of negroes in another hundred years—only by then the name won't mean anything. The people then will be as proud of their negro blood as they are today of their English and German and Italian and Norwegian blood. . . . If you can get used to THAT idea, maybe you can get used to the idea that BEING one isn't so awful.")

After his Wallace dream rumination was published, Rap had a fascinating exchange of letters with an African-American reader who had written before about the plight of blacks in America, always signing his letters "A. Human." In his critique of Rap's dream about Wallace, A. Human commented that it was odd that Palmer had a "consistent fascination for certain types of 'deros,' both political and religious such as Wallace and Goldwater." He went on to say "the flag has one meaning for whites and another for blacks. In the pledge of allegiance to the flag, the part about 'Liberty and Justice for all' really meant for whites only." Washington was a racist and a bigot who relied on slaves who "helped him save his little candy striped rag." He continued, "Wallace is a racist and bigot not because of what he says, but by his deeds in his own state." The reader added that should some "skin worshipping idiot murder me" he would come back and haunt him. He concluded, "What in hell is the white man going to do when he meets his crucified victims as a spirit without his mace and machine gun? Think about it Rap. I sure have."[37]

Rap gave a seven-page answer defending himself against charges of bigotry. He noted that as a child he grew up near the Negro district in Milwaukee and had black playmates. At age twenty, he also had a Negro roommate in the tuberculosis sanatorium in Wauwatosa, Wisconsin, who "died in my arms because there was no orderly on the floor that night to help him." On his own in Chicago, he often wandered the black neighborhoods of the South Side, ate frugally in coffee shops, and felt accepted.

Rap went on to insist that neither Goldwater nor Wallace was a dero. He saw Goldwater as opposed to the war in Vietnam and reasonable in pointing out that the Civil Rights bill was unnecessary as it merely repeated guarantees already in the Bill of Rights. Palmer then gave a unique reason for supporting Wallace. "Neither Humphrey or Nixon had any firm resolve to get us out of Viet Nam. Wallace might not have been ABLE to do it, but at least he was FOR it." He went on to criticize Nixon for "saying the peace had to be 'honorable.' I say, to HELL with honor, in ANY war! The only honorable thing to do is to STOP THE KILLING." He chose Wallace because "I am forced to vote for the ONLY man who tells me he will fight to prevent the great octopus of centralized government to take over." He added that he would hold Wallace accountable for his racial attitudes.

As for A. Human's plan to haunt racists, "How do you propose to advance the cause of justice by becoming one of those very 'dero' you say I am obsessed with?" He also questioned A. Human's disdain for the flag. "It seems to turn out to be a 'white' flag, much too often. But when YOU wave it, it turns out to be a 'black' flag in the eyes of whites. Why can't we both wave it as a red white and blue flag, INTENDED equally for all of us?" Rap went on to argue that of course there has never been "liberty and justice for all—and there never will! . . . True justice is a hard lesson to learn." Echoing Martin Luther King Jr., Rap argued that his reader should not give in to hate. "Because someone else messes his own bed, must you do the same foul thing?"

He concluded by arguing that it is not only black people who face prejudice and hostility. "You are black, and have great odds against succeeding in your pursuit of liberty and happiness. I am a cripple, and I have had to pit myself against able-bodied men all my life, who looked down on me because I am a hunchback. They have even fought me with their fists." But, he added, "Brawn is never the victor in the long run over brains. . . . Forget those muscles and use your brain. It's as good as mine, and it can get you all you want." His response continued in its confessional tone—Rap rarely referred to himself as a cripple or made mention that he was a hunchback. He said he could identify with A. Human's bitterness. "Want to know a secret? I'm a bitter man myself; it isn't 'just' that one man should suffer so much pain in one lifetime! But I have my pride also, and I think I can 'out-suffer' any man on the face of this Earth!"[38]

A. Human's provocative letter forced the slumbering long view of science fiction back into the open air of Rap's thoughts. As the period had for others, the 1960s triggered in Palmer a "long, strange, trip." Neither superhero nor villain, he comes across as a deeply flawed, bewildered tour guide. His ideas were an unstable compound: the same underlying impulses to speculate, to embrace the unexpected, and to reject the "official" story led him all over the map. He could be a right-wing crank, a left-wing progressive, or a full-blown mystic. He rejected dogma but often fell under the spell of conspiracy. Yet Rap still had the power to enter into dialogue, to talk openly and passionately. Those who wrote him letters reminded him that the best conspiracy theory, like a well-designed spaceship, should have escape hatches.

PROFESSOR PALMER'S INTERGALACTIC MEDICINE SHOW

9

U.F.O. Detector. This is not a toy. Guaranteed response to an approaching magnetic field. No N-S orientating. Certified reacting time: 1 millionth of a second! Fully assembled. For serious researchers. Hermetically sealed component. Audio and visual alarm systems. Completely portable. For each ready to operate detector, send only $10.00. Aerial Research Systems, Dept. FS, P.O. Box 715, Banning, California 92220.

— *Search*, September 1969

I detect in your letter a liking for Glenn Miller's music. Well, Alex, would your heaven be heaven without some marvelous, better-than-ever Glenn Miller compositions? And wouldn't you like a REALLY GOOD jukebox to play these selections for your eager ear?

—Rap, *Forum*, March 15, 1967

Although Rap was fascinated with the space age, the contours of his thought and his emphasis on mystery belonged to an older context—that of the wonder cabinet or dime museum stuffed with marvels large and small, authentic and dubious (or "gaffed" in carny parlance). Over the years many people commented on the peculiar circus, sideshow, or dime museum of which Ray Palmer long had been sole proprietor. In the 1950s, fanzine writer Joe Gibson wrote an article titled "Ray Palmer's Medicine Show," in which he claimed that Palmer resembled a "character who rambled around in an old wagon with 'Medicine Show' burnt on the tailboard by a hot running iron. He had a little she-jackass that could dance to a Jew's-harp (when she had a mind to) and he peddled a cure-all remedy that was guaranteed to take the warts off a toad or foal a dry mare, among other things. The thing was, this feller actually believed his remedy did some good because it sold well."[1] Gibson went on to reflect that it was Palmer's "instinct" and not "personality" that helped sell *Amazing Stories*, even before the Shaver Mystery and then the flying saucer emerged as added attractions in the medicine show.

Struck by Palmer's ability to generate "hokum," critics such as science writer Martin Gardner placed him in the lineage of the nineteenth-century showman P. T. Barnum, who had concocted tongue–in-cheek promotions of attractions such as the Fiji Mermaid and the Grand Egress. Allies also saw Palmer's resemblance to such showmen whose ballyhoo blurred the boundaries of the real. In the mid-1970s, a faithful reader of *Search* who respected Palmer for his daring, but wondered about the sources he depended on, wrote, "Hate to tell you this, but you remind me at times of a 'Barker' outside a side-show! Believe it or not *you* rob the respectability from the product you sell by your own methodology. . . . In spite of what I've just said I will continue to 'buy' part of what you 'sell.' . . . The ice is very thin on your lake, Ray and I skate only in the relative safety of the shore line."[2]

Medicine show or freak show? As the 1960s progressed, during times of despair, Rap wondered if all the talk about the New Age or the Rise of Aquarius and interest in ESP and the prophecies of Edgar Cayce indicated a genuine shift in consciousness. At one such moment he concluded no. "As always, people love a circus; they will stare popeyed at a FREAK! We aren't being accepted, we are kooky creeps! THEY don't believe us! They not only don't believe us, but they intend to take steps to cure us (of our delusions). For the moment we are curiosities, but don't believe that they will tolerate us upsetting their tight little world of 'reality.' Martians are, by very tradition, invaders! They are to be repelled, destroyed, defeated."[3]

Yet he also could set aside this sense of freakiness to declare himself an opener of minds, a self-confessed lover of fantasy and wonder. In 1963, Palmer wrote about visiting the Niagara Falls Museum on a family vacation several years earlier; it was a dime museum over one hundred years old stuffed with historical oddities and exhibits. A simple sign outside the museum, SEE THE EGYPTIAN MUMMIES, gave him a chuckle. He wrote, "Because Egyptology and mummies have been of great interest over the years, I was intrigued, and rather amused, because it seemed rather outré to consider that this little museum should contain any mummies of any importance, but rather most probably completely worthless bundles of rags, bones, and dust." But while his family wandered through the displays of stuffed animals, a humpback whale skeleton, bird eggs, minerals, Native American artifacts, coins, and other attractions, Rap spent hours wandering the mummy exhibit, in thrall. His long inspection "only served to increase the sense of shock and amazement, because each and every one of them was far superior to the best on exhibit anywhere else in the world."[4] (In classic Palmer fashion, he went on to insist that during a later museum visit he was dumbfounded to see that the better mummies had been spirited away and replaced with cheap substitutes. He was unable to confirm this but gained some hints he was correct from museum personnel.)

Like the curators of the Niagara Museum, Palmer was a collector and promoter of wonders. He had his own collection of Native American artifacts, not to mention a piece of a certified Maury Island flying saucer fragment as a paperweight and many of Shaver's "rock books"; he also fancied himself an amateur anthropologist. But more important, his publications offered the wonders of "gee whiz" astronomy and science, artistic renderings of space rocket voyages, tales of "real" visits to underground caverns, and purported photographs of flying saucers. He affirmed his role as a peddler of curiosities. Regarding his flying saucer interests, Rap wrote, "Perhaps it has been a mistake on my part even to allow the term 'researcher' to be applied to my activities. I am definitely not researching flying saucers. . . . What I do is quite different. I am probably only a 'collector,' plus being a 'disseminator.' I pick up everything that comes my way, and I publish it. I also theorize about it. I argue and debate about it. I become the devil's advocate in many cases."[5]

A photograph of a flying saucer—genuine or forged—was acceptable because it could start a conversation. In the first issue of *Flying Saucers from Other Worlds*, in 1957, he noted, "If there is a picture taken of a flying saucer, and we can get hold of it, we'll print it. If we can prove that such a photo is a fake, we will prove it." Rumors, whether of little green men or of men in black, had a place in his modern wonder cabinet. "In these pages you will find rumors reported also, together with the source, or lack of source, and plainly labeled as such." Rather like an anthropologist collecting folklore, or Carl Jung approaching the UFO legend, he presented these reports. Whether true or false, such accounts had their own validity, as they indicated trends in human belief and mapped the fears and dreams of the age.

As a collector and sole proprietor of a medicine show, his goal was not only to entertain but also to provide a safe haven for speculation, however odd. As to the selling of a cure-all, a key to a medicine show, science fiction zealots such as Gernsback and his many offspring believed they had that cure in progress. Progress was the elixir that would aid the salvation of the human race. It was powerful medicine. To this concoction, many SF fans added in liberal draughts of Technocracy, Esperanto, Communism, General Semantics, and Dianetics. Rap's fellow mystics in the late twentieth century also believed themselves an evolutionary avant-garde, a vision reinforced in Psi-Fi and flying saucer circles. Likewise, the community Rap forged did allow some healing for those who felt stigmatized because of their beliefs.

Yet for all his ruminations about the New Age, Rap was not so much in the business of healing as he was of "blowing minds." As a wonder cabinet proprietor, Rap spent his days casting around for the perfect exhibit. As such, he longed for another trophy or fetish object to offer alongside super science, the Shaver Mystery, the flying saucer, and assorted unexplained phenomena. His protégé Rog Phillips had become an excellent science fiction writer, but as a "mystery," he was a bust. There were new candidates Rap casually noted but didn't lavish attention on: Bigfoot, for example. Or the Loch Ness monster. Such evolutionary holdouts didn't fascinate Rap any more than the scandal-prone Hollywood celebrities with which such monsters had begun to share the front page of supermarket tabloids. (By the late 1960s, in order to be acceptable for supermarkets, the *National Enquirer* and other tabloids were dropping coverage of excessively violent crime and relying on a mix of celebrity scandal and the paranormal.)

As the supermarket tabloids began to resemble Rap's *Search* and *Flying Saucers*, he also sought out other sensations. In a brief foray into celebrity shock news, he revisited his story that in the late 1940s he had met with outlaw Jesse James. In "Visit with Jesse James," Rap explained that the old outlaw had faked his death. The corpse displayed was actually of fellow outlaw Charlie Bigelow, while the real Jesse was a pallbearer at his own funeral and remained alive until 1951. When Rap began to write James's story, he learned that the "outlaw" had contracts with several other writers. While this news had made a stir for Rap in the late 1940s, reviving this story in 1968 did not set the newsstands on fire. Such a concept came straight from the world of dime magazines and had no space age angle.

Palmer wanted something that struck at the base of our belief system, something that made us, in his frequent refrain, "think for the first time." Something like the Shaver Mystery with its fabulous paranoia and dread assurance that the ground we treaded on was unstable. Like the driven showman depicted in the movie *King Kong*, he searched for something that would amaze and evoke fear. He did not seek out monsters but monstrous notions, and his taste ran toward cosmology, first principles.

Rap's last doozy was the "hole in the pole"—his theory that there was an entrance for flying saucers at the North Pole—an idea that he offered variations on throughout the 1960s and 1970s, and one that James Oberg, his new associate editor at *Flying Saucers* and *Space World*, who had an interest in UFOs but a highly skeptical bent, kindly did not comment on.

Flight into an Unknown Land

"The Hole in the Pole," of course, had precedent in the long line of hollow earth literature that predated the Shaver Mystery. John Cleves Symmes, to name but one link in this great chain of underground being, issued a circular in 1818, addressed "To all the World," insisting, "I declare the earth is hollow and habitable within; containing a number of solid concentric spheres, one within the other, and that it is open at the poles twelve or sixteen degrees." He added, "I pledge my life in support of this truth, and am ready to explore the hollow, if the world will support and aid me in this undertaking."[6] In addition to nineteenth-century adventurers and utopian writers, the hollow earth theory also excited many of the best romance writers of early science fiction and fantasy, including Edgar Rice Burroughs and H. P. Lovecraft.

Rap periodically revisited this notion. In December 1959, in *Flying Saucers from Other Worlds* he ran the popular article "Polar Exploration Proves Saucers from This Earth!" The article relied on Amadeo F. Giannini's curious work *Worlds Beyond the Poles* (1959), an amplification of an earlier self-published work, *Physical Continuum*. Giannini, to be fair, did not exactly believe in a hollow earth. No, as the first paragraph of his book explains,

"There is no physical end to the Earth's northern and southern extent. The earth merges with land areas of the universe about us that exist straight ahead beyond the North Pole and the South Pole 'points' of theory. It is now established that we may at once journey into celestial land by customary movement on the horizontal from beyond the Pole points." To make it even clearer, this new geographer noted, "When one goes beyond the Poles one is moving, as the colloquial aptly describes, 'out of this world.' One then continues to move over land extending beyond the Earth."[7] Land routes, full of water and vegetation, stretched throughout the universe, connecting Earth to other planets and stars. Comparing himself to other greats scorned in the past such as Socrates, Christopher Columbus, Thomas Edison, and Louis Pasteur, Giannini calmly reported that the astronomical theories of all ages were false. There were no "globular and isolated bodies to be found throughout the whole Universe: they are elements of lens deception." The universe was entirely connected. As Shaver did with his rock books, Giannini was creating a new cosmology. Here was bold thought.

Giannini's evidence for these land routes were extracts from the diaries of the pilot and polar explorer Admiral Richard E. Byrd, who first flew over the North Pole in 1926, and in 1929 flew over the South Pole. Giannini insisted that in addition to these flights, Byrd had flown a mission over the North Pole in February 1947. Giannini reported that in one entry in Byrd's diary, the famous explorer had noted, "I'd like to see that land beyond the Pole. That area beyond the Pole is the center of the great unknown." Giannini reported that on Byrd's forgotten mission, "As progress was made beyond the pole point, iceless land and lakes, mountains covered with trees, and even a monstrous animal moving through the underbrush, were observed and reported via radio." Giannini also noted that in January 1956, a "U.S. Naval air unit penetrated to the *extent of 2,300 miles beyond* the assumed South Pole end of the Earth."

Palmer sniffed a good story. As good as a Shaver yarn. To bolster Gi-

Several decades after the Shaver Mystery, Palmer once again took up the hollow earth cause. *Department of Special Collections, Davidson Library, University of California, Santa Barbara*

annini, he discussed the topographic figure of the Mōbius strip, a folded piece of paper with only one side, and said, "Maybe it is true that by introducing a very simple 'twist' into our 'space topography,' we can travel to Mars or anywhere by a sort of 'sidestep and fifty paces ahead.'"[8] Aspects of Giannini's connected landmass universe, however, were a bit too bizarre even for Palmer. But it offered a new angle for speculation. Why not a doughnut-shaped earth? The correct analysis was that land extended beyond the poles because it was folding into the hollow earth. In *Flying Saucers* magazine, Palmer asked, "What if the Earth is not spherical, but actually doughnut-shaped, exactly as its surrounding Van Allen Belt?" This would then account for the unaccountable added miles that explorers, including Byrd and even Perry in one of his voyages, found when they traveled beyond the pole. Now Palmer arrived at one of his pet ideas. The flying saucers were not from outer space, "but rather from 'inner space!'" He added, "Evidence is extremely strong," and insisted that the "polar origin of the flying saucers will now have to be factually disproved. . . . More than a simple denial is necessary."[9]

Two months later, in the February 1960 issue of *Flying Saucers*, a somewhat contrite Palmer noted, "The one big flaw in our now 'most-talked-of' issue ever . . . is the non-existent North Pole Flight of Admiral Byrd in 1947." He went on to insist that he had published the theory as a sort of "fishing expedition, for which we hope our readers will pardon us." He claimed—rather unconvincingly—that he was trying to determine the validity of Byrd's North Pole flight and believed his readers' responses would help ferret out the truth. He then shifted to assert that even if he had not been near the North Pole, Byrd had made a flight 1,700 miles beyond the South Pole that year. He also added that he suspected that Giannini had deliberately falsified his book, perhaps as part of a confidence game to ridicule the flying saucer community and Palmer's own developing theory of the doughnut Earth.

Palmer then challenged the U.S. military to plan a flight in a straight line over the North Pole to prove or disprove the doughnut, or lands beyond, theory once and for all. "The Air Force is not . . . averse to flying millions of miles, spending millions of dollars of the taxpayers' money to chase down NON-EXISTENT (so they insist) flying saucers; so why should they object to a simple $100,000 flight across the Pole on a straight line?"[10] (Palmer's challenge, like that of Colonel Symmes a century earlier, was not taken up.) In this rambling editorial Palmer went on to note, "As a rather random point, let us assure our readers that we did not say the Moon was square! We only said that if it WAS, you couldn't prove it." He concluded with a vow to understand the "mystery lands at the Poles!"

This editorial reveals Palmer's standard techniques, though more weakly employed than usual. He enjoyed admitting he was "wrong" about a matter only to conclude that it was actually right or that it was all part of his strategy to elicit the truth. Like a hero in a space opera, a theory could be destroyed, yet somehow spring back to life (i.e., "work that twist, brother"). Paradoxes were encouraged. Here, however, he failed to convince the reader he was on to some secret knowledge. And while he was capable of admitting he was wrong about some of his theories—such as his later query "Why don't we have photographs of stars taken from outer space?"—the Hole in the Pole, for a time, was too much fun.

Five years later, even Palmer was bored with the story. In April of 1965, he ran Delmar H. Bryant's "The Hollow Earth Hoax" which spent much time refuting the theories of hollow earthers who had attempted to build on Giannini's dubious "research," including the concocted quotes from Byrd's diary. Bryant insisted that documentation proved that Byrd was not in the Arctic Circle, but in Antarctica during the entire month of February 1947. His flight from his base camp in Antarctica to the South Pole, while indeed 1,800 miles long, was simply a round trip from his base to perhaps 100 miles beyond the pole and back.

Bryant's article traced the lore that followed Giannini's account through Palmer, Gray Barker, and yet another publication, Raymond Bernard's *The Hollow Earth* (1964), which added even more fanciful details to the phantom Byrd expedition. (Bernard, like Palmer, did not expound on the "endless land routes into space" notion of Giannini but focused on entrances to the hollow earth.) Palmer noted that Bernard, with his purported academic background, was actually Walter Siegmeister, an operator who sold people land parcels off Cape Horn in South America where he claimed "there was an entrance to the inner world" that could serve as a refuge from atomic warfare. According to Palmer, Siegmeister "intended to found a colony with himself as the boss," and he owed Palmer advertising revenue.[11]

Even after running Bryant's piece in *Flying Saucers*, Palmer couldn't entirely reject the doughnut theory. In January 1966, Rap said, "The idea of an actual opening into the interior of the Earth at either or both of the poles is also difficult to swallow. . . . Why can't we . . . say the 'hole' is not a hole in the dictionary sense of the word, but in a more abstract sense, such as the much-misused and misconstrued 'fourth dimension' sense? There may well be a hole there, and a hollow earth where the bogies came from." Traveling through it might be akin to a "'ghost' that travels through a closed door that would give us a 'black eye' if we tried it."

Satellite composite photo that Palmer insisted provided evidence for the "Hole at the Pole" theory. *Department of Special Collections, Davidson Library, University of California, Santa Barbara*

In June 1970, undoubtedly in a bid to improve sales, Palmer returned to the controversy. The cover of *Flying Saucers* ran a satellite photograph of the earth with a black hole at its center where the North Pole should be, with the title "First Photos of the Hole at the Pole! Satellites ESSA-3 and Essa-7 Penetrate Cloud Cover! Mariners also Photograph Polar Opening!" He noted in his editorial, "We do not see any ice fields in a large circular area directly at the geographic pole. Instead we see—THE HOLE!" He added, "How many more photos will we require to establish a fact? . . . If there is a hole at the pole, and our scientists know it, why don't they tell us?" He added other photographs, of the South Pole, that did not show a hole but instead showed white cloud cover.

Palmer went on to add that cosmologists seeking to explain the formation of planets had begun to "adopt the 'vortex' or 'whirlpool' theory. . . . Thus, in this theory, quite widely held by astronomers and physicists, many planetary bodies still have this typical hole at the center of the whirl that formed them." Why not Earth too? And perhaps there were indeed underground civilizations.

He was bombarded by letters. Some supported him. Most pointed out that the photograph, although real, was a composite, made from numerous overlapping shots. The entire pole area could not be in sunlight, as the sun only shines on one side of the earth at a time. Further, the hole, if real as depicted, would include more than half of Greenland. Reader Dennis Kier concluded, "I suppose all this has occurred to you, and that you have some other motive in printing it in this way." Other readers, prone to accept Palmer's assertion, queried the fine points of hollow earth theory. One asked, "If there is a 'sun' at the center of the earth as most accounts of the hollow earth describe, why didn't some of its light show through the polar holes in the satellite photographs? As a romantic I hope that you are right." Another reader also noted that the "hole," or dark area, was a result of a composite—even at noon at winter, part of the pole is always in darkness. He added, "In my opinion, if there is a hole in the polar regions, it is in the head of the propounder of the idea." Palmer's long answer concluded, "Our planet is a tremendous mystery, and the more we find out about it, the more mysterious it gets. . . . Maybe you don't want any answers, but I do! And don't think that I want the answer to be a hole! Any ANSWER will do, rather than the baffling mystery that makes the bump of curiosity on my head swell until it seems likely to burst."

Delighted to be barraged with letters—evidence of the planet's "mass mind"—for several issues Palmer jousted with readers: he noted that the satellites had infrared cameras that could make it appear daylight even in shadow, and so on. He added that he was not trying to trick anyone. "Many of the things I have presented have later fallen flat on their faces, but not because I lied about them! I *presented* them. I gave you a chance to see for yourself, decide for yourself, refute or support me if you could!"

In a response to a member of the National Investigations Committee on Aerial Phenomena who also debunked the photograph as a composite with the darkness indicating nighttime shadow, Rap brought in a new wild card: a missing newsreel of the Byrd flight over the North Pole. "In 1929," he wrote, "a newsreel could be seen in America's theaters which . . . showed newsreel photos of the 'land beyond the pole (north) with its mountains, trees, rivers, and large animal identified as a mammoth.' Today this newsreel apparently does not exist, although hundreds of my readers remember, as I do, seeing this movie short."[12] What had become of that newsreel? He and his readers debated. A year and a half later, the controversy of the photograph of the hole had run its course. No copies of the newsreel were uncovered.

How to Build a Heaven

Like a NASA rocket shedding stages as it leaves the atmosphere for interplanetary travel, illness forced him to trim back his responsibilities. In 1971, a bout with a deadly strain of flu returned Rap to the hospital. He put his wife, Marjorie, formerly head of his business operations, in complete charge of *Search* magazine. Now his only duties would be to write an editorial and one article per issue on a topic Marjorie assigned and to answer readers' letters. Although he had hoped to be around for the return of Halley's Comet in 1986, his health was failing. To further trim his responsibilities, in 1976 he and his wife merged *Search* and *Flying Saucers* into one large-format two-part magazine and hired James Oberg to edit both *Flying*

Saucers and *Space World*. Palmer's territory had now shrunk to that of a capsule hurtling through outer space or, as he would argue, à la *Oahspe*, through the far reaches of Earth's atmosphere. Like any person reaching his biological end, he was preparing to face eternity.

In the October 1970 *Forum*, as well as a subsequent issue, Palmer ran portraits of himself as a charming three-year-old with a starkly blond pageboy haircut. One showed him posed behind a coffee table with two stacks of alphabet blocks on the polished top, a hand on the knee of his white knickers. He commented, concerning the passage of time, "We went through our file of pictures to try to find the most recent one that did not portray us in such a bad light as to frighten anyone off. . . . It seems that this editor has deteriorated rapidly with the passage of time, and from nine years on, he fully qualifies for the lead in any Boris Karloff horror movie. Also, the picture on this page presents the last time this editor looked partially intelligent, or even human."

His failure to launch the lavish multivolume autobiography "Martian Diary," and the impossibility of even telling what he really knew, had him flummoxed. He was seeing the end of his life's work with some disappointment. He recalled that he had made a "twenty-year deal" with his maker when he survived the fall in the basement in 1950, and that twenty years had come and gone.

As he aged, Palmer became fixated on two issues: the origins of flying saucers and notions of heaven. He believed the two were connected via the mysteries of the earth's atmosphere. He was intrigued by the idea that the earth's atmosphere reached far higher in outer space than commonly believed—up 180,000 miles, or 50,000 shy of the moon—a notion propounded in *Oahspe*. Tucked away in this energized field were possible heavens. Spiritualists believed that departed souls took up living again on various planes, or "plateaus." The particular plateau depended on the person's moral advancement in life.

Oahspe listed several groups of intelligent beings as inhabitants of these plateaus: the "corporeans," trapped in bodies; the "atmosphereans," no longer bound in bodies but limited in movement; and the even more rarefied "etherians," who dwell in Etherea. From this mysterious extended atmosphere, flying saucers might also materialize. Dwellers on these plateaus constructed roadways to connect the various levels. *Oahspe* reported that atmosphereans built "arrow ships" and other craft resembling UFOs to travel the roadways between plateaus. If UFOs could appear, vanish, and tremble, didn't it make as much sense to assume they came from the atmosphere as from some distant star system?[13]

Between waves of Hole in the Pole promotions, Rap pushed his atmospheric origins theory of flying saucers. He was among the first ufologists to express disenchantment with the "extra-terrestrial hypothesis" (ETH), indicating his doubts from the very first sightings. As early as 1947, Palmer noted the saucers might come from Shaver's caves or have some other explanation. Similarly, in his study first published in English in 1959, Carl Jung had noted that the saucers reportedly maneuvered in a weightless manner that suggested they were neither entirely of this world, nor from another "real" planet or star system in the known universe. By the 1970s, many theorists had begun to argue that the ETs might actually be mythic visitors, rather like the elves and faeries of folklore. A major proponent of this viewpoint was ufologist John Keel who, in *Our Haunted Planet* (1971), proposed that the "aliens" be thought not of as extra-terrestrials, but as "ultraterrestrials"—shape-shifters from another mythic dimension.

The most notable researcher questioning the ETH was Jacques Vallée. The character that Francois Truffaut played in the film *Close Encounters of the Third Kind* (1977) was based on this French scientist turned ufologist. Beginning in the 1970s, Vallée became intrigued by the idea that UFO sightings were part of a feedback or control system to train humanity in a new approach to life on the planet and, perhaps, in the cosmos. His 1989 paper "Five Arguments Against the Extraterrestrial Origin of Unidentified Flying Objects" addressed the problem with the ETH and mentioned some of the newer hypotheses. Vallée noted that the ETs might even be time travelers returned to correct our course and added, "The 'Extraterrestrials' can be from anywhere and any time, and could even originate from our own Earth."

Rap was fixated on the atmosphere. In a 1965 article that promoted his atmospheric origins theory of UFOs, he proposed that humanity's knowledge of the universe was as limited as a fish's knowledge of the world as viewed from a pond—that is, it ended at the surface. How could a fish be aware of the land and sky and all its organisms? "The moment he realizes that all the emptiness between him and the clouds is real, physical, and capable of being inhabited, his search can culminate in discovery."[14] We had to look not to the depths of outer space but to the mysteries of our own atmosphere.

Palmer traced his own fascination with this idea to a science fiction story he had read as a child, "Islands in the Sky," that featured an adventurer who crashed his airplane into a hidden city in the clouds, which was invisible from the earth's surface because it did not register on the visible light spectrum, but which was nevertheless solid. Rap also referred to the work of Grote Reber, a pioneer of radio astronomy, who, while living in suburban Chicago in the late 1930s, built a radio array in his Wheaton, Illinois, backyard to gather signals from the skies. In the 1940s Reber began to map the skies based on his data. After studying Reber's antenna array, Palmer concluded that Reber was wrong; the signals weren't originating in outer space, but within the earth's atmosphere. "Our flying saucers aren't from Mars, or outer space. They are from Earth, from that very full and real area extending from the 4,000 mile mark to the 180,000 mile mark, some 50,000 miles shy of the moon."[15]

Palmer obtained these figures from *Oahspe*, calculations that he said closely matched the limits of the Earth's electromagnetic reach. He wasn't precisely arguing, as did Giannini, that the land extended into the sky, but that the atmosphere had room for all the heavens we could imagine. "Your author likes to think that all of Space is inhabited by intelligent beings, intelligent beings who are related, have the same common origin." He added, "If we are all part of a big family, there would be some sort of provision for a 'family reunion' some day."[16]

Worlds were hidden within worlds. If *Oahspe* and the Shaver Mystery provided two divergent models for Rap's Hidden World, he doggedly sought a synthesis. *Oahspe* followed Spiritualist beliefs, while Shaver had been a dedicated materialist. For Shaver, there were no "spirits" and no "magic," just dero and tero and their remarkable mech. The gods were humans who had been zapped into immortality thanks to amazing technology. Without special shielding and technology, when a person died, his or her molecules dispersed. Eventually they disintegrated into exd. There was nothing else. Rap and Shaver had given physical immortality a shot, with dietary plans, attempts to ward off dis or to recover health-inducing mech, but now Palmer, ill and aging, continued to contemplate the afterlife, and, to some extent, he borrowed Shaver's idea that even spirit was physical.

Palmer's own experiences—which included meetings with his dead brother and many others who were no longer alive—convinced him that there was an afterlife. In fact, it was possible we were already in it. In 1967, returning to an old theme, he wrote the essay, "How Do I Know I Am Alive?" It recounted his nighttime habit of falling asleep by conjuring a rich fantasy, in this case of hurtling in a jet above the clouds and over a stunning landscape. He would periodically return to his room and his bed and then resume the fantasy, flying over mountains, feeling a tremendous sense of speed and awareness. Then he began examining a painting full of human figures. "Beautiful figures. Peopled dressed in exotic costumes such as I had never seen before. And I could continue my control—I could 'zoom' in on any particular portion of the painting, until I could even examine the brushmarks." He then began to worry about which world was genuine, that of his imagination with all its detail or the world where he lay in bed at night next to his wife. What was real? Was he in fact alive? Had he in fact died in that basement fall in 1950? In the essay he wrote, "What if I died seventeen years ago, and DON'T KNOW IT!" After his "recovery," had he really moved to Wisconsin, or "was it really my wife and her three children who moved there [alone]. . . . Does she really set a place for me at the table or do I only imagine that she does, unwilling to consider that I am actually dead?"[17] This train of thought matched his theory that many of the newly dead would not know it because the afterlife was "extremely close in similarity" to this life.

According to Rap, heaven might be the sort of place you wandered into when driving well off the beaten path—say beyond the North Pole—and found your way onto one of Giannini's endless land routes. Palmer asserted in one of the last articles before he died that "Heaven Is Solid." He referred to the experiment of a psychic researcher who had weighed a dying man and determined that his spirit's departure deducted about three ounces from his weight. Palmer thought that in the earth's surrounding atmosphere there was room for these spirits, and that the spirit continued to mimic the molecular structure of the original body. In this way, we "'fit right in' to our new environment, with no need to face the problem of being unable to 'relate.' . . . If you so choose, you could kick me in the pants and I'd probably let out a yell."[18]

Not only was heaven solid but it closely resembled life on earth—forget clouds and harp-playing cherubs. A decade earlier, while musing on the nature of the afterlife, Rap concluded there were likely factories in the afterlife and workers and money to propel them. In heaven, social workers could keep themselves busy trying to find useful employment for deceased drifters or bums. He doubted the Spiritualists' (or was it the television series *Bewitched*'s?) concept of the Summerland, where "all you have to do is wrinkle your nose and think a new suit into being."[19] Just because one died, why should one suddenly develop new skills like "thinking ice cream cones into existence"? In his heaven, Glenn Miller tunes would play on the jukebox. There would be no prostitution because there would be no marriage, and free love would reign. Palmer argued that since the standard marriage vow ended with "until death do us part," no marriage pacts survived in the afterlife, and everyone, sensibly, would become a free agent. He hoped he was correct and that heaven didn't conform to the common description, noting, "I can't seem to bring myself to believe that the afterlife is so foreign that nothing familiar remains in it at all, except a lot of sourpusses (with ecstatic and senseless smirks on their faces) walking around in a white kimono, claiming they have attained the ultimate in all WPA programs, Nirvana, or At-One-Ment."[20]

But this was just the first stage of Rap's concept of heaven. Following Spiritualist notions, he thought that a person's tenure on earth was like a visit to a school to learn important lessons. These weren't simply moral lessons. No, people must acquire important crafts and skills. "In this little world of ours we learn primitive things. . . . We have to learn our simple lessons here, then graduate to that expanded 'world' where the lessons are harder, the jobs more complex." Progress meant gaining more skills and knowledge. Ultimately, he thought we could learn to build people (that is, "a physical habitat for a 'spirit'"), then go on "to fashion a WHOLE WORLD, and after that a Solar System, and even an Island Universe. Why not eventually a Cosmos?"[21]

A man, then, was not, as Ralph Waldo Emerson put it, a god in ruins, but one in training. Science fiction of the 1920s and 1930s had abounded with "supermen"—mutated or genetically improved specimens—this superman was actually us, as we made a slow and tedious transformation from man to god, or Ray Palmer to the Atom. Rap thought he'd ease in gently. In an interview with a college radio station, Palmer said he knew that heaven was a real place, but once there he would go on "publishing books or magazines, or running a press. . . . I'm not going to be suddenly translated to a harp player, or singing at a throne."[22]

He also scaled back his theorizing about flying saucers. A year before his death, in the Fall 1976 *Search* he simply noted, "It is still true, as I predicted in 1947, that no flying saucer has ever been 'captured' or even 'proved.' They are as real as Shaver's caves, and just as 'psychic.' They are the unknown, the hidden world, that all of us at one time or another are aware exists, and which intrudes into our lives to make us think."

It is appropriate that in one of the final issues of *Forum*, Rap, true to his roots as an early Gernsback convert, was launching a contest. He announced up to $9,000 in prizes, including a $250 first prize, to the reader with the best response to the prompt "If I Were Editor . . ." ("Nothing to buy! Just tell us what you would do if you were editor of *Forum*—in 50 words or more.") Other prizes included copies of various Amherst Press books including Palmer and Shaver's *The Secret World* and William A. Hyman's *Magna Carta of Space*. ("One of the most important developments in the history of Law. The entire future of mankind's justice may depend on the protection of mankind's legal rights in Space.")

In late July 1977, Rap and his wife, Marjorie, left home to drive to Tallahassee to visit a newborn grandson. Only thirty miles down the road, he pulled the car over to the roadside. He felt numbness. During the long drive south, he had another bout of numbness. Three days later, on the morning of Sunday, July 31, they arrived at their daughter Jennifer's house in Florida. It was very hot. The proud grandparents admired their daughter's baby boy who was not yet a week old. That afternoon, Rap collapsed to the floor. He recovered and once again insisted he was fine. The next day, August 1, his birthday, his daughter insisted Rap go to Tallahassee Memorial Hospital. After four days of tests, he was diagnosed with a blocked artery in his neck and underwent surgery.

The operation, according to Marjorie, "did not go well." Within a week he had suffered two more strokes. At that point, his doctors thought he would only survive another twenty-four hours, but he struggled on. On August 15, 1977, he died in the intensive care unit. His wife noted of his final days, "Although it was difficult to understand when he attempted to talk, we did communicate and he fought a terrific fight to live."[23] Four days after his death in Florida, his funeral took place in Amherst, Wisconsin.

The next issue of *Search* was bundled with not only *Flying Saucers*, but also the final issue of *Forum* and a group of affectionate letters from readers and friends, titled "Bon Voyage, Ray." The letters included a message from Howard Browne, who credited Palmer for all his success: Browne had gone from assisting Rap (and throwing Shaver's first letter into the trash) to editing *Amazing Stories* and a career writing screenplays and mystery novels.

It was clear that someone else had put this issue together—there were no notes from A. R. Steber, Rae Winter, Frank Patton, G. H. Irwin, Morris Steele, Alexander Blade, or anyone borrowing a house pseudonym. Marjorie concluded the issue with a quote from Rap's recent essay on the afterlife: "It seems to me that Heaven is a very *solid* place, and it also seems to me that any more complicated concept is totally unnecessary to an eternal existence. Here's hoping I see you there, and that we can shake hands with *feeling*."

INTO THE VORTEX

Rap's short novel "The Vortex World," was serialized in 1934 in *Fantasy Magazine*. In the series, hoping to gain information about the fourth dimension, the crew of the spaceship *Bluebird* seeks to penetrate a vortex. Their effort does not involve splashy special effects or battles with titanic forces; instead, once the ship is caught in the "clutches of this whirlpool" the crew relies on mysterious globes that feed on their mental powers to guide them. The result, as a crew member announces, is to shift into a "universe whose vibrations are exactly opposite our own. It is as if we had stepped into mirror-land and a double, or rather the original, had remained on the other side."

As in this story, Palmer often sought out a realm where expectations were reversed, a vortex into which he would ultimately be swept. He would propose a wild idea for its shock value, defend it, and eventually succumb to its truth. The whirlpool of time, however, awaits all truths and their proponents, to render them into dust then, perhaps, exd. Statues of grand leaders topple, temples fall to ruin, and pulp editors who commissioned artists to depict strange worlds where beautiful women are threatened by Martian space octopi are completely forgotten.

As he approached his final days as a corporean, Rap also stripped down some of the layers of hyperbole. At a UFO conference in Chicago in 1977, during a discussion of the possible connection between Jules Verne stories and the strange airship sightings of the turn of the twentieth century, Rap argued that fiction often shapes our perception of reality, particularly of the extraordinary. Trying to define the relationship between imagination and cognition, he vacillated between the notions of suggestion and influence, but concluded, "It's a basic weakness that we like to fool ourselves. We go out and catch a big fish. It's always a big fish, and the bigger it is the more it gets away."[1]

Was he announcing that all his efforts amounted to a fisherman's tall tale? Or was he suggesting that the big fish he was after, the contour of a hidden world, by its very nature tends to remain hidden, its murky details fleshed out only by seers and pulp writers? His fellow panelists at the First International UFO Congress in Chicago did not attempt to coax out his position. In fact, they largely chose to ignore him, as he seemed to imply that sightings of UFOs might well be written off as cases of hypnotic suggestion.

Palmer's big fish statement had the appearance of a confession, suggested a slipping of a confidence trickster's mask, or so thought Martin Gardner, a founding member of the skeptics' organization the Committee for the Scientific Investigation of Claims of the Paranormal (CSICOP). In 1988, Gardner proposed that Rap's handicaps had inculcated Palmer with a desire for revenge or, at least, a joy in perpetrating flimflams. Palmer, Gardner claimed, was "a strange little man, chuckling to himself as he wrote, somehow getting enormous kicks out of hornswoggling people bigger than he was."[2]

Such a view of Palmer as a flimflam man emerged earlier when many cast the Shaver Mystery as the Shaver Hoax. At a SF conference in the early 1950s, writer Harlan Ellison announced that Palmer had told him that he had created the Shaver Mystery merely as a "publicity grabber to gain circulation." This recounted conversation made the rounds with almost the same impact as L. Ron Hubbard's statement at the 1948 Eastern Science Fiction Association Conference, "You don't get rich writing science fiction. If you want to get rich, you start a religion." (Though Scientologists frequently challenge this quote, Sam Moskowitz allegedly signed an affidavit to indicate it was correct.) As for Palmer's statement to Ellison, in a long letter to fellow ufologist Gray Barker in 1957, Palmer explained that he did intend the Shaver Mystery as a "publicity grabber" but that did not make it a hoax. He insisted that the Shaver Mystery reverberated too deeply for too many, including himself. To Barker he wrote that Shaver's uncanny ideas served as "positive evidence that man's thinking to date has been inadequate in his understanding of the nature of the universe."[3]

What of Gardner's theories of Palmer's psychological motivation? Was Rap, like the "Lone Wolf of Space," an angry man hell-bent on revenge? However tilted Gardner's interpretation, the arch-skeptic was probably right in fixating on the possible psychological consequences of Palmer's physical disabilities. Handling jeers and stares for much of his life surely hardened him. According to Gardner's reasoning, Palmer was embittered, had a carnival operator's view of the world, and, fueled by contempt, sought to fleece the rubes. Rap certainly seemed more inured to public ridicule than most, hence had the makeup to be a bold hoaxer. But Palmer's motivation could not have been so simplistic. To A. Human, the African-American correspondent who vowed he would haunt racists after his death if murdered, Rap confessed that he also was bitter about the pain he felt and the prejudice he navigated daily, yet he urged A. Human not to give in to hatred (in this case, of white people). As for Gardner's suspicion that Palmer's career was a form of revenge, in 1963 Rap wrote, "I have handicaps—I consider them blessings, and valuable experience, a problem to be solved."[4] Revenge could not have been the only motive for his life's work. His personality would be described better as ambitious than as "vengeful."

It is not plausible that Palmer, a fearless individual, would spend three decades churning out editorials, articles, and magazines—millions of words—that all added up to a gigantic hoax; that is, nothing. He may well have had some of the instincts of a carny offering cheap thrills, but this cannot fully explain his preoccupations. As he pointed out frequently, if he really had no moral qualms, no interest in investigating mysteries, and was only governed by a desire for the dollar, he could have jumped into the sleaze-publishing racket along with his Chicago colleagues Hugh Hefner and William Hamling. Such a career would not only be profitable but he could also ennoble it—as did Hefner and Hamling—by championing free speech.

While Rap undoubtedly had many a trick up his sleeve, he believed that the universe had far more tricks tucked away. His outsider status allowed him to reject everyday norms and to look at others as Shaver viewed his elder stones—as containers for hidden knowledge. He relished the flood of letters he received at *Amazing Stories*, *Fate*, and *Mystic*, because to Rap they represented the mass mind of humanity.

The case against Palmer then proceeds: if not a flimflammer, then a hack. Unless they were former members of his stable at *Amazing Stories*, or shared his Psi-Fi instincts, most SF writers have heaped scorn on Palmer for his hack aesthetic and his defection from the Gernsbackian vision. Few science fiction critics appear aware of the wit he displayed in his burlesques on the SF genre in the 1930s, or of his skill as an essayist and the care with which he wrote his hundreds of editorials. For example, Everett F. Bleiler in *Science Fiction: The Gernsback Years* (1998) took the scorched earth approach, assessing Rap's impact on SF as follows, "As a science-fiction editor, Palmer was of no historical importance, except as a force for the worse; as an occult proponent, he stands behind much of the modern outgrowth of irrationality; as a writer, he could well be ignored." Of Palmer's first story, "The Time Ray of Jandra," Bleiler noted, "Confusing exposition, and of no interest." Another he summarized as "routine at best," and a third, probably fairly, "a tawdry performance."[5]

Mike Ashley, a historian of SF magazines was kinder, rejecting the "pure hack" label to point out that Palmer as an editor offered some daring and innovative SF when he began *Other Worlds*. Ashley's praise, however, was mixed, noting that while in the past Rap had sought "to pander to the lunatic fringe, now Palmer was seeking to shock the newly enlightened science fiction audience, and for once he was able to prove what a good editor he was."[6] In *Science Fiction of the 20th Century* (1999), Frank M. Robinson, a Chicago colleague of Rap's, commented, "Palmer knew what good writing was," and, as had Ashley, Robinson praised Rap's edgy editing of *Other Worlds* and *Universe*. Another recent assessment by fanzine editor Hank Luttrell, also focused on *Other Worlds*, was complimentary to both Rap and his associate editor Bea Mahaffey. "Palmer was clearly some kind of strange genius, as well, but I remain convinced that Mahaffey brought her own considerable talents to the collaboration."[7]

While it is not surprising that hard-core SF critics or skeptics often downplay Palmer's impact, skipping from Gernsback to Campbell then on to other editors such as Frederik Pohl and Michael Moorcock in discussing the genre's development, it is peculiar that Palmer often is not even acknowledged as an important influence on the flying saucer and modern New Age movements. In the first, and to some extent, only academic study of the early flying saucer movement, *The UFO Controversy in America* (1975), David M. Jacobs never mentioned Palmer at all—quite an omission for a book focused on controversy. In contrast, early and energetic UFO debunker Donald H. Menzel, an astronomer at Harvard University, was happy to detail Palmer's stratagems in the chapter titled "Hoaxers and Jokers" in his book *Flying Saucers* (1953).

Others have likely overemphasized Palmer's importance. Peter Kor, who contributed the skeptical "Critic's Corner" to *Flying Saucers* and was one of Rap's intellectual sparring partners, insisted in 1974 that Ray Palmer, Donald Keyhoe, and George Adamski were the crucial figures that shaped the flying saucer movement. Without Keyhoe's championing of the extraterrestrial hypothesis, Adamski's concoction of the contactee genre, and Palmer's general probing, Kor argued, "The coming of the saucers would have been marked merely by a series of nonintegrated happenings of an extraordinary nature. As a result of the activities of these men, the flying saucers have become a modern mythological mystery."[8] Shortly before Palmer's death in 1977, Kor shifted the emphasis fully to Palmer, "His greatest achievement is the one he gets the least credit for: The 'making' of the flying saucer mystery. For years, there was no 'flying saucer field.' There was only Ray Palmer. He battled government pressure and public apathy to rescue flying saucers from almost certain oblivion. Almost single-handedly, he put flying saucers on the intellectual map."[9]

Kor's assessment was echoed by John Keel, in his often circulated 1983 *Fortean Times* article "The Man Who Invented Flying Saucers." Keel insisted that Palmer from the first "converted UFO reports from what might have been a Silly Season phenomenon into a [real] subject. . . . From 1957 to 1964, ufology in the United States was in total limbo. This was the Dark Age. . . . It was Palmer, and Palmer alone, who kept the subject alive during the Dark Age and lured new youngsters into ufology."[10] Even Martin Gardner gave Palmer a nod as a promoter of this new mystery, noting, "It would be foolish to suppose that UFOmania would never have gathered steam without Palmer's aid; yet no one can deny that he played an enormous role, now almost forgotten, in tirelessly promoting the craze."[11]

Palmer's partners at *Fate* magazine also tended to be silent about his other clear achievement: originating a new genre, the paranormal pulp magazine (a feat Rap first achieved within the pages of *Amazing Stories*, to the horror of SF fans, before he went on to create *Fate*). *Fate*'s lasting success in opening this field led to knockoffs, including James L. Quinn's *Strange: The Magazine of True Mystery* (that ran for three issues in 1952); *If: Worlds of Science Fiction* (a companion science fiction magazine that included writing by Palmer and Shaver that later merged with *Galaxy Science Fiction*); many comic books chronicling strange phenomena such as *Journey into Mystery*; the British publication *Fortean Times*; and *Omni*, which included a mixture of science news, cyborg fetishism, and SF weirdness and debuted in 1978, the year after Rap's death.

Rap's fellow pioneers, Curtis Fuller and in particular Curtis's wife, Mary, had a mixed opinion of their former partner. In 1977, to celebrate *Fate*'s thirtieth anniversary, there was a spate of interviews in Chicago newspapers in which the Fullers recounted the offbeat history of *Fate*. In many of these articles, Ray Palmer is not mentioned at all, giving the impression that the quirky yet upscale Fullers had created the magazine on their own. To his credit, Curtis Fuller mentions in one interview that he began the magazine with "his friend" Ray Palmer, but beyond that one sentence reference, in these interviews—some published just shortly after Palmer's death—there was near total silence about his role.

Behind the scenes, however, the Fullers were gracious enough to keep on staff at *Fate* the former *Amazing Stories* writer and Shaver Mystery Club editor Chester S. Geier, who was totally deaf and whose career as a SF writer had dwindled in the early 1950s. The Fullers also hired Rap to help with mailings and distribution from his base in Wisconsin. Likewise, in the introduction to the 1980 *Proceedings of the First International UFO Congress*, a production of the *Fate* editorial department, a nod was given to Palmer for originating the magazine. Yet there is a sense that the Fullers preferred to rewrite the history of *Fate* magazine with the outlandish persona and monstrous tastes of Palmer exiled.

Palmer could charm and delight but he also made people uncomfortable. As he noted to one letter writer, "I am sometimes a bit rough because I've learned that nobody listens to a polite man. They stand murmuring 'very interesting' but they aren't even listening."[12] He wanted people to listen, he wanted to provoke, he wanted to shock minds open—or just to shock. He didn't want to claim the label normal. No one, in his opinion, was normal. Palmer believed everyone had a touch of psychosis, and he would not have denied being somewhat unhinged himself. In an affectionate tribute in *Locus*, Frank M. Robinson, who had served as a copy boy at Ziff-Davis before becoming a SF writer, editor, and screenwriter, noted that Palmer was a gifted editor and one of a kind. "With time I realized that few great editors played with a full deck, that for better or worse God had made them individualists and it was that individualism that was their great value."[13]

While the standard history of science fiction delegates Palmer to a tawdry footnote, interest in Palmer and Shaver has increased in recent years, along with interest in the paranormal, alternative religions, conspiracy theories, and outsider art. Even Palmer and Shaver's joint literary production *I Remember Lemuria* has a curious legacy. In a 1996 vote, it was among four nominees for the Retro Hugo Award for novellas for 1946, losing to George Orwell's *Animal Farm*. As of 2012, Mutan Mion's narrative was also among the assembled texts on sacredtexts.com, a website that includes tracts and gospels from major and alternative religions (*Oahspe* can also be found on the site).

Over the decades, a core group of Shaver devotees that has included true believers as well as amused aficionados of crankdom has maintained Shaver-related newsletters and websites (a prime example is Richard Toronto's Shavertron—essentially the *Shaver Mystery Magazine* with an added underground comics aesthetic). A renewed interest in Shaver's art has accompanied the growing taste for outsider art—a genre first recognized when artist Jean Dubuffet and Surrealist André Breton set up a foundation in 1948 to collect and exhibit what they called Art Brut: the obsessive paintings of untrained and solitary "folk" artists and the mentally ill. As decades passed and rock-and-roll fans embraced low culture, snapped up albums decorated with the visionary folk art of Reverend Howard Finster, and sought out tattoos, the taste for outsider art also spiked. In 1994, Richard Shaver's art was shown at the Santa Monica Museum of Art, and in 2002, the Christine Burgin Gallery in New York offered "Weird and Wonderful Art: Rokfogos, Paintings and Books." Although no household name, Shaver has gained a presence in the ranks of gifted outsider artists.

As scholars became intrigued by conspiracy theory and the paranormal, Ray Palmer also has been rediscovered. Jeffrey J. Kripal, a scholar of religion, accorded Ray Palmer a central place in his study of the connection between popular culture and the paranormal, *Mutants and Mystics: Science Fiction, Superhero Comics, and the Paranormal* (2011). In this work, Kripal traced the life stories of creative people in science fiction and comic books who first explored fantasy realms via the imagination and then had full-blown mystic experiences. Kripal argued that Palmer forged the way as the first major defector from science fiction and fantasy to Psi-Fi.

The Plot Thickens

Palmer's greatest impact has been in the murky world of conspiracy theory. When consensus reality is denied, new narratives rush in to fill the void. As an early impresario of the paranormal, Palmer shares in much of the credit—or the blame—for the development of contemporary conspiracy theory culture, particularly its cross-fertilization with popular culture and entertainment. Two sturdy branches of conspiracy theory have Palmer's fingerprints all over them: the flying saucer community's certainty of a governmental cover-up, and the hollow earth tradition as elaborated via the writings of Richard Shaver and Rap. Often these two blueprints combine.

One example of such a combination is the high-profile conspiracy legend focused on Dulce, New Mexico. If you take Shaver's hollow earth dero theory and then fold in a race of hypnotic lizards straight out of Edgar Rice Burroughs, a secret pact between aliens and U.S. agencies, and underground laboratories, and then, to make the recipe more toxic, add anti-Semitic theories of the origins of the lizard race, one arrives at the Dulce, New Mexico, legend, still thriving on the Internet as of 2012.

One of the first to give the basic framework of the Shaver Mystery a push toward Dulce was the dedicated pulp magazine reader Maurice Doreal, the founder of the Brotherhood of the White Temple. In his 1950s pamphlets, Doreal (born Claude Doggins) described his Shaveresque meeting with Atlanteans beneath Mount Shasta. According to Doreal, the Atlanteans relied on an energy source that "blended the rays of the sun and the moon" but that—in a nod to Shaver's greatest worry—"had all the harmful rays in it extracted and only the life-giving and beneficial energies left." Doreal also reported that after a long battle, the Lemurians, the Atlanteans' rivals, had sealed themselves underground in a vast empire of "pleasure places" (roughly below San Francisco). Here Doreal departed from Shaver, adding an anti-Semitic touch—the swarthy, smart, and not altogether trustworthy Lemurians, with their dero-like fixation on pleasure, were the ancestors of all the Semitic peoples. But the Lemurians weren't mankind's worst problem. In another of Doreal's pamphlets, he reported that the South Pole had hatched a race of serpent demons with "illusionary powers" that made them appear human. (They also, curiously, were unable to pronounce the word *kinninigan*.) Most, but not all, of the shape-shifting serpents were defeated via atomic warfare.[14] What would have been laughable, if somewhat creepy, as a comic book plot apparently recruited new members to the Brotherhood of the White Temple.

Conspiracy theorists began to seed New Mexico with the remnants of Doreal's lizard race in the early 1980s. This began when UFO researcher Paul Bennewitz, who lived near the Kirtland Air Force Base in southeast

Albuquerque, met a local woman who insisted she had UFO encounters; under hypnosis, she reported that on several occasions she had been taken to an underground research base that included vats with human body parts floating in them—a dero scene right out of a Shaver story. Bennewitz rigged up electronic equipment and concluded that UFOs were in contact with a large underground research center run by the Department of Defense's Sandia Laboratories. This secret underground facility was apparently one hundred miles north, at Dulce, near the Colorado border.

In a free-form version of the round-robin novel *Cosmos* that Ray Palmer had orchestrated with sixteen other authors in the 1930s, other conspiracy theorists added to the Dulce saga. In the early 1980s, Thomas Edwin Castello, who claimed he had been part of the security force at Dulce, announced that the aliens working underground were "reptoid" shape-shifters. (His inspiration may have been the human-masked lizard race known as Visitors featured in the 1980s television series *V*.) Then a writer from Utah who called himself Branton posted material on the web in 1999 and 2000 insisting that the aliens' base, which he called Dreamland, was beneath much of the western territory of the United States. He believed the U.S. government was not the guilty party. The government was actually secretly battling the "Bavarian Illuminati's New World Order"—a clandestine society of long pedigree—that had joined forces with the reptoids to take over the world.

Other authors, adding religious motifs, began to cast the struggle between humans and serpents as a prelude to Armageddon. Then came the leap to anti-Semitism (with a dash of added misogyny); according to this embellishment, the biblical serpent had actually impregnated Eve, and the ensuing line of reptoids, via Cain, represented the ancestry of Jews. The other "purely human" line (i.e., the white race) fathered by Adam could yet save the human race from impurity and treachery.[15] To cap off the saga, former BBC sports announcer David Icke explained that Reptilian Overlords were locked in battle with the grays of alien lore, had been

around since the age of Babylonia, and, yes, were determined to establish
a one-world government. According to Icke and his followers, many influential people were secret reptilians, including the country singer Boxcar
Willie, Kris Kristofferson, Rowan Atkinson (Mr. Bean), Al Gore, the British
royal family, George W. Bush, Tom Cruise, and Donald Rumsfeld. Unwittingly, the entire bizarre theory was anchored in one specific outpost of
Dreamland: the collaboration of Rap with Richard Shaver that appeared in
Amazing Stories more than half a century earlier.

When You Meet the Buddha

While vital strands of conspiracy theory struggled free from the pages of
pulp magazines, especially *Amazing Stories*, in recent decades such theories
also have been reabsorbed by the entertainment culture from which they
sprang. The conspiracy theory can be enjoyed as either fact or fiction—or
as an inhabitant of the twilight zone in between.[16] Palmer developed this
blend with his promotion of the Shaver Mystery as "true" but also as
"entertaining fiction." In this way, the Shaver Mystery helped begat the
ironic pleasures of such "mocku-conspiracy" television series as *Twin Peaks*
and *The X-Files*, just as the proliferation of religious cults—many of them
with origins in 1950s flying saucer religions—led to mock religions of the
1980s, such as the Church of the SubGenius that highlighted its pipe-
puffing salesman named Bob.

Yet beneath the ironic appreciation of conspiracy theory or instant religions is the theme of betrayal. Who can we trust? What is being hidden?
A proponent of free inquiry, Palmer believed something was wrong with
the official stories. Perhaps while driving home that night in Wisconsin he
had seen a brownie and not a rabbit running across a farm field. Maybe
nuclear fallout really was something to be alarmed about. Wasn't it con-

ceivable that at least one UFO sighting was inexplicable and not simply a
faked photo of a deftly tossed pie pan?

Conspiracy reasoning and its hardened assurances can undermine such
healthy skepticism. At his worst, as when he saw his American Dream
threatened and so blamed the Department of Natural Resources, Ray
Palmer was a true believer, as concerned about one-worlders as the typical
John Birch Society member. He was, of course, one of the few such believers who loved the song "The Age of Aquarius" from the musical *Hair* and
mocked those with conventional notions about religion. This Palmer was
someone for whom the conspiracy was complete, a done deal. This Palmer
has a lot to answer for, such as forging the template of the Dulce legend
with its increasingly toxic payload.

But at his best, Rap kept asking "What if?" What if the government has
kidnapped your editor and replaced him with a replica that will write in-
sipid editorials? What if Richard Shaver is not a raving lunatic but the
bearer of secret knowledge? What if there is no such thing as mental illness? What if we never get to the bottom of the "what if" reflex? At his
best, he knew that people who *knew* were full of baloney. That included
those who clung to religious or scientific orthodoxy. And it included himself. He was not a hoaxer but someone who wondered if all belief was
ultimately a sort of hoax. This prompted his further suspicion that the insane were not insane, but merely explorers of the psychic wilds.

At his most intriguing, Rap was a master of paradox who hinted that
multiple interpretations coexisted as true. In 1970, he wrote, "While I believe every word he [Shaver] says, that he has presented it honestly, in reality it is a complete fraud! Except that while I swear by the reality of flying
saucers, there is no such thing! Except that while I believe in the spirit
world, there is no such thing as a spirit! Except that while I disbelieve in
reincarnation, there are billions of reincarnates! Except that while space
travel is a demonstrable fact, real space travel is impossible!"[17] When a

truth was discovered, as with any false idol, it had to be admired then smashed.

After his initial failure to launch "Martian Diary," Palmer recognized the danger of the trap of knowing. As he said, "That book I was going to write wasn't like my magazines, which only STIMULATED thinking—it was a book that would PATTERN THOUGHT. Therein lies the frustration. Now that I KNOW, I can't tell you. Nor would you accept it." He further developed this meditation by way of a parable. Rap asked what would happen if he came to the conclusion that there was "a pot of gold at the end of the rainbow." He could write this truth but it would be rubbish. "We both know that you can't go to the end of the rainbow and pick up that pot of gold. It is inaccessible! The truth is UNTELLABLE! Once you know, you are stuck with it, your lips are sealed, and worse, it may be true only for you!"[18]

He continued to elaborate on his rejection of not just telling but knowing during the last year of his life, while plugging his magazine *Search*, "The most stupid thing in the world is to say: 'Eureka,' which means 'I have found it.' . . . Quite the reverse is true. SEARCH goes on eternally. It is the PURPOSE of existence. Always, over that next hill, is a new valley to be discovered. . . . No matter how much we see, there is more to see. No matter what we learn, there is more to learn. . . . Not to think, is not to *be*!"[19]

His last focus was not on finality or on airtight systems, but on process. He was prepared to admit that throughout his life he had been searching not just for truth, but also for big fish. In that search, Rap found first Richard Shaver, then, several years later, Kenneth Arnold and the flying saucer. Along the way, in *Amazing Stories* and *Fate* and his other publications, he developed the uncomfortable blend of science fiction and true mystery—leavened with irony—that has continued to shape our culture and entertainment industries. This legacy can be regarded either as a great act of mischief or as a gift. Yet to dupes of conspiracy theory, of which he could

be one, he would note, quite rationally, "I don't ask you to believe anything! I do ask you to challenge everything!" Proprietors of a medicine
show needed a big fish; audience members needed to think for themselves.

Palmer pushed boundaries. His search for the ultimate amazing story
often landed him in a "universe whose vibrations are exactly opposite our
own." But he lived his life on his own terms, and accepted nothing on faith.
To the old Zen saying, "If you meet the Buddha on the road, kill him," he
would add, "Then throw another body through the skylight." When necessary, this visitor from Mars would dive through the skylight himself, risking
the broken glass to enjoy his moment in the light.

Palmer in July 1950, leaning
on his red automobile. *Photo
courtesy Margaret Ford Kiefer*

NOTES

★ ★ ★

CHAPTER ONE—BIRTH OF A FAN

1. Hugo Gernsback, "A New Sort of Magazine," *Amazing Stories*, April 1926, 3.
2. This account comes from Palmer's son, Raymond B. Palmer, interviewed by the author on February 8, 2011.
3. Much of this account of Palmer's illness comes from his own short autobiographical work "Martian Diary, Book 1," in Raymond Palmer and Richard Shaver, *The Secret World* (Amherst, WI: Amherst Press, 1975). He also discusses his injury in "As the Twig Is Bent . . ." *Hidden World,* A-13 (Spring 1964): 2175–76.
4. Gernsback's financial difficulties with *Amazing Stories* are detailed in many works, including Mark Richard Seigel, *Hugo Gernsback: Father of Modern Science Fiction* (San Bernardino, CA: Borgo Press, 1988).
5. Mike Ashley and Robert A. Lowndes, *The Gernsback Days: A Study of the Evolution of Modern Science Fiction from 1911 to 1936* (Holicong: PA: Wildside Press, 2004): 119.
6. The development of fanzines is discussed in Sam Moskowitz, *The Immortal Storm: A History of Science Fiction Fandom* (Westport, CT: Hyperion Press, 1954): 8–12. The quote is from Moskowitz's essay "The Origins of Science Fiction Fandom: A Reconstruction" in Joe Sanders, ed., *Science Fiction Fandom* (Westport, CT: Greenwood Press, 1994): 30.
7. Quoted in Eric Leif Davin, *Pioneers of Wonder: Conversations with the Founders of Science Fiction* (Amherst, NY: Prometheus Books, 1999): 65.
8. Hugo Gernsback, *Science Wonder Stories* 1, no. 1 (Fall 1929): 3.
9. Palmer, "Martian Diary," 26.
10. Raymond Palmer, "Where the Reader Has His Say," *Search*, March 1969, 70.

11. Raymond Palmer to Lloyd A. Eshbach, March 6, 1934. Eshbach Papers, Temple University Library.

12. Eshbach to Palmer, June 1934. Eshbach Papers, Temple University Library.

13. Palmer to Eshbach, July 6, 1934. Eshbach Papers, Temple University Library.

14. "Skylaugh of Space," *Fantasy Magazine*, May 1934, 16–18. The story is signed with an alias, "Omnia," but the style suggests that Rap, the fanzine's literary editor, was the author.

15. Robert Bloch, *Once Around the Bloch* (New York: Tor, 1993). Bloch discusses his adventures with the Milwaukee Fictioneers on pages 74–78.

16. Information on Shade Publishing can be found in Mike Ashley, *Time Machines: The Story of Science-Fiction Pulp Magazines from the Beginning to 1950* (Liverpool, UK: Liverpool University Press, 2000): 93–94.

17. Ralph Milne Farley to Raymond Palmer, May 17, 1935. Weinbaum Papers, Temple University Library.

18. The Scarlett Adventuress series is discussed in Eric Leif Davin, *Partners in Wonder: Women and the Birth of Science Fiction, 1926–1965* (Oxford, UK: Lexington Books, 2006): 141.

19. Palmer, "Martian Diary," 26.

CHAPTER TWO—AMAZING STORIES

1. T. O'Conor Sloane, "Discussions," *Amazing Stories*, April 1938, 141.

2. T. O'Conor Sloane, "Space Travel," *Amazing Stories*, March 1935, 11.

3. Raymond Palmer, "Palmer Tears His Hair . . . Out and Down," *Stardust*, November 1940, 12.

4. Earl Binder to Otto Binder, February 20, 1938. Otto Binder Collection, Texas A&M University, Science Fiction and Fantasy Research Collection.

5. Raymond Palmer, "Observatory," *Amazing Stories*, June 1938, 8.

6. Phil Klass, quoted in "John W. Campbell's Golden Age of Science Fiction; Text Supplement to the CD," 29. http://www.sfcenter.ku.edu/JWC_Study_Supplement.pdf.

7. For an introduction to pulp art, see Robert Lesser, ed., *Pulp Art: Original Cover Paintings for the Great American Pulp Magazines* (Edison, NJ: Castle Books, 2003).

8. Palmer, "Palmer Tears His Hair," 12. Robert Moore Williams promoted the Palmer method in his article "Corpse Through the Roof," *Writer's Digest*, July 1949, 13–18.

9. B. G. Davis, "Notice to Contributors," October 10, 1938. Eshbach Papers, Temple University Library.

10. B. G. Davis, "Notice to Contributors." Not dated. Eshbach Papers, Temple University Library.

11. Donald A. Wollheim, "Commentary on the November 'Novae Terrae,'" *Novae Terrae* 20 (January 1938), 13; http://www.fiawol.org.uk/fanstuff/then%20archive/newworlds/NT20.htm.

12. Howard Browne, "A Profit Without Honor," *Amazing Stories*, May 1984, 74.

13. Palmer, "Palmer Tears His Hair," 24.

14. Palmer, "Observatory." *Amazing Stories*, November 1941, 6.

15. "Meet the Authors," *Amazing Stories*, September 1943, 87.

16. Raymond Palmer, "Where the Reader Has His Say," *Search*, March 1969, 72.

17. Quoted in Eric Leif Davin, *Partners in Wonder: Women and the Birth of Science Fiction, 1926–1965* (Oxford, UK: Lexington Books, 2006): 141.

18. Browne, "A Profit Without Honor," 73.

19. For the details of Ray Palmer's courtship with Marjorie, I am indebted to their son Raymond B. Palmer's pamphlet printed in 1998 for his mother's memorial. It also included Frances Yerxa's reminiscences about that period.

CHAPTER THREE—THE ALPHABET FROM OUTER SPACE

1. Richard Shaver, "An Ancient Language?" in "Letters," *Amazing Stories*, January 1944, 206.

2. Howard Browne, "A Profit Without Honor," *Amazing Stories*, May 1984, 80–81.

3. Raymond Palmer, "Observatory," *Amazing Stories*, July 1939.

4. Palmer's correspondence with Richard Shaver for the years 1943–45 is reproduced in "The Secret Shaver-Palmer Letter File" sections offered in Palmer's *Hidden World*, volumes A-13, A-14, A-15, A-16, all published in 1964. Volume A-4, published in Winter 1961, pages 633–62, also features "My Correspondence with Richard S. Shaver," letters collected in the late 1940s by George Wentworth, a Shaver Mystery Club member. This quote is from a letter Shaver sent to Palmer in December 1944, prior to Christmas, in *Hidden World*, A-13 (Spring 1964): 2185.

5. Jim Wentworth, *Giants in the Earth* (Amherst WI: Palmer Publications, 1973): 14. For census information, I relied on the website Society of the Descendants of Johannes de la Montagne; http://wc.rootsweb.ancestry.com/cgi-bin/igm.cgi?op=GET&db=delamontagne&id=I36850.

6. Shaver to Palmer, December 25, 1943, *Hidden World*, A-13 (Spring 1964): 2186.

7. For some details of Shaver's early life, I have relied on Doug Skinner, "What's This? A Shaver Revival?" *Fate*, June 2005; http://www.fatemag.com/issues/2000s/2005-06.html.

8. Shaver to Palmer, March 18, 1944, *Hidden World*, A-13 (Spring 1964): 2246.

9. Shaver to Palmer, August 1944, *Hidden World*, A-13 (Spring 1964): 2386.

10. Shaver to Palmer, March 5, 1945, *Hidden World*, A-15 (Fall 1964): 2609.

11. Author's interview with Richard Shaver's daughter Evelyn Bryant, March 22, 2012. She never knew her father and indicated much of her information was furnished to her by researchers, in particular, Richard Toronto, a journalist and the editor of *Shavertron* magazine. Toronto furnished Evelyn with copies of Shaver's May 6, 1943, discharge papers from Michigan's Ionia State Hospital for the Criminally Insane into the custody of his parents in Pennsylvania. Palmer may have confused this longer stay with his briefer hospitalization in Ypsilanti in the early 1930s.

12. Shaver to Palmer, January 26, 1945, *Hidden World*, A-15 (Fall 1964): 2574.

13. Shaver to Palmer, July 29, 1944, *Hidden World*, A-14 (Summer 1964): 2370.

14. Shaver to Palmer, March 18, 1944, *Hidden World*, A-13 (Spring 1964): 2249–50.

15. David Standish, *Hollow Earth: The Long and Curious History* (Cambridge: MA: Da Capo Press, 2004): 64–67.

16. Symmes's call to action is reproduced in Standish, *Hollow Earth*, 40–41.

17. Standish, *Hollow Earth*, 218-24.

18. Ibid., 243–51.

19. Mike Ashley, *Time Machine: The Story of the Science-Fiction Pulp Magazines from the Beginning to 1950* (Liverpool, UK: Liverpool University Press, 2000): 37.

20. All quotes from Victor Tausk, "The Origin of the Influencing Machine in Schizophrenia." Reprinted in *Journal of Psychotherapy Practice and Research* 1, no. 2 (Spring 1992): 185–206.

21. Shaver to Palmer, September 16, 1944, *Hidden World*, A-14 (Summer 1964): 2414.

22. Raymond Palmer, "Flying Saucers and the Stymie Factor," *Search* (Summer 1977): 38.

23. Shaver to Palmer, January 27, 1945, *Hidden World*, A-15 (Fall 1964): 2586.

24. Raymond Palmer, "Martian Diary, Book 1," in Ray Palmer and Richard Shaver, *The Secret World* (Amherst, WI: Amherst Press, 1975): 39–40.

25. Shaver to Palmer, March 5, 1945, *Hidden World*, A-15 (Fall 1964): 2607.

CHAPTER FOUR—SHAVER MANIA

1. Raymond Palmer, "The New Fandom," *Fantasy News* 9, no. 3 (February 18, 1945), 176.

2. Shaver to Palmer, July 23, 1944, *Hidden World*, A-14 (Summer 1964): 2368.

3. Shaver to Palmer, June 8, 1944, *Hidden World*, A-14 (Summer 1964): 2341.

4. *Amazing Stories*, September 1945, 29.

5. Richard Shaver, "I Enter the Caves," *Hidden World*, A-1 (Spring 1961): 41.

6. Shaver to Palmer, *Hidden World*, A-14 (Summer 1964): 2407.

7. Shaver to Palmer, May 4, 1944, *Hidden World*, A-14 (Summer 1964): 2323.

8. Shaver to Palmer, July 29, 1944, *Hidden World*, A-14 (Summer 1964): 2370.

9. Shaver to Palmer, July 10, 1944, *Hidden World*, A-14 (Summer 1964): 2362.

10. Jeffrey J. Kripal, *Mutants and Mystics: Science Fiction, Superhero Comics, and the Paranormal* (Chicago: University of Chicago Press, 2011): 2.

11. Mitch Horowitz, *Occult America* (New York: Bantam Books, 2009): 204–7.

12. Shaver to Palmer, April 19, 1944, *Hidden World*, A-14 (Summer 1964): 2315.

13. Alden M. Scrum, "Amazing Letter," *Amazing Stories*, September, 1945, 173.

14. *Amazing Stories*, June 1946, 96.

15. Shaver to Palmer, June 8, 1944, *Hidden World*. A-14 (Summer 1964): 2336.

16. Shaver to Palmer, July 10, 1944, *Hidden World*, A-14 (Summer 1964): 2360.

17. Shaver to Jim Wentworth, *Hidden World*, A-4 (Winter 1961): 754.

18. Richard Shaver, "The Facts on Deros," *Hidden World*, A-4 (Winter 1961): 755.

19. Shaver to Palmer, July 29, 1944, *Hidden World*, A-14 (Summer 1964): 2411–12.

20. Shaver to Palmer, December 25, 1944, *Hidden World*, A-13 (Spring 1964): 2186.

21. "He Doesn't Hear Voices," *Amazing Stories*, October 1946, 173.

22. Forrest Ackerman, *Voice of the Imagi Nation* 41, April 1945, 4.

23. Walter Dunkelberger, "An Open Letter to RAP," *Fanews*, August 10, 1945.

24. Raymond Palmer, "Ray Palmer Answers Dunk," *Fanews*, August 23, 1945.

25. Geoffrey Giles, "The Palmer Hoax," *Science-Fantasy Review*, Winter 1949–50, 10–14; http://efanzines.com/FR/sfr17.htm.

26. Ibid.

27. Kenneth Slater, "Goodbye to All That—Readers Vote on the Shaver Mystery," *Science-Fantasy Review*, April–May 1949, 11; http://efanzines.com/FR/fr14.htm.

CHAPTER FIVE—THE MAN WHO INVENTED FLYING SAUCERS

1. John Keel, "The Man Who Invented Flying Saucers." *Fortean Times* 41 (Winter 1983): 52–57.

2. E-mail from Jerome Clark to author, November 2, 2011. This account also relies on Jerome Clark, "60 Years of Fate Magazine," *Fortean Times* 237 (2008).

3. James Webb, *The Occult Underground* (Chicago: Open Court Publishing, 1974).

4. "The Strange Secret of Highland Park," *Chicago Reader*, August 12, 1977.

5. Mentioned in Richard Toronto, "The Man from Tomorrow," *eI41*, December 2008; http://efanzines.com/EK/eI41/index.htm#man.

6. "Dr. Newbrough's 'Oahspe,' " *New York Times*, October 21, 1882.

7. Newbrough remarks from article in *The Banner of Light*, January 21, 1883, as quoted in Sean Casteel, "Oahspe and the Remarkable Mr. Newbrough—a UFO Digest Book Review," December 18, 2009; http://www.ufodigest.com/news/1209/OAHSPE-print.php.

8. "The Press: Psychic Tomorrow," *Time*, September 16, 1946.

9. From National Archives Microfilm Publication T1206: Project Blue Book, Roll 1: Contains Case Files of Individual Sightings: Index and File Nos. 1–54 for Summer 1947: July 9, 1947 (1976), 541; http://www.bluebookarchive.org/page.aspx?PageCode=NARA-PBB1-563.

10. Frank M. Brown's report, Project Blue Book, Roll 1, 562–63.

11. Project Blue Book, Roll 1, 535.

12. Martin Shough, "Return of the Flying Saucers: A Fresh Look at the Sighting That Started It All," *Darklore* 5, no. 76; darklore.dailygrail.com.

13. Kenneth Arnold and Raymond Palmer, *The Coming of the Saucers* (Amherst, WI: Palmer, 1952): 20.

14. Ibid., 34.

15. Ibid., 57.

16. Ibid., 69.

17. Project Blue Book, Roll Maxwell 2, 903; http://www.bluebookarchive.org/page.aspx?PageCode=MAXW-PBB2-897.

18. FBI Report, August 18, 1947, Project Blue Book, Roll Maxwell 2, 899.

19. Raymond Palmer, *Forum*, November 1973, 12.

20. David Michael Jacobs, *The UFO Controversy in America* (Bloomington: Indiana University Press, 1975): 49–51.

21. Project Blue Book, Roll 1, 532.

22. Donald Keyhoe, *The Flying Saucers Are Real* (New York: Fawcett Publications, 1950): 175.

CHAPTER SIX—TRAPPED IN THE HOLLOW EARTH

1. Raymond Palmer, "The Dead Doctor Operated," *Mystic*, May 1956, 28–34.

2. Raymond Palmer, "How Do I Know I Am Alive?" *Forum*, April 1967, 14–19.

3. Author's interview with Helga Onan, March 23, 2012.

4. Palmer to Shaver, June 11, 1945, *Hidden World*, A-16 (Winter 1964): 2768.

5. Kenneth Arnold and Raymond Palmer, *The Coming of the Saucers* (Amherst, WI: Palmer, 1952): 158.

6. Geoffrey Giles, "The Palmer Hoax," *Science-Fantasy Review*, Winter 1949–50, 13; http://efanzines.com/FR/sfr17.htm.

7. Wilkie Connor, "Konner's Corner," *Spacewarp*, March 1950, 22.

8. Quoted in Rob Latham, "Worlds Well Lost: Male Homosexuality in Postwar Science Fiction," *eI* 8, no. 5 (October 2009); http://efanzines.com/EK/eI46/index.htm#worlds.

9. Paul Meehan, *Saucer Movies: A Ufological History of the Cinema* (Lanham, MD: Scarecrow Press, 1991): 15.

10. Desmond Leslie and George Adamski, *Flying Saucers Have Landed* (New York: British Book Centre, 1953): 195.

11. Michael Barkun, *A Culture of Conspiracy: Apocalyptic Visions in Contemporary America* (Berkeley: University of California Press, 2003): 155.

12. George Williamson, *Other Tongues—Other Flesh* (Amherst, WI: Amherst Press, 1953): 387–88; http://www.sacred-texts.com/ufo/otof/otof00.htm.

13. Jerome Clark, "60 Years of Fate Magazine," *Fortean Times* 237 (2008): 48.

14. Carl Jung, *Flying Saucers: A Modern Myth of Things Seen in the Skies* (New York: Signet Books, 1959, reprinted 1969): 84.

15. Ibid., 26.

16. Ibid., 126–27.

17. Orfeo Angelucci, *The Secret of the Saucers* (Amherst, WI: Amherst Press, 1955): 6.

18. Ibid., 13.

19. Ibid., 24.

20. Ibid., 34.

21. Jung, *Flying Saucers*, 50.

22. Angelucci, *Secret of the Saucers*, 83.

23. Raymond Palmer, *Flying Saucers from Other Worlds*, June 1957, 4.

24. Raymond Palmer, *Flying Saucers*, September 1963, 2.

CHAPTER SEVEN—PALMER AND SHAVER INC.

1. Richard Shaver, "Carvings on Rocks Mean Something." *Hidden World*, A-16 (Winter 1964): 2723.

2. Richard Shaver, "The Shaver Mystery No. 3 Why Do We Die? The Real 'Sin' of Adam and Eve," *Mystic*, March 1956, 8.

3. Shaver to Ray Palmer, May 16, 1944, *Hidden World*, A-14 (Summer 1964): 2331.

4. Shaver to Palmer, *Hidden World*, A-14 (Summer 1964): 2312.

5. Ibid., 2409.

6. Shaver to Palmer, *Hidden World*, A-13 (Spring 1964): 2216.

7. Shaver, "Carvings on Rocks Mean Something," 2724.

8. Richard Shaver, "The Ancient Earth, Its Story in Stone," in Raymond Palmer, *The Secret World* (Amherst, WI: Amherst Press, 1975): 58.

9. Shaver discusses his techniques for rokfogos in Palmer, *Secret World*, 80–89, and in "How to Make a Portrait of Dero Activity," in Palmer, *Hidden World*, A-8 (Winter 1962): 1349–53.

10. Palmer, *Secret World*, 56.

11. Ibid., 80.

12. Shaver, "Carvings on Rocks Mean Something," 2725.

13. Richard Shaver, "My Painting of Adam and Eve," *Hidden World*, A-8 (Winter 1962): 1399.

14. Ibid., 1400.

15. Stephen Jay Gould, "Velikovsky in Collision." In Gould, *Ever Since Darwin: Reflections in Natural History* (New York: W. W. Norton, 1977): 153.

16. Palmer, *Secret World*, 53.

17. Ibid.,52.

18. Shaver, "The Ancient Earth," 49.

19. See Earl Kemp, "Have Typewriter, Will Whore for Food," *eI* 1, no. 2 (April 2002); http://efanzines.com/EK/eI2/index.htm.

20. Robert W. Wells, "Where Is Publisher of Smut Literature?" *Milwaukee Journal*, April 4, 1963, 1, 14.

21. Palmer, *Hidden World*, A-16 (Winter 1964): 2789.

22. Palmer, *Hidden World*, B-2 (Spring 1962): 934.

23. Shaver, "The Secret Cave of the Dero," *Mystic*, May 1956, 69.

24. Earl Kemp, "Fear and Loathing in Evanston," *eI* 2, no. 6 (December 2003): 14; http://efanzines.com/EK/eI11/eI11.pdf.

25. For the history of Hamling's legal battles, see Earl Kemp, editor, *eI* 1, no. 4 (October 2002). Articles include Kemp "The Season of the Game," "Futting with the F.B.I. Futter," "Beauty and the Beast Otra Vez," and Stephen J. Gertz, "Earthlings, Beware! A Galaxy of Porn in San Diego"; http://efanzines.com/EK/eI4/index.htm.

26. Rog Phillips, "Christ an Autobiography," in Earl Kemp, ed., *eI31* 6, no. 2 (April 2007) (reprinted from *Spacewarp* 42); http://efanzines.com/EK/eI31/index.htm.

27. Ibid.

28. The letters between Palmer and Shaver regarding Rog Phillips are undated. Most likely

they are from late 1945. *Hidden World*, A-16 (Winter 1964), 2779–2807. This quote is from page 2784.

29. Shaver to Palmer, *Hidden World*, A-16 (Winter 1964), 2786.

30. Palmer to Shaver, *Hidden World*, A-16 (Winter 1964), 2791.

31. Ibid., 2795.

32. Ibid., 2803.

33. Raymond Palmer, *Search*, May 1957, 73.

CHAPTER EIGHT—ESP, OR THE ELDER STATESMAN OF PULP

1. Julius Schwartz, *A Man of Two Worlds: My Life in Science Fiction and Comics* (New York: Harper, 2000): 88–89.

2. Jeffrey J. Kripal suggested this "superhero origins" concept in *Mutants and Mystics*, 16.

3. Raymond Palmer, *Fate* 2, no. 1 (May 1949): 5.

4. Raymond Palmer, "Editorial," *Fate* 1, no. 3 (Fall 1948): 4.

5. Catherine Caufield, *Multiple Exposures: Chronicles of the Radiation Age* (Chicago: University of Chicago Press, 1989): 118.

6. Raymond Palmer, *Mystic*, March 1956, 51.

7. From the FBI file on Raymond Palmer that included copies of letters from an informant dated December 15, 1952, and an agent's subsequent reports filed on March 11, 1953, and April 22, 1953.

8. From the FBI file on Raymond Palmer. Perlman's letter to Hoover is dated September 29, 1954. Hoover's response is dated October 5, 1954.

9. Raymond Palmer, "Editorial," *Mystic*, August 1954, 6–7, 21, 79–83.

10. FBI dossier on Raymond Palmer. Report dated May 14, 1964.

11. Raymond Palmer, "Editorial," *Forum*, January 1968, 2–7.

12. Raymond Palmer, "Editorial," *Search*, September 1970, 5.

13. Raymond Palmer, *Forum*, July 1971, 4.

14. Raymond Palmer, "Richard S. Shaver—In Memorium," *Flying Saucers*, June 1976, 4.

15. Raymond Palmer, "Editorial," *Search*, March 1960, 7.

16. Raymond Palmer, *Search*, November 1965, 6.

17. *Forum*, August 1, 1966.

18. Raymond Palmer, advertisement for *Forum* in *Flying Saucers*, March 1966, inside cover.

19. Raymond Palmer, *Forum*, September 1969, 6.

20. Raymond Palmer, "Editorial," *Forum*, October 1972, 2–4.

21. Raymond Palmer, *Forum*, June 1970, 2.

22. Raymond Palmer, "Letters," *Forum*, August 1967, 12.

23. *Forum*, August 1, 1966, 16–18.

24. Raymond Palmer, *Search*, March 1976, 20.

25. Raymond Palmer, "Editorial," *Search*, March 1969, 5.

26. Raymond Palmer, "No Place to Go," *Search*, March 1969, 29–30.

27. Raymond Palmer, "Letters," *Forum*, September 1970, 28.

28. Raymond Palmer, "Editorial," *Search*, September 1973, 2.

29. Raymond Palmer, "Editorial," *Search*, May 1968, 19.

30. Michael Barkun, *A Culture of Conspiracy: Apocalyptic Visions in Contemporary America* (Berkeley: University of California Press, 2003): 37.

31. Palmer's original editorial was in *Forum*, July 1968. Shadel's letter (and Palmer's response) appeared in *Forum*, January 1969, 21–22.

32. *Forum*, May 1969, 24–25.

33. Ted Steinberg, *Acts of God: The Unnatural History of Natural Disaster in America* (New York: Oxford University Press, 2000): 132–39.

34. Raymond Palmer, "The Plot to Destroy the Constitution," *Forum*, August 1975, 2–4.

35. *Forum*, March 15, 1967, 27.

36. Raymond Palmer, "George Wallace and a Vision of Destiny," *Search*, January 1969, 17.

37. A. Human, "Where the Reader Has His Say," *Search*, March 1969, 68–70.

38. Raymond Palmer, *Search*, March 1969, 70–75, 92.

CHAPTER NINE—PROFESSOR PALMER'S INTERGALACTIC MEDICINE SHOW

1. Joe Gibson, "Ray Palmer's Medicine Show," *Inside and Science Fiction Advertiser*, July 1955, 21.

2. Jacquelinn A. Randolph, "You Remind Me of a Sideshow, Ray," *Search*, July 1974, 63–64.

3. Raymond Palmer, "Editorial," *Forum*, January 1968, 5.

4. Raymond Palmer, "The Mystery of the World's Most Unusual Mummies," *Search*, April 1963, 14.

5. Raymond Palmer, *Forum*, March 1974, 8.

6. As quoted in David Standish, *Hollow Earth* (Cambridge, MA: Da Capo Press, 2006): 40.

7. Amadeo Giannini, *Worlds Beyond the Poles* (New York: Vantage Press, 1959): 57.

8. Raymond Palmer, *Forum*, August 1967, 18.

9. Raymond Palmer, "Saucers from Earth! A Challenge to Secrecy," *Flying Saucers*, December 1959, 21.

10. Raymond Palmer, "Editorial," *Flying Saucers*, December 1959, 31–32.

11. Raymond Palmer, "Where the Reader Has His Say," *Flying Saucers*, September 1970, 38.

12. Ibid., 33–34.

13. Raymond Palmer, "Flying Saucers and the Stymie Factor," *Search*, Summer 1977, 34–44.

14. Raymond Palmer, "Editorial," *Flying Saucers*, August 1965, 4.

15. Ibid., 5.

16. Ibid., 9.

17. Raymond Palmer, "How Do I Know I Am Alive?" *Forum*, April 1967, 14–19.

18. Raymond Palmer, "Heaven Is Solid," *Search*, Summer 1977, 18–19.

19. Raymond Palmer, "Letters," *Forum*, March 15, 1967, 29.

20. Ibid., 28.

21. Raymond Palmer, *Forum*, August 1, 1966, 22.

22. "The *Caveat Emptor* Interview: Ray Palmer," *Caveat Emptor* 1 (Fall 1971): 12.

23. "Bon Voyage, Ray," *Search*, Fall 1977, 4.

CHAPTER TEN—INTO THE VORTEX

1. Curtis Fuller, Jerome Clark, et al., eds., *Proceedings of the First International UFO Congress* (New York: Warner Books, 1980): 349.

2. Martin Gardner, *The New Age: Notes of a Fringe Watcher* (Buffalo, NY: Prometheus Books, 1998): 215.

3. Raymond Palmer to Gray Barker, February 4, 1957, Gray Barker Collection, Clarksburg-Harrison Public Library, Clarksburg, West Virginia.

4. Raymond Palmer, *Forum*, August 1, 1966, 23.

5. Everett F. Bleiler, *Science Fiction: The Gernsback Years* (Kent, OH: Kent State University Press, 1998): 318–19.

6. Mike Ashley, *The Story of the Science Fiction Magazines from 1950 to 1970* (Liverpool: Liverpool University Press, 2005): 9.

7. Hank Luttrell, *Vegas Fandom Weekly* 49 (October 2005) 16; http://efanzines.com/VFW/VFW49.pdf.

8. Peter Kor, "The Palmer Method," *Forum*, March 1974, 4.

9. Peter Kor, "Back Talk—Where the Reader Has His Say," *Search*, Winter 1977, 61.

10. John Keel, "The Man Who Invented Flying Saucers," *Fortean Times*, Winter 1983, 52–57.

11. Gardner, *The New Age*, 214.

12. Raymond Palmer, "Letters," *Forum*, March 15, 1967, 27.

13. Frank N. Robinson, "Raymond, I Hardly Knew Ye . . ." *Locus*, September 1977, 16.

14. Maurice Doreal, *Mysteries of the Gobi* (Sedalia, CO: Brotherhood of the White Temple, not dated): 6–10.

15. The evolution of the Dulce legend with its many players is discussed in Michael Barkun, *A Culture of Conspiracy*, (Berkeley, University of California Press, 2003): 111–25.

16. This enfolding of conspiracy theory into entertainment is discussed in Peter Knight, *Conspiracy Nation: The Politics of Paranoia in Postwar America* (New York: New York University Press, 2002): 6.

17. Raymond Palmer, *Search*, July 1970, 5.

18. Raymond Palmer, "Editorial," *Forum*, February 1969, 2–5.

19. Raymond Palmer, "Editorial," *Search*, Fall 1976, 2.

BIBLIOGRAPHY

★ ★ ★

When rendering the life of Ray Palmer, it is tempting to take the advice of the newspaperman in the 1962 movie *The Man Who Shot Liberty Valance* and choose to simply "print the legend." Palmer's use of poetic license in describing his own experiences makes it difficult to sift fact from fiction about key events, including details of his friendship with Richard Shaver. A group of articles about Palmer and Shaver frequently reposted on the Internet, including those of John Keel, Doug Skinner, Richard Toronto, and Bruce Lanier Wright, helped give direction to my initial research. While I have sifted out some of the myths from the facts of Palmer's life story, undoubtedly I've allowed a few legends to slip through into my own account.

No university library currently holds the "Ray Palmer Papers," or, for that matter, the "Richard Shaver Collection," so the primary sources I turned to are the numerous articles and editorials that Ray Palmer published in the magazines for which he served as literary editor, editor, or publisher; these include: *Time Traveller*, *Science Fiction Digest*, *Fantasy Magazine*, *Amazing Stories*, *Fantastic Adventures*, *Fate*, *Other Worlds Science Stories*, *Universe Science Stories*, *Mystic*, *Search*, *Flying Saucers*, *Forum*, and the sixteen-volume *The Hidden World*.

Only a handful of Palmer's letters are available to researchers in university collections. Fortunately, Palmer published his extensive 1943–45 correspondence with Richard Shaver in "The Secret Shaver-Palmer Letter File," offered in the final four issues in his series, *The Hidden World*, A-13, A-14, A-15, A-16 (Palmer Publications, 1964). Palmer also cowrote two books that include autobiographical material: Kenneth Arnold and Ray Palmer, *The Coming of the Saucers* (Amherst,

WI: Palmer Publications, 1952); and, more important, Ray Palmer and Richard Shaver, *The Secret World* (Amherst, WI: Amherst Press, 1975), which includes Palmer's autobiographical "Martian Diary, Book I."

Other sources I relied on include telephone interviews or e-mail exchanges with Jerome Clark, a journalist and former editor of *Fate*; Helga Onan, a former employee of Palmer's; Evelyn Bryant, who is Richard Shaver's daughter; and Raymond B. Palmer, who is Ray Palmer's son. Raymond B. was also kind enough to furnish a copy of a booklet he compiled for his mother's memorial that provided some basic information about their family history.

The staff at the following archives aided my research: the American Religions Collection, Special Collections, Library of the University of California at Santa Barbara—scholar J. Gordon Melton donated much of this collection, which includes nearly full runs of many of Palmer's publications; the Eaton Collection of Science Fiction and Fantasy, Tomas Rivera Library, University of California, Riverside, which includes the finest collection of SF fanzines in the world; the Paskow Science Fiction Collection, Temple University Library; the Science Fiction and Fantasy Research Collection, Cushing Library, Texas A&M University; the Gray Barker Collection, Clarksburg-Harrison Public Library, Clarksburg, West Virginia; and the FBI file on Raymond Palmer.

My thanks to Peter Armenti at the Library of Congress, who aided me, long distance, in securing a difficult to find edition of *The Hidden World*. My thanks also to Andrew Porter and Brian Emrich for providing photographs, to Bud Webster for providing contact information, and to Rob Latham and Earl Kemp, who reviewed portions of this manuscript. My gratitude goes out as well to my two editors at Tarcher/Penguin: Gabrielle Moss and editor in chief Mitch Horowitz, who, with great cheer, helped to launch and complete this project. I am fortunate that my brother Steve Nadis, a science journalist, had the patience to aid me throughout. Finally, my love and thanks to Kate, and our children, Saul and Rose.

BOOKS CONSULTED

Angelucci, Orfeo. *The Secret of the Saucers*. Amherst, WI: Amherst Press, 1955.

Arnold, Kenneth, and Ray Palmer. *The Coming of the Saucers*. Amherst, WI: Palmer Publications, 1952.

Ashley, Mike. *Time Machines: The Story of Science-Fiction Pulp Magazines from the Beginning to 1950*. Liverpool, UK: Liverpool University Press, 2000.

———. *Transformations: The Story of the Science Fiction Magazines from 1950 to 1970*. Liverpool: Liverpool University Press, 2005.

Ashley, Mike, and Robert A. Lowndes. *The Gernsback Days: A Study of the Evolution of Modern Science Fiction from 1911 to 1936*. Holicong, PA: Wildside Press, 2004.

Barkun, Michael. *A Culture of Conspiracy: Apocalyptic Visions in Contemporary America*. Berkeley: University of California Press, 2003.

Bleiler, Everett F. *Science Fiction: The Gernsback Years*. Kent, OH: Kent State University Press, 1998.

Bloch, Robert. *Once Around the Bloch*. New York: Tor, 1993.

Caufield, Catherine. *Multiple Exposures: Chronicles of the Radiation Age*. Chicago: University of Chicago Press, 1989.

Davin, Eric Leif. *Partners in Wonder: Women and the Birth of Science Fiction, 1926–1965*. Oxford, UK: Lexington Books, 2006.

———. *Pioneers of Wonder: Conversations with the Founders of Science Fiction*. Amherst, NY: Prometheus Books, 1999.

Fuller, Curtis, Jerome Clark, et al., eds. *Proceedings of the First International UFO Congress*. New York: Warner Books, 1980.

Gardner, Martin. *The New Age: Notes of a Fringe Watcher*. Buffalo, NY: Prometheus Books, 1998.

Gould, Stephen Jay. *Ever Since Darwin: Reflections in Natural History*. New York: W. W. Norton, 1977.

Horowitz, Mitch. *Occult America*. New York: Bantam Books, 2009.

Jacobs, David Michael. *The UFO Controversy in America*. Bloomington: Indiana University Press, 1975.

Jung, Carl. *Flying Saucers: A Modern Myth of Things Seen in the Skies*. New York: Signet Books, 1959, reprint 1969.

Keyhoe, Donald. *The Flying Saucers Are Real*. New York: Fawcett Publications, 1950.

Knight, Peter. *Conspiracy Nation: The Politics of Paranoia in Postwar America*. New York: New York University Press, 2002.

Kripal, Jeffrey J. *Mutants and Mystics: Science Fiction, Superhero Comics, and the Paranormal*. Chicago: University of Chicago Press, 2011.

Leslie, Desmond and George Adamski. *Flying Saucers Have Landed*. New York: British Book Centre, 1953.

Lesser, Robert, ed. *Pulp Art: Original Cover Paintings for the Great American Pulp Magazines*. Edison, NJ: Castle Books, 2003.

Meehan, Paul. *Saucer Movies: A Ufological History of the Cinema*. Lanham, MD: Scarecrow Press, 1991.

Moskowitz, Sam. *The Immortal Storm: A History of Science Fiction Fandom*. Westport, CT: Hyperion Press, 1954.

Nadis, Fred. *Wonder Shows: Performing Science, Magic, and Religion in America*. New Brunswick, NJ: Rutgers University Press, 2005.

Palmer, Ray, ed. *The Hidden World*. 16 volumes. Amherst, WI: Palmer Publications, 1961–1964.

Palmer, Ray, and Richard Shaver. *The Secret World*. Amherst, WI: Amherst Press, 1975.

Robinson, Frank M. *Science Fiction of the 20th Century: An Illustrated History*. New York: Barnes and Noble Books, 1999.

Sanders, Joe, ed. *Science Fiction Fandom*. Westport, CT: Greenwood Press, 1994.

Schelly, Bill. *Words of Wonder: The Life and Times of Otto Binder*. Seattle, WA: Hamster Press, 2003.

Schwartz, Julius. *A Man of Two Worlds: My Life in Science Fiction and Comics*. New York: Harper, 2000.

Siegel, Mark Richard. *Hugo Gernsback: Father of Modern Science Fiction*. San Bernardino, CA: Borgo Press, 1988.

Server, Lee. *Danger Is My Business: An Illustrated History of the Fabulous Pulp Magazines*. San Francisco: Chronicle Books, 1993.

Standish, David. *Hollow Earth: The Long and Curious History*. Cambridge: MA, Da Capo Press, 2004.

Steinberg, Ted. *Acts of God: The Unnatural History of Natural Disaster in America*. New York: Oxford University Press, 2000.

Vallée, Jacques. *Revelations: Alien Contact and Human Deception*. New York: Ballantine Books, 1991.

Warner, Harry. *A Wealth of Fable: An Informal History of Science Fiction Fandom in the 1950s*. Van Nuys, CA: Scifi Press, 1976, reprint 1992.

Webb, James. *The Occult Underground*. Chicago: Open Court Publishing, 1974.

Wentworth, Jim. *Giants in the Earth*. Amherst WI: Palmer Publications, 1973.

Westfahl, Gary. *Hugo Gernsback and the Century of Science Fiction*. Jefferson, NC: McFarland and Company, Inc., 2007.

Williamson, George. *Other Tongues—Other Flesh*. Amherst, WI: Amherst Press, 1953.

ARTICLES CONSULTED

Baring-Gould, William S. "Little Superman, What Now?" *Harper's Magazine*, September 1946, 283–88.

Browne, Howard. "A Profit Without Honor," *Amazing Stories*, May 1984, 71–81.

"The *Caveat Emptor* Interview: Ray Palmer," *Caveat Emptor* 1 (Fall 1971): 9–12, 26.

Clark, Jerome. "60 Years of *Fate* Magazine," *Fortean Times*, 2008, 44–49.

Gardner, Thomas S. "Calling All Crack-pots: An Analysis of the Lemurian Hoax in *Amazing Stories*," *Fantasy Commentator* 1, no. 6 (Spring 1945):115–18.

Gertz, Stephen J. "Earthlings, Beware! A Galaxy of Porn in San Diego," *eI* 1, no. 4 (October 2002). http://efanzines.com/EK/eI4/index.htm.

Gibson, Joe. "Ray Palmer's Medicine Show," *Inside and Science Fiction Advertiser*, July 1955, 21–23.

Giles, Geoffrey. "The Palmer Hoax," *Science-Fantasy Review* 4, no. 17 (Winter 1949–50): 10–14. http://efanzines.com/FR/sfr17.htm.

Keel, John. "The Man Who Invented Flying Saucers." *Fortean Times* 41 (Winter 1983): 52–57.

Kemp, Earl. "Fear and Loathing in Evanston," *e.I* 2, no. 6 (December 2003): 14. http://efanzines .com/EK/eI11/eI11.pdf.

———. "Beauty and the Beast Otra Vez," *e.I* 1, no. 4 (October 2002). http://efanzines.com/ EK/eI4/index.htm.

———. "Futting with the F.B.I. Futter," *e.I* 1, no. 4 (October 2002). http://efanzines.com/ EK/eI4/index.htm.

———. "The Season of the Game," *e.I* 1, no. 4 (October 2002). http://efanzines.com/EK/ eI4/index.htm.

Latham, Rob. "Worlds Well Lost: Male Homosexuality in Postwar Science Fiction," *eI* 8, no. 5 (October 2009). http://efanzines.com/EK/eI46/index.htm#worlds.

Palmer, Ray (as "Omnia"). "Skylaugh of Space," *Fantasy Magazine*, May 1934, 16–18.

———. "Flying Saucers and the Stymie Factor," *Search*, Summer 1977, 34–44.

———. "Palmer Tears His Hair . . . Out and Down," *Stardust*, November 1940, 11–13, 24.

———. "As the Twig Is Bent . . ." *Hidden World*, Spring 1964, 2173–79.

Palmer, Raymond B. "Marjorie Palmer: 1917–1998." Memorial pamphlet.

Phillips, Rog (Roger Phillips Graham). "Christ an Autobiography," in Earl Kemp, ed., *eI* 31 6, no. 2 (April 2007) (reprinted from *Spacewarp* 42). http://efanzines.com/EK/eI31/index .htm.

Robinson, Frank N. "Raymond, I Hardly Knew Ye . . ." *Locus* 204 (September 1977): 15–16.

Sargeant, Winthrop. "Through the Interstellar Looking Glass," *Life*, May 21, 1951, 127–40.

Shough, Martin. "Return of the Flying Saucers: A Fresh Look at the Sighting that Started It All," *Darklore* 5, no. 76. http://darklore.dailygrail.com.

Skinner, Doug. "What's This? A Shaver Revival?" *Fate* 58, no. 6, issue 662 (June 2005). http:// www.fatemag.com/issues/2000s/2005-06.html.

Tausk, Victor. "The Origin of the Influencing Machine in Schizophrenia," reprinted in *Journal of Psychotherapy Practice and Research* 1, no. 2 (Spring 1992): 185–206.

Toronto, Richard. "The Man from Tomorrow," *eI* 41, December 2008. http://efanzines .com/EK/eI41/index.htm#man.

———. "The Shaver Mystery;" *Fate*, March, 1998. http://www.fatemag.com/ issues/1990s/1998-03-ShaverMystery.html.

"2001: Words or Less, an Interview with Ray B. Palmer." http://www.theufoforum.org/2001 WordsOrLessRayPalmer.html.

Walker, Paul. "Paul Walker Interviews Robert Bloch." http://mgpfeff.home.sprynet.com/ interview_walker.html.

Williams, Robert Moore. "Corpse Through the Roof," *Writer's Digest*, 29, no. 8 (July 1949): 13–18.

Wright, Bruce Lanier. "Fear Down Below: the Curious History of the Shaver Mystery." http:// www.softcom.net/users/falconkam/feardownbelow.html.

INDEX

★ ★ ★

Ackerman, Forrest J, 16–17, 20, 21, 40
  on Shaver Mystery, 88, 106–107, 109–10
Adam and Eve in Space (Shaver), 176–78
Adamski, George, 151–54, 156, 159–60, 163, 254
  Flying Saucers Have Landed, 152
"Age of Aquarius" (song), 213–14, 261
Agharti legend, 96–97, 98 (illus.), 100
Air Force Materiel Command, 122
Amazing Stories, 1–4, 8, 9, 10, 11, 19, 28, 124,
    188–90, 247, 252, 260
  all-Shaver issue of, 89, 103, 105, 111
  first issue of, 2–3
  Gernsback's vision for, 2–3
  and Maury Island hoax, 132–33
  occultist content in, 97–98, 110–11
  Palmer's early repositioning of, 31–33, 35–40,
    42–46
  T. O'Conor Sloane as editor of, 29–30, 32
*Amazons Defending Against the Attack of the
    Ape Bats* (Shaver), 176, 181 (illus.)
American Dream, 215–16, 261
American News Company, 164, 185–86
American Rocketry Club, 30
Amherst, Wisconsin, 140, 143–45
Amherst Press, 148–49, 154–56
Amsbury, Clifton, 11
"Ancient Earth, Its Story in Stone, The"
    (Shaver), 167, 175–76
Ancient Symbols of Mu (Churchward), 156
Anderson, Wing, 117–18, 119
Angelucci, Orfeo, 157
  bigoted responses to, 158–59
  The *Secret of the Saucers*, 159–64
Anti-communism, 104–105
Anti-communist denunciations of Palmer,
    202–205

Anti-Semitism, 155, 156, 258, 259
  conspiracy theory and, 104, 218
  Ray Palmer and. *See under* Palmer, Raymond
    A., conspiracy beliefs and
Arnold, Kenneth, x, 113, 119–22, 124–25, 132,
    134, 165, 262
  Coming of the Saucers, The, 125–31, 154
  honesty of, 123
Art Brut (Outsider Art), 256–57
Art Institute of Chicago, 34
Ashley, Mike, 79
Asimov, Isaac, 36–37, 52
  fan letters to *Amazing Stories* of, 36
Astounding Science Fiction, xi, 18, 26, 28, 33, 35,
    36, 42–43, 76, 88, 90–91, 107,145, 147,
    149, 164, 190
*Astounding Stories (Astounding). See Astounding
    Science Fiction*
Astrology, 150–51, 165, 183
Atlantis, myth of and occultists, 61–62, 72, 92,
    96, 97, 107, 156
Atmosphereans, 241
Atom (comic book), 197–200, 210, 245
Atomic bomb. *See* Nuclear weapons and power

Ballard, Guy and Edna, 97, 155
Barker, Gray, 236, 251
Barnum, Phineas Taylor, 228
Barto, Pennsylvania, 68, 83–85
Bates, Harry, 149
Bavarian Illuminati's New World Order, 259
Beckham, Tom, 133
Bedside Books, 183
Bennewitz, Paul, 258–59
Bernard, Raymond, 236
Bethurum, Truman, 152, 153

Bigfoot, 231
Binder, Earl, 31, 32–33, 36–37
Binder, Otto, 32–33, 36–37, 47, 166
    and sale of *Space World* to Palmer, 166
Black Mask, 25
Blavatsky, Madame Helena, 61, 95–96, 97
Bleiler, Everett F., 252–53
Bloch, Robert, 23–24, 34, 39, 198
    first meeting with Palmer of, 23
    parody of Palmer of, 39
Block, Lawrence, 183
Bok, Hannes, 165
Bonfils, Robert, 184
Bradbury, Ray, 37, 146
Bradley, Marion Zimmer, 183, 184
Brand, Stewart, 213
Branton, 259
Breton, André, 256–57
Brotherhood of the White Temple, 97, 98, 99,
    119, 258
Brown, Governor Jerry, 213
Brown, Lieutenant Frank M., 125, 129
    assessment of Arnold of, 123
    death in plane crash of, 129
Browne, Howard, 42, 43, 48, 49 (illus.), 57–58,
    61, 112–13, 193, 247
    on *Amazing Stories'* plots, 42
Brundage, Margaret, 33–34, 35, 64
Buford, John Carson, 142, 168
Bug-Eyed Monster (BEM), 26, 34, 42, 147
Bulwer-Lytton, Edward, *The Coming Race*, 96
Burroughs, Edgar Rice, 8, 23, 35, 37, 42, 48, 60,
    62, 76
    Pellucidar series of, 78–79
Burroughs, William S., 176
Byrd, Admiral Richard E.
    missing newsreel of, 239
    pole flight legend and, 233–36

Cage, John, 176
Campbell, John W., xi, 18, 33, 36, 42–43, 88,
    90–91, 146, 147, 253
    Palmer's criticism of, 43
Carson, Rachel, *Silent Spring*, 201
Casanova, Jacques, *Icosameron Or, the Story of
    Edward and Elizabeth*, 77–78
Central Intelligence Agency (CIA), 133, 217,
    221
Chicago, 46–47, 48, 50–51, 58, 64, 85, 97, 109,
    116, 129, 141–42, 144, 148, 149, 163, 182,
    187, 189, 190, 219, 223, 242, 250, 255

Christian Science, 95
Christianity, 76, 150, 151, 158, 162, 175, 215
Christianity, in Angelucci's contactee tale, 158,
    162
Christine Burgin Gallery, 257
Church of the SubGenius, 260
Churchward, James, 62
    Ancient Symbols of Mu, 156
Cinvention, Ray Palmer and, 112 (illus.), 144
    (illus.), 145
Clark, Jerome, 157
Clark Publishing Company, 116, 140, 143, 145,
    156
Clements, Aubrey, 17
Close Encounters of the Third Kind (movie), 241
"Club House, The" (column), 112, 190
Cold War, 100, 217
    domestic anti-Communism and, 202–205
    flying saucer craze and, 150, 155, 159
    paranoia and, 104–105
Comet, The (fanzine), 10, 11, 13
Coming of the Saucers, The (Arnold and Palmer),
    125–31, 136, 143, 154
Coming Race, The (Bulwer-Lytton), 96
Committee for the Scientific Investigation of
    Claims of the Paranormal (CSICOP),
    250
Connor, Wilkie, 146
Conspiracy theory, xii, 103–105, 225
    Dulce. *See* Dulce conspiracy theory
    and one-world fear, 215–19
    Potamac River basin compact and, 219–20
Contactees, 97, 148–50, 254
    George Adamski and, 151–52
    Orfeo Angelucci and, 157–64
    subculture of, 152–53, 157
    George Hunt Williamson and, 154–56
Corporeans, 241
Cosmology (fanzine), 1
Cosmos, 18–19
Crisman, Fred, 125, 126, 128–30, 131, 132
    possible CIA links of, 133
Criswell, Jerome "The Amazing," 163, 183
Curtis, Edward S., 213

Dahl, Harold, 125–29, 130, 131, 132–33
Davenport Brothers, 95
Davidson, Captain William, 125, 129
Davis, Bernard, x, 29, 37–38, 61, 75, 113, 194
*Dawn of Flame: The Stanley G. Weinbaum
    Memorial Volume* (Ruppert), 27

Day the Earth Stood Still, The (movie), 149–50, 151

DC Comics, 197–98

"De and te" theory. *See under* Shaver, Richard S., "de and te" theory of

"Dear Devil" (Russell), 146–47

Deegan, Frances, 47–48

Dennis, Walter, 10, 13, 14 (illus.), 37 (illus.)

Dero, Shaver's theory of, 60, 62, 65, 66–68, 81, 90, 98, 99, 101–104, 142, 175, 178, 186, 243, 258

Detroit Institute of Arts, 64

Dianetics, 88, 230

Dick, Philip K., 171, 190

Dill Pickle Club, 64

Dime museums, 227, 228, 229

Doc Savage, 43, 164

Doggins, Claude. *See* Doreal, Maurice

Donahoe, J. Bruce, 26

Donnelly, Ignatius, 96

Doreal, Maurice, 97, 99, 258

Dubuffet, Jean, 256

Dulce, New Mexico, 258

Dulce conspiracy theory, 258–60, 261

Dunkelberger, Walter, 109

Elder Races, The, 60, 68, 73, 142, 168–69, 173, 174–75, 178, 180, 181, 186, 191

Electrical Experimenter, 1, 2

Ellison, Harlan, 105, 183, 251

England, George Allan, 2

Eshbach, Lloyd Arthur, 19–20

ESP (extrasensory perception). *See* Paranormal

Esperanto, 41, 55, 110, 155, 230

Essa-3 and Essa-7 satellite photos of Earth, 237–39

Etherians, 241

Etidorhpa (Lloyd), 78

Extra-Terrestrial Hypothesis (ETH), The, 241–42

Fascism and the occult, 97, 155–56

Fan culture. *See* Science fiction fan culture

Fantastic Adventures, 35, 36, 37, 38–39, 48, 89, 115, 188, 190, 200

Fantasy Commentator, 107, 110

Fantasy Magazine, 17 (illus.), 19, 20–21, 24, 26, 249

Fantasy News, 87, 106

Fanzines, 10–11, 16–17, 40, 41, 164

Farley, Ralph Milne, 18, 20, 23–26, 29–31

Fate (magazine), 143, 145, 151–52, 156, 169, 254–55

early history of, 116–20

first issue of, 121–25

Palmer's departure from, 156–57

return of Fullers to, 157

FBI (Federal Bureau of Investigation), ix–xi, xii, 132–33, 139, 203–204, 206

Finney, Jack, *Invasion of the Body Snatchers*, 101

Finster, Reverend Howard, 257

First International UFO Congress, Chicago, 250

"Five Arguments Against the Extraterrestrial Origin of Unidentified Flying Objects" (Vallée), 241–42

Flying saucers, xii, 113–14

Kenneth Arnold and, 119–25

Day the Earth Stood Still and, 149–51

early controversy over, 134–37

hollow earth theory and, 232–39, 240–42

hostility of Palmer's critics regarding, 163–64

Maury Island hoax and, 125–34

Palmer's role in promotion of, 116–17, 119, 136–37, 253–54

See also Contactees; Adamski, George; Angelucci, Orfeo; Jung, Carl; Williamson, George Hunt

Flying Saucers (magazine), 164–66, 211, 215, 230, 231, 232, 247

Flying Saucers (Menzel), 253–54

"Flying Saucers Are Real" (Keyhoe), 135–36, 254

Flying Saucers from Other Worlds. See Flying Saucers (magazine)

Flying Saucers Have Landed (Adamski and Leslie), 151–52

Flying Saucers: A Modern Myth of Things Seen in the Skies (Jung) 159–60, 162–63

Fortean Times, 254, 255

Forum, The, 210–12, 240, 246, 247

Fox, Gardner, 198–99

Freedom Publishing, 183–88

in *Milwaukee Journal*, 184–85

Fuller, Curtis, 116–18, 119, 121, 123, 135, 156–58, 255

Fuller, Mary, 157, 255

Fuqua, Robert (Joseph Tillotson), 98 (illus.)

Futurians, 40–41

Gaenslen, Dr. Herman, 140

Gardner, Martin, 228, 250–52, 254

Gardner, Thomas S., 107, 113

Garrett, Eileen, 118–19

Gay and lesbian paperbacks, 183–84
Geier, Chester, 89, 100, 255
General Semantics, 41, 230
Gernsback, Hugo, 2–4, 16, 27, 29–30, 33, 35, 38,
    42–43, 69–70, 108, 110, 112, 116, 230,
    246, 252, 253
    and creation of SF fandom, 10–12, 13–14
    publications and enterprises of, 2, 8–9, 25, 29
Giannini, Amadeo F., *Worlds Beyond the Poles*,
    232–34, 236, 242, 244
Gibson, Joe, 228
Ginna, Robert E., 151
Gold, Jon (pseudonym). *See* Crisman, Fred
Glasser, Allen, 16
Gnosticism, 171
Goldwater, Barry, 210, 221, 223
Graham, Roger Phillips. *See* Phillips, Rog
Great Society, 216, 221
"Green Man, The" (Sherman), 76, 148–49, 150
"Green Man Returns, The" (Sherman), 76,
    148–49, 150
Greenwich Village, 84, 194
Gridley Dairy Company, 4, 5 (illus.)
Gurvitch, Sophie, 64, 65–66

Haggard, H. Rider, 8, 12, 79
Hair (musical), 213–14, 261
Halley, Edmond, hollow earth theory of, 77
Halley's Comet, 4–5, 189, 239
Hamling, William, 31, 50, 54, 141, 193, 195, 252
    court battles of, 187–88
    shift from SF to smut publishing of, 182–86
Hansen, L. T., 35, 143
    Navajo relief campaign and, 200
    "Scientific Mysteries" and, 111
Hauser, Heinrich, 100, 105
Hefner, Hugh, 182, 252
Hidden World series, xii, 67 (illus.), 83 (illus.),
    169, 175, 178 (illus.), 182, 193, 210, 249
Hippies, 212–15
Hoar, Roger Sherman. *See* Farley, Ralph Milne
Holberg, Baron Ludvig, hollow earth tale of,
    77–78
Hole in the pole theory, 232–39
"Hollow Earth Hoax, The" (Bryant), 236
Hollow earth lore, 76–78, 96, 114, 211
    flying saucers and, 232–39, 240–43
    occultists and, 96–98, 99, 257–60
    science fiction and, 76, 78–80
    See also Dulce conspiracy theory; Shaver
    Mystery

Hoover, J. Edgar, 139, 187, 203–204
Hornig, Charles D., 11, 18, 69
Houdini, Harry, 191
House Un-American Activities Committee
    (HUAC), 105
"How Do I Know I Am Alive?" (Palmer), 141,
    243–44
Howard, Robert E., 39, 62
Hubbard, L. Ron, 76, 88, 171, 251
Hugo Awards, 190, 256
Hynek, Allen J., on Kenneth Arnold sighting,
    122–23
Hypnotism. *See* Mesmerism and hypnotism

"I Am" (religious movement), 97, 155
Icke, David, 259–60
I Remember Lemuria (Shaver and Palmer), 60–62,
    71–73, 82, 86, 88, 89, 119, 141, 188, 190,
    193, 256
    Palmer's promotions of, 61, 69–71, 74
    reception of, 74–76, 87, 107, 108, 109
    See also Shaver Mystery
If: Worlds of Science Fiction, 255
Inferno (Dante), 32, 77
Influencing machines. *See* Tausk, Victor
Invasion of the Body Snatchers (Finney), 101
Ionia State Hospital, 68, 82
"Islands in the Sky" (short story), 242

Jacobs, David M., *The UFO Controversy in
    America*, 253
James, Jesse, 231
Jensen, Johannes V., 100
Jesus movement, 215
John Birch Society, 218, 261
John Reed Club, 64
Johnson, Lyndon B., 216, 221
Jones, Robert Gibson, 35, 70 (illus.), 85, 89, 91
Joshua Tree National Park, 152
Jules Verne Prize Club, 17–18
Jung, Carl, 165, 230, 241
    *Flying Saucers: A Modern Myth of Things Seen
    in the Skies*, 159–60
    interest in *The Secret of the Saucers* of, 159,
    160, 162–63

Keel, John, 241
    on first flying saucer convention, 116
    on Palmer's importance to UFO subculture,
    137, 254
Kemp, Earl, 164, 184, 187–88

Kepner, James, 107–108, 109
Keyhoe, Donald, 254
    "Flying Saucers Are Real," 135–36
Kirtland Air Force Base, 258
Kor, Peter, 220, 254
Kripal, Jeffrey J., 94, 257

Lasser, David, 30
Layne, Meade, 99
Leinster, Murray, 3
Lemuria (Mu), 71, 107
    early scientific theory of, 61–62
    in occult lore, 96–97, 152–53, 258
    See also I Remember Lemuria; Shaver Mystery
Le Plongeon, Augustus, 61–62
Leslie, Desmond, Flying Saucers Have Landed, 152
Ley, Willy, 11, 163–64
Liddy, G. Gordon, 217
Life (magazine) and treatment of UFOs, 135 (illus.), 151
Lily Lake, Illinois, 142
Lloyd, John Uri, Etidorhpa and hollow earth literature, 78
Loch Ness Monster, 231
"Lone Wolf of Space, The" (Palmer), 29, 48, 49–50, 251
Lost civilizations, 61–62, 71, 92–93, 96–97, 107, 152–53, 156, 258. See also Atlantis; Lemuria (Mu)
Lovecraft, H. P., 39, 62, 78, 80, 85, 124, 232
Lowell, Percival, 11
LSD (lysergic acid diethylamide), 11, 214–15
Luttrell, Hank, 253

Macfadden, Bernarr, 9
Mac Girls, 53, 145, 184
Mahaffey, Bea, 41, 145–46, 147 (illus.), 148 (illus.), 157, 164, 203, 253
Mammoth Detective, 35, 37, 48, 75
Mammoth Western, 37, 200
Mantong, 57, 58, 59, 60, 84, 89, 155
"Man Who Invented Flying Saucers, The" (Keel), 137, 254
Marcel, Major Jesse, 122
"Man Who Walked Through Mirrors, The" (Bloch), 39
Mars (Lowell), 11
"Martian Diary, The" (Palmer), 175, 206–10
"Martian Odyssey, A" (Weinbaum), 26
Maury Island, Washington, 127

Maury Island hoax, 125–34
McCauley, Harold, 34–35, 38, 44–45, 184
McKenna, Bob, 85, 88
Medicine shows, 228, 230, 263
Mencken, H. L., pulp publishing and, 25
Men's adventure magazines, 186
Men's soft-core magazines, 182, 183, 184, 187, 194
Menzel, Donald H., Flying Saucers, 253–54
Meredith, Scott, 183
Merritt, Abraham, 18, 19, 60, 62, 78, 79
Mesmerism and hypnotism, 94–95, 207, 259
Michelism, 40–41
Midnight Reader, 183
Millennialism, 150–51
Miller, P. Schuyler, 18
Milwaukee, 2, 4–8, 10, 14, 22–23, 46
Milwaukee Fictioneers, 23–28
Milwaukee Journal, 184, 185
Milwaukee Sentinel, 184
Mind Magic (magazine), 24–25
Mocku-conspiracy genre, 260
Modern Electrics, 2, 5
Moorcock, Michael, 253
Morello, Ted, 128, 130–31, 132
Moskowitz, Sam, 11, 40, 88, 110, 251
Muirdale Sanitorium, 14–16, 21, 171, 223
Mummies, 229
Murder Mysteries (magazine), 25
Mystery plays, 72, 77
Mystic (magazine), xii, 139, 157–58, 160, 165, 169, 202, 203, 204, 211, 252

National Investigations Committee on Aerial Phenomena (NICAP), 239
National Speleological Society, 99–100
Navajo Indians, 200–201
Nebel, Long John, 153
New Age, 148, 150–51, 156, 228, 231, 253
New Deal, The, 63–64, 245
New Thought (positive thinking), 94–95
Newbrough, John Ballou, 118. See also Oahspe
Niagara Falls Museum, 229
Nightstand Books, 183–84
1980 Proceedings of the First International UFO Congress, 250
Nixon, Richard, 210, 217, 224
Northwestern University, 116
Nuclear weapons and nuclear power, xi, 53, 88, 117, 148–49, 150, 152, 179, 192, 218, 260
    Palmer's campaign against testing, 201–203

Oahspe (Spiritualist bible), 94, 105, 118, 119, 143, 189, 191, 256
.Wing Anderson and, 117–18
John Ballou Newbrough and, 118
Palmer and, 143, 170, 173, 192, 210, 240–41, 242, 243
Oberg, James, 232, 239–40
"Observatory, The" (column), 32, 44, 45, 48, 52, 69, 87, 93, 111
Occultism, xii, 61–62, 148–51, 152–53
bigotry in, 154–56, 158–59, 258–60
Palmer and, 70–71, 75, 76, 78, 92–98, 117–19, 136–37, 192, 214, 253
See also Agharti legend; Atlantis; Hollow earth lore; Lemuria (Mu); Psi–Fi; Shaver Mystery; Theosophy
Olmsted, Frederick Law, 6
Omni magazine, 255
Onan, Helga, 141, 206
One-world conspiracy theory. *See under* Conspiracy theory, and one-world fear
O'Neill, Gerard, on space colonization, 213
"Origin of the Influencing Machine in Schizophrenia, The" (Tausk), 80–81
Orwell, George, 256
Ossendowski, Ferdinand, 96
Other Tongues, Other Flesh (Williamson), 154–56
Other Worlds Science Stories, 115, 116, 140, 141,145–47, 164
"Outlaw of Space" (Palmer), 48–49
Outsider art. *See* Art Brut

P. J. Lavies & Company, 10, 16, 28
Palmer, Helen Martha (mother), 6, 7–8, 200, 209
Palmer, Jennifer (daughter), 52, 246
Palmer, Linda (daughter), 51, 58, 84
Palmer, Marjorie (wife), 50–51, 58, 118, 140, 141, 144, 182, 239, 246–47
Palmer, Raymond A. (Alfred)
ability to hear music of spheres, 6
anti-military beliefs of, 201, 202–203, 224
and anti-Semitism, 218–19
anti-unionism of, 16
atmospheric theory of flying saucers of, 240–42
childhood in Milwaukee of, 4–8, 9–10
The Comet and, 10–11
The Coming of the Saucers and, 125–31, 132, 136, 143, 154
conspiracy beliefs and, 105, 129, 133–34, 171, 200, 204–205, 210–11, 215, 217–21, 225, 257
contact with Kenneth Arnold of, x, 124–25, 129
courtship of Marjorie of, 50–52
on daily life in Wisconsin, 140, 142–45, 195
on dangers of pesticides, 201
death of, 246–47
death threat to, 206
denunciation of psychics of, 205, 214
early backing of world unity of, 55
early days in Chicago, 46–48
early tricks in *Amazing Stories* of, 44–46, 74, 75 (illus.)
far right and libertarian politics of, 16, 73, 156, 205, 215–16, 218–25, 245
first crippling injury of, 7–8
first meeting with Shaver of, 83–86
friendship with Richard Shaver of, 141–42, 170–75
feud with Richard Shaver of, 191–94
on good pulp writing, 38
on heaven, 227, 240–41, 242–45, 247
"How Do I Know If I Am Alive?," 141, 243–44
on human perfectibility, 245
and launch of *Fate* magazine, 115–20
and launch of *Flying Saucers* magazine, 164–66
and launch of *Mystic* magazine, 157–58
legacy of, 206, 250–57
"Martian Diary" and, 175, 206–10, 221, 240, 262
memorial to, 247
Milwaukee Fictioneers and, 23–28, 37
move to Wisconsin of, 140
1950 accident of, 140–41
on 1960s counterculture, 212–15
one-world conspiracy and, 217, 218–20
opposition to nuclear weapons of, 201–203
"Outlaw of Space" and, 48–49
and paranoia, 60, 103, 104, 200, 217, 221
promotion of Shaver Mystery of, xi, 55, 57–61, 62, 69–71, 73–76, 85–86, 87, 89–90, 93–94, 97–98, 100–101, 103, 105–106, 109, 110–14
psychic experiences of, 21, 209–10, 243–44
rejection of dependency of, 205, 214–16
rejection of LSD of, 214–15
rejection of traditional religion of, 171

Palmer, Raymond A. (Alfred) (cont.)
   response to bigotry of, 158–59
   sanitorium stay of, 14–15, 21
   scientifiction spoofs of, 21–22
   The Secret World and, 175, 208, 246
   on self as collector, 229–30
   on self as "Man from Mars," 200, 206–208,
      229
   on Shaver's "rock books," 169–70
   on Shaver's writing ability, 194
   "Skylaugh of Space" and, 21–22
   space colonies and, 213
   start at Amazing Stories of, 31–38
   support for George Wallace of, 210–11,
      221–25
   "Time Ray of Jandra, The," and, 1, 8, 12–13,
      21, 253
   UFO sightings of, 59, 143
   on U.S. Department of Natural Resources,
      216–17, 218, 221, 261
   use of pseudonyms of, 21, 28, 45–46, 74, 116,
      247
   Vietnam War opposition of, 144, 206, 213,
      224
   visits from fans of, 205
   as young pulp writer, 8, 12–14, 16–28
   on Zionism, 218–20
Palmer, Raymond B. (Palmer's son), 52, 143–44,
   167–68
Palmer, Roy Clarence (father), 6, 7–8, 209
Paranoia, 101–105, 171, 217–21, 232–32. See also
   Cold War; Conspiracy theory; Shaver
   Mystery
Paranormal, xii, 58–59, 76, 88, 94, 111, 143, 153,
   163, 189, 200, 205, 206–207, 209–10, 214,
   231, 244, 250, 254, 256, 257
   in Fate magazine, 116, 117, 119
   See also Occultism; Psi–Fi; Telepathy
Paris Nights, 25
Parisienne, 25
Patton, Frank (Palmer pseudonym), 28, 46, 53,
   247
Paul, Frank, 2, 34, 35–36, 40
Pelley, William Dudley, 155
Pep!, 25
Perlman, V. T., 203–205
Phenix Publications, 187
Phillips, Rog (Roger Phillips Graham), 89, 103,
   105, 112, 186, 188–91, 192, 194, 231
Physical Culture (magazine), 9
Poe, Edgar Allan, 2, 19

Pohl, Frederik, 253
Positive Thinking Movement, 94–95
Potomac River Basin Compact and Conspiracy
   theory, 219–20
Propaganda, 36, 52, 202–203, 204, 205
Project Blue Book, 122, 160
Project Grudge, 122
Psi-Fi, 88, 148, 190, 230, 252, 257
Psychics, 205
Pulp magazines, xii, 8–9, 23, 25, 37–40, 42–43,
   52–54, 76, 78–80, 110–11, 183–84, 198,
   200–201
   cover art of, 25, 34–36
   demise of, 164–65, 174, 185–86
   Forum as "anti-pulp," 210–13
   Palmer's creation of occult pulps and, 116,
      117, 118–20

Queens Science Fiction League, 110
"Quest of Brail, The" (Shaver), 89–90, 91–92

Racial memory and the Shaver Mystery, xi, 59,
   61, 71, 74–75, 85, 113, 193, 194
Radio News, 2, 9, 29, 59
Rainier, Mount, 113, 120 (illus.), 121
Rape of (Jewish) Palestine, The (Ziff), 219
Reber, Grote, 242
Robinson, Frank M., 253, 256
Rockefeller, Nelson, and plan to take over
   United States, 220
Rogers, Margaret, 100
Rogue (magazine), 50, 182, 183, 184, 187, 194
Rokfogos. See under Shaver, Richard S., and
   rokfogos
Root races in Theosophy, 61, 96
Ross, John C., 123–24
Ruppert, Conrad H., Dawn of Flame: The Stanley
   G. Weinbaum Memorial Volume, 27
Russell, Frank, "Dear Devil," 146–47

Saint Germain, 97
Sander, Major George, 131
Sandia Laboratories, 259
Saucy Stories, 25
Scarlet Adventuress, 25, 26, 27–28
Scarlet Gang Stories, 25–26, 34
Schuster, Sharon, 212
Schwartz, Julius, 16–17, 20, 37
   and creation of Ray Palmer as Atom,
      198–99
Science Correspondence Clubs, 10, 13, 40

Science fiction
  demise of pulps and, 164–65, 174, 185–86
  early history of genre of, 2–3, 8–9, 10–12, 18,
     29–30, 33–34, 42–43
  Gernsback's contribution to, 10–12, 13–14
  gnosticism in, 171
  hollow earth narratives in, 76, 78–80
Science fiction conventions, 4, 40, 41, 112
     (illus.), 145, 146, 163, 190
Science Fiction Digest (fanzine), 16–19, 20, 27, 37,
     198
Science fiction fan culture
  development of, 4, 10–12, 13–14, 16–18, 20,
     21, 33, 40, 44, 47, 69, 112–13, 190
  fads in, 40–42, 76
  minorities and, 20
  and Shaver Mystery, 106–10
  and women, 17, 41, 145–46
Scientifiction (stf), 2, 12, 17, 41, 146
Scientology. See Dianetics
Sclater, Philip, 61
Search (magazine), xii, 125 (illus.), 169, 170, 193,
     197, 211, 212–13, 214, 220 (illus.), 227,
     228, 231, 239–40, 246, 247, 249, 262
Secret of the Saucers, The (Angelucci), 159–64
Secret World, The (Palmer and Shaver), 175, 208,
     246
Sexology (magazine), 9
Shade Publishing Company, 24–28
Shadow, The, 43, 164
Shalett, Sidney, 134–35
Shamanism, 66, 67, 163
Shasta, Mount, and occult writings, 92, 97, 258
Shaver Mystery Club, 100–101, 142, 168, 194, 255
Shaver Mystery
  initial fan reaction to, 62, 75–76, 92–94, 106–107
  Mantong alphabet and, 57–59
  outline of, 60, 64–65, 66–68
  reaction of occultists to, 97–99
  reader hostility to, 107–10, 111–13
  See also under Palmer, Raymond A.,
     promotion of Shaver Mystery
Shaver, Dorothy (Dottie), 69, 82, 83–86, 141–42,
     168, 193
Shaver, Evelyn Ann (daughter), 64, 66
Shaver, Richard S.
  admiration for Velikovsky, of, 179–80
  Amazons Defending Against the Attack of the
     Ape Bats and, 176, 181 (illus.)
  The Ancient Earth, Its Story in Stone and, 167,
     175–76

anger towards establishment science of,
     179–82
  on Bible's falsity, 171–72, 175, 177–78
  and brother's death, 64–65
  on dero, 60, 65, 66–67, 68, 81, 90, 98, 102,
     175, 177–78, 186
  "de and te" theory of, 172–74, 189, 191
  Detroit years of, 63–66
  and doubts about evolution, 180
  drifter period of, 66–69
  early correspondence with Palmer of, 57–58,
     170–74
  feud with Palmer of, 191–94
  first psychotic episode of, 64–66
  on gaining immortality, 92, 172, 173–74,
     177–78, 243
  Gnosticism and, 171
  on hell, 66–68, 81, 90
  Hidden World manuscript and, 169–70, 175–76
  institutionalization of, 65–66, 68, 82
  and loss of custody of daughter, 66
  move to Arkansas of, 182, 185, 193, 194
  move to Illinois of, 141–42
  move to Wisconsin of, 141–42
  paranoia of, 101–103
  participation in radical politics of, 63–64
  participation in sleaze publishing of, 183,
     184–85, 186–88
  psychic initiation of, 64–68
  return to Pennsylvania of, 68–69
  revision of the sciences of, 172–74, 179–82
  rivalry with Rog Phillips of, 188–93
  and rokfogos, 175–78, 194, 208, 257
  The Secret World and, 175, 208, 246
  on sex in science fiction, 90–91, 186–87
  on tamper, 68, 102–103, 142, 168
  theory of elder races of, 60, 67–68, 168,
     174–75, 176–79, 180–82
  theory of the cosmos of, 81–82, 90, 170–73,
     175, 177–80
  training as artist of, 63–64
  youth of, 63
  See also I Remember Lemuria
Shaver, Taylor (brother), 63, 64–65, 193
Sherman, Harold M., 149, 150
  The Green Man, 76, 148
  The Green Man Returns, 76, 148
  Thoughts Through Space, 148, 149
Shuster, Joe, 21
Siegel, Jerome, 21
Silent Spring (Carson), 201

Silver Legion, 155
Silverberg, Robert, 183, 184
Skylark of Space, The (Smith), 22
"Skylaugh of Space" (Palmer), 22
Slan subculture, 42, 76
Sloane, T. O'Conor, 29–30, 32, 43–44
Smart Set, 25
Smith, Edward E. "Doc." *See The Skylark of Space*
Smith, Emil, 125, 128–31
Smith, Malcolm H., 145, 203
Smut publishing, 182–88
Solar Sales Service, 37, 198
South Sea Stories, 39–40
Southern, Terry, 187
Space colonization, 213
Space opera, i, 18, 22, 42–43, 48, 62, 146
Space World, xii, 166, 206, 232, 239–40
Spicy Adventure, 25
Spicy Detective, 25, 27, 34
Spicy Mystery, 25
Spicy Western, 25
"Spilling the Atoms" (column), 16–17, 21, 32, 69
Spiritualism, 94–95
St. Ann's high school, 8, 10
St. John, J. Allen, 34–35, 47
Stapledon, Olaf, 165
Star Guests (Pelley), 155
Steber, Alfred (Palmer pseudonym), 6, 28, 29,
    48, 247
   mock biographies of, 45–46, 74, 75 (illus.)
Strange Adventures, 24–25
Strange: The Magazine of True Mystery, 255
Street and Smith, 43, 164
Summerland, 244
Summit, Arkansas, 182
Surrealists, 176, 256
Symmes, John Cleves, 78, 232, 235

Tabloid newspapers, 231
Tacoma, Washington, x, 125–32
Tacoma Times and reporting of Maury Island
    incident, 128, 130
Taff, Master Sergeant Elmer L., 129, 130
Tausk, Victor, 80–81
Technocracy, 41, 230
Telepathy, 66, 68, 76, 78, 79, 88, 109, 147, 149, 169
Theosophy, 61, 62, 94, 95–96, 155
Thoughts Through Space (Sherman and Wilkins),
    148, 149
"Time Ray of Jandra, The" (Palmer), 1, 8,
    12–13, 21, 253

Time Traveller (fanzine), 11, 16, 198
Tomorrow (magazine), 118–19
Toronto, Richard, 256
Tremaine, F. Orlin, 18
True Confessions, 9
True Detective, 9
True Gang Life, 25, 26, 209–10
True Romances, 9
True Story, 9
Twin Peaks, 260

UFO Controversy in America, The (Jacobs), 253
Ufologists, 153, 241, 251
UFOs. *See* Flying saucers
Underworld, myths of journeys to, 67, 76–78
United States Department of Natural
    Resources, 216, 217, 218, 221, 261
University of Chicago, 132
University of Michigan, 133
Urantia, 76, 149

V (television series), 259
Vallée, Jacques, 241–42
Valor (magazine), 155
Van Tassel, George, 152
Van Vogt, A. E., 42, 76, 88
Velikovsky, Immanuel, *Worlds in Collision*,
    179–80
Verne, Jules, 2, 3, 8, 17, 19, 78, 250
Vest, Paul M., 139, 158, 160
Vietnam War and counterculture, 144, 206, 213,
    215, 217, 223, 224
Vision literature, 67
   "Vision of Drythelm" and, 76–77
Vogel, Ernie, 132
Von Däniken, Erich, 154–55
Vortex World, The (Palmer), 21, 249

Wallace, George, 210, 222–24
War of the Worlds. See Welles, Orson, *War of the
    Worlds* (broadcast)
Warner, Harry, 88
Washington, George, 222, 223
"Way in the Middle of the Air" (Bradbury), 146
Webb, James, 117
Weinbaum, Stanley, 23, 25, 26–27, 37, 198
Weird Tales, 8, 20, 23, 33–34, 37, 64, 79, 165,
    198
Weisinger, Mort, 16, 37
Welles, Orson, *War of the Worlds* (broadcast), 59
Wells, H. G., 2, 3, 8, 12

Wertenbaker, G. Peyton, 2–3
Westlake, Donald, 183
WGN, 149
"What Have I Done to Spread Science Fiction?"
    (contest), 13
"Who Killed Science Fiction?" (Kemp), 164
Wilkins, Sir Hubert, *Thoughts Through Space*,
    148, 149
Williams, Robert Moore, 38
Williamson, George Hunt, *Other Tongues, Other*
    Flesh, 154–56
Wilson, Marjorie. *See* Marjorie Palmer
Winchell, Walter, 203
Witchcraft and Shaverism, 65, 68, 84
Wonder cabinets, 168
Wood, Ed, Jr., 183
World War One, 5
World War Two, 34, 87–88, 218
    in *Amazing Stories*, 52–55
    death of Palmer's brother Dave in, 54–55
    Palmer's psychic experiences related to, 209
Worlds Beyond the Poles (Giannini), 232–34, 235,
    236, 242, 244

World's fairs
    Century of Progress Exposition, Chicago,
        1933–34, 64
    New York World's Fair, 1939–40, 40
Worlds in Collision (Velikovsky), 179–80
Works Progress Administration (WPA), 245
Wright, Farnsworth, 20, 33
Wright-Patterson Air Force base, 122, 125, 130
WRNY, 9

X-Files (television series), 260

Yerxa, Frances, 50–51, 182
Yerxa, Leroy, 39, 50, 54
Your Body (magazine), 9
Ypsilanti State Hospital, 66, 82

Ziff, William B., 218–19
    The Rape of (Jewish) Palestine, 219
Ziff-Davis publishing company, 29–33, 34,
        47–48, 75, 84, 112, 116–17, 123, 182
Ziff-Davis pulp story guidelines, 38, 39–40
Zionism, 218–19

ABOUT THE AUTHOR

★ ★ ★

Fred Nadis writes about popular culture, popular religion, and science. He has been a visiting associate professor of American studies at Doshisha University in Japan, as well as a freelance journalist, publishing articles and essays in *The Atlantic* and other magazines. He is the author of *Wonder Shows: Performing Science, Magic, and Religion in America*. A past fellow at the Smithsonian, Nadis has a PhD in American studies from the University of Texas at Austin. He lives in California.